Contents

PHARMACOTHERAPEUTICS-III

A CLINICAL APPROACH FOR PHARM.D

DR. NAGA LATHA,DR. VEENA ,DR. VARUN

Made with ♥ on the Notion Press Platform
www.notionpress.com

Textbook Of Pharmacotherapeutics–iii

A Clinical Approach for Pharm.D
AUTHORS
Dr. D. Naga Latha, Pharm.D. (P.B.), Ph.D.
Associate Professor & Head of the Department,
Department of Pharmacy Practice,
Sri Indu Institute of Pharmacy (Autonomous),
Sheriguda (V), Ibrahimpatnam (M),
R.R. District, Hyderabad, Telangana - 501510, India
Dr. Veena Gadicherla, M.Pharm., Ph.D.
Professor & Head of the Department,
Department of Pharmacology,
Sri Indu Institute of Pharmacy (Autonomous),
Sheriguda (V), Ibrahimpatnam (M),
R.R. District, Hyderabad, Telangana - 501510, India
Dr. D. Varun, M.Pharm., Ph.D., PGDDRA
Professor & Principal, Head of the Department,
Department of Pharmaceutics,
Sri Indu Institute of Pharmacy (Autonomous),
Sheriguda (V), Ibrahimpatnam (M),
R.R. District, Hyderabad, Telangana - 501510, India
Editor
Dr. A. Muralidhar Rao, M.Pharm., PhD.
Principal,
St. Mary's College of Pharmacy,
Secunderabad, Telangana, India

Published by Notion Press

Notion Press, Inc.
800, West El Camino Real #180,
California, USA 94040

Notion Press Media Pvt Ltd
#7, Red Cross Road,
Egmore, Chennai, Tamil Nadu 600008
Email ID: publish@notionpress.com
Phone Number: +91 44 46315631
FEBRUARY 2025

Preface

The field of pharmacotherapeutics serves as the cornerstone of clinical pharmacy practice, equipping healthcare professionals with the knowledge and skills required to make informed decisions in drug therapy management. This book, "Pharmacotherapeutics-III: A Clinical Approach for Pharm.D," is designed to provide comprehensive, evidence-based insights into the pathophysiology, pharmacological interventions, and patient-centered management of various diseases.

Pharmacists play a pivotal role in optimizing therapeutic outcomes, minimizing adverse effects, and ensuring the rational use of medications. This book focuses on the clinical application of pharmacotherapeutics, enabling students to bridge the gap between theoretical knowledge and real-world patient care. Each chapter is structured to provide a systematic understanding of disease management, covering essential topics such as the gastrointestinal system, hematological disorders, neurological conditions, psychiatric illnesses, and pain management.

A distinguishing feature of this book is its emphasis on evidence-based medicine (EBM), ensuring that treatment recommendations align with the latest clinical guidelines and research findings. Case studies, dosage regimens, and clinical considerations have been integrated throughout the chapters to facilitate critical thinking and clinical decision-making.

This book is tailored to meet the curriculum requirements for Pharm.D students and serve as a practical resource for pharmacy professionals, clinical practitioners, and academicians. The content is structured to align with Pharm.D examination patterns, incorporating important concepts, commonly asked questions, and essential clinical pearls.

We extend our gratitude to students, faculty, and healthcare professionals whose valuable feedback and clinical experiences have contributed to shaping this book. It is our sincere hope that this resource enhances learning, strengthens clinical acumen, and inspires future pharmacists to take an active role in evidence-based patient care.

Dr. D. Naga Latha
Dr. Veena Gadicherla
Dr. D. Varun

Chapter Wise Contents

- **Definition and Principles:**

  - Define **EBM** as the integration of:

    - Best available evidence.
    - Clinical expertise.
    - Patient preferences and values.

  - Discuss the importance of EBM in improving **clinical outcomes** and **rational prescribing**.
  - Include a workflow diagram summarizing the **5-step EBM process**:

    - **Ask** a clinical question.
    - **Acquire** relevant evidence.
    - **Appraise** the evidence quality.
    - **Apply** findings to clinical practice.
    - **Assess** therapeutic outcomes.

  7.2 Hierarchy of Evidence

- Explain the **Pyramid of Evidence**, highlighting:

  - **Systematic Reviews and Meta-Analyses**: Most robust evidence.
  - **Randomized Controlled Trials (RCTs)**: Gold standard for evaluating interventions.
  - **Observational Studies**: Cohort, case-control, and cross-sectional studies.
  - **Expert Opinion and Case Reports**: Least reliable evidence.

- Include examples:

  - **Systematic Review**: Use of statins in preventing cardiovascular events.
  - **RCT**: Efficacy of new anticoagulants (DOACs) vs warfarin.

- Provide a table summarizing the strengths and weaknesses of each evidence type.

7.3 Formulating Clinical Questions

- Introduce the **PICO Framework**:

  - **P**: Patient/Population (e.g., elderly with hypertension).
  - **I**: Intervention (e.g., ACE inhibitors).
  - **C**: Comparator (e.g., ARBs or no treatment).
  - **O**: Outcome (e.g., reduction in stroke incidence).

- Provide an example of a well-formulated PICO question:

  - "In patients with atrial fibrillation (P), does warfarin (I) compared to aspirin (C) reduce the risk of stroke (O)?"

7.4 Application of EBM in Pharmacotherapeutics

- **Steps in EBM Application**:

  - Identifying reliable evidence sources:

    - PubMed, Cochrane Library, clinical guidelines (e.g., ADA, WHO).

  - Evaluating evidence:

    - Assessing validity (study design, randomization, blinding).
    - Interpreting clinical outcomes (e.g., **Relative Risk Reduction (RRR), Absolute Risk Reduction (ARR)**).

  - Applying findings to specific patient populations:

    - Case example: Use of SGLT2 inhibitors in diabetic patients with cardiovascular risks.

- **Statistical Tools:**

7.5 Pharmacist's Role in EBM

- **Literature Appraisal:**

- ◦ Skills for evaluating clinical trials and systematic reviews.
- ◦ Example: Critiquing a study on the efficacy of a new antipsychotic.

- **Patient-Centric Application**:

  - ◦ Educating patients on the risks and benefits of therapy.
  - ◦ Adjusting dosages and regimens based on the latest guidelines.

- **Team Collaboration**:

  - ◦ Working with physicians and other healthcare professionals to implement EBM.

7.6 Challenges in Implementing EBM

- **Common Barriers**:

  - ◦ Lack of access to high-quality evidence in resource-poor settings.
  - ◦ Time constraints in busy clinical environments.
  - ◦ Variability in patient preferences and cultural values.

- **Overcoming Challenges**:

  - ◦ Use of summarized evidence sources (e.g., guidelines, clinical summaries).
  - ◦ Incorporating decision support tools in clinical practice.
  - ◦ Promoting continuing education on EBM principles.

7.7 Case Studies in EBM

- Example 1: Use of EBM in selecting anticoagulation therapy:

  - ◦ Clinical question: Should rivaroxaban be preferred over warfarin for stroke prevention in atrial fibrillation?
  - ◦ Evidence: RCT showing **25% lower risk of major bleeding** with rivaroxaban.

- Example 2: EBM for chronic pain management:

- ○ Decision to use gabapentin vs pregabalin based on patient-specific parameters and cost-effectiveness.

7.8 Future Directions in EBM

- **Integration of Real-World Evidence (RWE):**

  - ○ Combining observational data with traditional RCTs.

- **Artificial Intelligence (AI) in EBM:**

  - ○ Use of AI for evidence synthesis and personalized medicine.

- **Global Trends:**

  - ○ Expansion of open-access evidence databases to support resource-limited settings.

Authors' Profiles

Dr. Dhulipalla Naga Latha

Dr. Dhulipalla Naga Latha is an accomplished academician and researcher, presently serving as Associate Professor and Head of the Department of Pharmacy Practice at Sri Indu Institute of Pharmacy (Autonomous), Hyderabad. With over 10 years of experience in teaching, research, and administration, she has made significant contributions to the field of pharmaceutical sciences.

Dr. Latha completed her Bachelor of Pharmacy (B.Pharm) degree in the year 2005, and her Pharm.D (Post Baccalaureate) in the year 2014. She was awarded a Doctor of Philosophy in the year 2022.

A prolific scholar, Dr. Latha has authored over 21 publications in esteemed national and international peer-reviewed journals, reflecting her commitment to advancing pharmaceutical research. She is an active Life Member of the Indian Pharmaceutical Association (IPA) Additionally, she contributes her expertise as a member of the IPA Local Branch – Ibrahimpatnam (Telangana State), Institutional Quality Assurance Cell (IQAC) for NAAC, and the Institutional Ethical Committee.

Dr. Latha plays a pivotal role as Coordinator for the ADR Monitoring Center (AMC), recognized by the Pharmacovigilance of India (PvPI), and as a committee member of the Institutional Research & Development Cell. In recognition of her contributions to science and education, she received the

Young Scientist Award at the International Scientist Awards on Engineering, Science, and Medicine in 2022.

In addition to her academic and administrative roles, Dr. Latha serves as a reviewer for the Indian Journal of Pharmaceutical Sciences and Dove Medical Press, further cementing her reputation as a respected voice in the pharmaceutical community.

Through her dedication to education, research, and professional excellence, Dr. Dhulipalla Naga Latha continues to inspire future generations of pharmacists and researchers.

Dr. Veena Gadicherla

Dr G Veena is a distinguished expert in the field of Pharmaceutical sciences with a wealth of experience in both academic and clinical settings. Holding a Ph.D. in Pharmacology, Dr G Veena has spent many years researching, teaching, and contributing to the advancement of Pharmacological knowledge. With a focus on drug mechanisms, therapeutic applications, and the clinical use of pharmaceuticals, the author has written extensively to bridge the gap between theory and practice. Dr G Veena has published numerous research articles that are widely used as citations. Her passion for educating future healthcare professionals is reflected in the clear, concise, and engaging style of writing that aims to make complex concepts accessible to students and practitioners alike. In addition to her academic contributions, Dr G Veena has also been involved in clinical practice, pharmaceutical industry collaborations and continuing education programs.

Dr. G Veena is a creative intellectual with over 21 publications in prestigious national and international peer-reviewed journals along with 3 Patent Publications and 2 Design Patents. Dr. G Veena is an active Life Member of the Indian Pharmaceutical Association (IPA), the Association of Pharmacy Teachers of India (APTI), and a was awarded a Summer Research Fellowship by CSIR-CCMB. She also served as Mentor for CSIR-SRTP organized by CSIR-NEIST, Jorhat, India. She is the Coordinator for several esteemed committees, including the IPA Local Branch in Ibrahimpatnam (Telangana), the Institutional Quality Assurance Cell (IQAC) for NAAC, and the Institutional Ethical Committee. As the Deputy Coordinator for the ADR Monitoring Center (AMC), recognized by the Pharmacovigilance of India (PvPI), and a key member of the Institutional Research & Development Cell, Dr. G Veena plays an integral role in promoting research and ensuring the safety and efficacy of Pharmaceutical Products.

Dr. D. Varun

Dr. D. Varun is a distinguished academician, researcher, and author with **19 years of teaching experience** in the field of pharmaceutical sciences. He currently serves as the **Ratified Professor, Principal, and Head of the Department of Pharmaceutics** at **Sri Indu Institute of Pharmacy (Autonomous), Hyderabad.**

A prolific researcher, Dr. Varun has **published over 90 research papers** in esteemed National and International peer-reviewed journals. His contributions to pharmaceutical innovation include **6 Patent Publications** and **3 Design Patent Grants**. As an author, he has written **5 books**, further enriching the field with his expertise and scholarly insights.

Dr. Varun's excellence has been widely recognized through prestigious awards. As a dedicated mentor, he has **supervised 6 Ph.D. scholars** and guided **around 150 research projects** at the UG and PG levels. His research interests span **Formulation Research & Development, Herbal Product Development & Evaluation, Advanced Drug Delivery Systems & In-vivo Characterization, Drug Regulatory Affairs, Pharmaceutical Management, and Clinical Research.**

Dr. Varun is an **approved Ph.D. supervisor** at various reputed Universities and actively contributes to academic discourse as a **Speaker**, having delivered **20 invited lectures.**He is a **Life Member** of esteemed organizations, including the **Association of Pharmacy Teachers of India (APTI), Indian Pharmaceutical Association (IPA), and the Association of Pharmacy Professionals.**

With a passion for research, education, and innovation, Dr. D. Varun continues to make significant contributions to pharmaceutical sciences, inspiring future researchers and professionals in the field.

CHAPTER ONE

Introduction

1.1 Scope and Objectives

1.1.1 Importance of Pharmacotherapeutics in Clinical Practice

Pharmacotherapeutics is the branch of pharmacology that focuses on the **rational use of drugs for the treatment, prevention, and management of diseases.** It plays a crucial role in modern medicine by ensuring that drug therapy is optimized for **maximum benefit with minimal risk.** Unlike pharmacokinetics, which deals with drug movement within the body, or pharmacodynamics, which studies the effects of drugs at the receptor level, pharmacotherapeutics integrates these concepts to achieve **effective patient-centered treatment strategies.**

The importance of pharmacotherapeutics lies in its ability to enhance **patient outcomes** by improving drug efficacy, reducing adverse effects, and preventing disease progression. The ultimate goal is to achieve **symptom relief, disease modification, and overall improvement in quality of life.** The correct selection of drugs, proper dosing, appropriate duration of therapy, and regular monitoring are all essential components of pharmacotherapeutic decision-making.

For instance, in **hypertension**, uncontrolled high blood pressure is a major risk factor for cardiovascular diseases such as stroke and heart attacks. Effective **pharmacotherapy with antihypertensive agents**, such as **angiotensin-converting enzyme (ACE) inhibitors** or **calcium channel blockers**, reduces the incidence of complications by nearly **35-40%.** Similarly, in **diabetes mellitus**, pharmacotherapeutic agents such as **metformin** and **SGLT2 inhibitors** significantly lower the risk of **microvascular and macrovascular complications** by controlling blood glucose levels and reducing insulin resistance.

A well-planned pharmacotherapeutic approach also plays a major role in the **management of epilepsy**, where uncontrolled seizures can lead to **brain damage, cognitive impairment, and even sudden unexpected death in epilepsy (SUDEP)**. The introduction of **antiseizure medications (ASMs)** such as **levetiracetam and valproate** has reduced seizure frequency in more than **70% of epilepsy patients**, allowing them to lead normal lives.

To further understand the impact of pharmacotherapeutics on patient health, consider the following statistics:

- **Diabetes management**: The use of **metformin** as a first-line therapy reduces HbA1c levels by approximately **1.5%**, significantly lowering the risk of long-term complications such as nephropathy and neuropathy.
- **Hypertension treatment**: Studies indicate that **every 10 mmHg reduction in systolic blood pressure (SBP) lowers the risk of cardiovascular disease by nearly 20%**.
- **Epilepsy control**: Patients on **antiseizure medications** have an estimated **80% reduction in seizure recurrence**, leading to an improved quality of life.
- **Reduction in hospital readmissions**: Effective pharmacotherapeutic management in chronic diseases like heart failure and COPD has been shown to **reduce hospital readmission rates by 15-20%**, thus decreasing the burden on healthcare systems.

Pharmacotherapeutics is also essential for **public health interventions**. For example, the use of **antibiotics in bacterial infections** prevents the spread of infectious diseases, while the proper implementation of **vaccination programs** has eradicated or controlled deadly conditions such as **smallpox, polio, and measles**. Similarly, the advancement in **targeted cancer therapies** has improved **5-year survival rates in cancers like breast cancer and leukemia by over 50%**.

A key aspect of pharmacotherapeutics is the **relationship between drug mechanism and clinical application**. Every drug acts by modifying **biochemical or physiological processes** within the body. For instance:

- **ACE inhibitors (e.g., Enalapril, Ramipril)** work by **blocking the conversion of angiotensin I to angiotensin II**, leading to **vasodilation and reduced blood pressure**. This is why they are commonly prescribed for **hypertension and heart failure.**

- **Metformin**, the most widely used drug for **Type 2 diabetes**, lowers blood glucose levels by **reducing hepatic glucose production and increasing insulin sensitivity in peripheral tissues.**
- **Statins (e.g., Atorvastatin, Rosuvastatin)** reduce cholesterol levels by **inhibiting HMG-CoA reductase**, thus preventing atherosclerosis and cardiovascular events.
- **Selective serotonin reuptake inhibitors (SSRIs) such as Fluoxetine and Sertraline** act by **blocking the reuptake of serotonin in the brain,** improving symptoms of depression and anxiety disorders.

The **pharmacodynamic and pharmacokinetic profiles** of drugs also play an essential role in determining their suitability for different patients. For example, **elderly patients** with impaired renal function may require **dose adjustments of renally excreted drugs** such as aminoglycosides or metformin to prevent toxicity. Similarly, **patients with liver dysfunction** should avoid drugs that undergo extensive hepatic metabolism, such as benzodiazepines, to prevent accumulation and adverse effects.

One of the critical aspects of pharmacotherapeutics is **therapeutic drug monitoring (TDM)**, which is essential for **narrow therapeutic index (NTI) drugs** such as **warfarin, lithium, and digoxin.** These drugs require **regular blood level assessments** to ensure they remain within the **therapeutic range** and to prevent toxicity. For example:

- **Therapeutic INR range for warfarin in atrial fibrillation: 2.0-3.0.**
- **Target lithium levels for bipolar disorder: 0.6-1.2 mEq/L.**
- **Digoxin therapeutic range: 0.5-2.0 ng/mL.**

Another essential consideration in pharmacotherapeutics is **adverse drug reactions (ADRs)** and **drug interactions**, which can significantly impact treatment outcomes. The **WHO estimates that nearly 5% of all hospital admissions are due to ADRs**, highlighting the importance of **careful drug selection, dose optimization, and monitoring.** Some common examples include:

- NSAIDs (e.g., Ibuprofen, Diclofenac) increasing the risk of **gastrointestinal bleeding when combined with anticoagulants (e.g., Warfarin).**

- **Grapefruit juice inhibiting CYP3A4 enzymes,** leading to elevated levels of drugs such as **Atorvastatin and Cyclosporine,** increasing the risk of toxicity.
- **Concurrent use of ACE inhibitors and potassium-sparing diuretics (e.g., Spironolactone) causing hyperkalemia.**

1.1.1 Importance of Pharmacotherapeutics in Clinical Practice

Pharmacotherapeutics is the branch of pharmacology that focuses on the rational use of drugs for the treatment, prevention, and management of diseases. It plays a crucial role in modern medicine by ensuring that drug therapy is optimized for maximum benefit with minimal risk. Unlike pharmacokinetics, which deals with drug movement within the body, or pharmacodynamics, which studies the effects of drugs at the receptor level, pharmacotherapeutics integrates these concepts to achieve effective patient-centered treatment strategies.

The importance of pharmacotherapeutics lies in its ability to enhance patient outcomes by improving drug efficacy, reducing adverse effects, and preventing disease progression. The ultimate goal is to achieve symptom relief, disease modification, and overall improvement in quality of life. The correct selection of drugs, proper dosing, appropriate duration of therapy, and regular monitoring are all essential components of pharmacotherapeutic decision-making.

For instance, in hypertension, uncontrolled high blood pressure is a major risk factor for cardiovascular diseases such as stroke and heart attacks. Effective pharmacotherapy with antihypertensive agents such as angiotensin-converting enzyme inhibitors or calcium channel blockers reduces the incidence of complications by nearly thirty-five to forty percent. Similarly, in diabetes mellitus, pharmacotherapeutic agents such as metformin and sodium-glucose co-transporter two inhibitors significantly lower the risk of microvascular and macrovascular complications by controlling blood glucose levels and reducing insulin resistance.

A well-planned pharmacotherapeutic approach also plays a major role in the management of epilepsy, where uncontrolled seizures can lead to brain damage, cognitive impairment, and even sudden unexpected death in epilepsy. The introduction of antiseizure medications such as levetiracetam and valproate has reduced seizure frequency in more than seventy percent of epilepsy patients, allowing them to lead normal lives.

To further understand the impact of pharmacotherapeutics on patient health, consider the following statistics. The use of metformin as a first-line therapy reduces glycated hemoglobin levels by approximately one point five percent, significantly lowering the risk of long-term complications such as nephropathy and neuropathy. Studies indicate that every ten millimeters of mercury reduction in systolic blood pressure lowers the risk of cardiovascular disease by nearly twenty percent. Patients on antiseizure medications have an estimated eighty percent reduction in seizure recurrence, leading to an improved quality of life. Effective pharmacotherapeutic management in chronic diseases like heart failure and chronic obstructive pulmonary disease has been shown to reduce hospital readmission rates by fifteen to twenty percent, thus decreasing the burden on healthcare systems.

Pharmacotherapeutics is also essential for public health interventions. The use of antibiotics in bacterial infections prevents the spread of infectious diseases, while the proper implementation of vaccination programs has eradicated or controlled deadly conditions such as smallpox, polio, and measles. Similarly, the advancement in targeted cancer therapies has improved five-year survival rates in cancers like breast cancer and leukemia by over fifty percent.

A key aspect of pharmacotherapeutics is the relationship between drug mechanism and clinical application. Every drug acts by modifying biochemical or physiological processes within the body. For instance, angiotensin-converting enzyme inhibitors such as enalapril and ramipril work by blocking the conversion of angiotensin one to angiotensin two, leading to vasodilation and reduced blood pressure. This is why they are commonly prescribed for hypertension and heart failure. Metformin, the most widely used drug for type two diabetes, lowers blood glucose levels by reducing hepatic glucose production and increasing insulin sensitivity in peripheral tissues. Statins such as atorvastatin and rosuvastatin reduce cholesterol levels by inhibiting hydroxy-methyl-glutaryl coenzyme a reductase, thus preventing atherosclerosis and cardiovascular events. Selective serotonin reuptake inhibitors such as fluoxetine and sertraline act by blocking the reuptake of serotonin in the brain, improving symptoms of depression and anxiety disorders.

The pharmacodynamic and pharmacokinetic profiles of drugs also play an essential role in determining their suitability for different patients. Elderly patients with impaired renal function may require dose adjustments of renally excreted drugs such as aminoglycosides or metformin to prevent toxicity. Similarly, patients with liver dysfunction should avoid drugs that undergo extensive hepatic metabolism, such as benzodiazepines, to prevent accumulation and adverse effects.

One of the critical aspects of pharmacotherapeutics is therapeutic drug monitoring, which is essential for narrow therapeutic index drugs such as warfarin, lithium, and digoxin. These drugs require regular blood level assessments to ensure they remain within the therapeutic range and to prevent toxicity. The therapeutic international normalized ratio range for warfarin in atrial fibrillation is two to three. The target lithium levels for bipolar disorder are between zero point six and one point two milliequivalents per liter. The therapeutic range of digoxin is zero point five to two nanograms per milliliter.

Another essential consideration in pharmacotherapeutics is adverse drug reactions and drug interactions, which can significantly impact treatment outcomes. The world health organization estimates that nearly five percent of all hospital admissions are due to adverse drug reactions, highlighting the importance of careful drug selection, dose optimization, and monitoring. Some common examples include nonsteroidal anti-inflammatory drugs such as ibuprofen and diclofenac increasing the risk of gastrointestinal bleeding when combined with anticoagulants such as warfarin. Grapefruit juice inhibiting cytochrome p four fifty enzymes, leading to elevated levels of drugs such as atorvastatin and cyclosporine, increasing the risk of toxicity. Concurrent use of angiotensin-converting enzyme inhibitors and potassium-sparing diuretics such as spironolactone causing hyperkalemia.

1.1.2 Bridging Pathophysiology with Treatment

Understanding the pathophysiology of diseases is essential in selecting appropriate drug therapy. Pathophysiology refers to the **functional and biochemical changes** that occur in a disease state, influencing the progression and severity of symptoms. By identifying the **underlying mechanisms** that drive diseases, clinicians can **target specific pathways** with pharmacological interventions. This approach ensures that treatments are not only symptom-relieving but also **disease-modifying**, ultimately improving long-term patient outcomes.

A clear understanding of disease mechanisms allows for **rational drug selection**, optimizing efficacy while minimizing adverse effects. For example, in **hypertension**, persistent elevation of blood pressure is largely mediated by the **renin-angiotensin-aldosterone system (RAAS)** and **vascular resistance**. Drugs like **angiotensin-converting enzyme (ACE) inhibitors** directly inhibit the production of **angiotensin II**, a potent vasoconstrictor, leading to **reduced blood pressure** and **decreased cardiac workload**. Similarly, in **asthma**, an exaggerated immune response results in airway inflammation and bronchoconstriction, necessitating the use of **corticosteroids** and **beta-agonists** to control inflammation and improve airflow.

Asthma: Pathophysiology and Drug Selection

Asthma is a **chronic inflammatory disease** of the airways, characterized by **bronchial hyperresponsiveness**, **mucosal edema**, and **excess mucus production**. The primary triggers include allergens, pollutants, respiratory infections, and stress, all of which activate the **immune system**, leading to airway narrowing and difficulty in breathing.

Pathophysiology of Asthma

1. **Trigger exposure** (e.g., allergens, dust, cold air) leads to **activation of immune cells**, including **mast cells and eosinophils**.
2. These immune cells release **pro-inflammatory cytokines and histamine**, leading to **airway inflammation and swelling**.
3. The release of **leukotrienes and prostaglandins** results in **bronchoconstriction** by stimulating smooth muscle contraction.
4. Chronic inflammation leads to **airway remodeling**, reducing lung function over time.

Pharmacotherapeutic Approach

- **Corticosteroids (e.g., Budesonide, Fluticasone)**: These drugs **suppress inflammation** by inhibiting cytokine release and reducing immune cell activation.
- **Beta-2 Agonists (e.g., Salbutamol, Formoterol)**: These drugs **relax bronchial smooth muscles** by stimulating beta-adrenergic receptors, relieving bronchoconstriction.
- **Leukotriene Receptor Antagonists (e.g., Montelukast)**: These agents block leukotriene-mediated inflammation and mucus secretion,

preventing airway narrowing.

- **Mast Cell Stabilizers (e.g., Cromolyn Sodium)**: These drugs prevent degranulation of mast cells, reducing histamine release and inflammatory response.

By addressing the **core pathophysiological mechanisms**, asthma medications not only relieve acute symptoms but also prevent long-term airway damage.

Hypertension: Role of RAAS and Pharmacological Intervention

Hypertension is a **multifactorial disorder** driven by excessive **vasoconstriction, sodium retention, and increased cardiac output**. A major contributor to hypertension is the **renin-angiotensin-aldosterone system (RAAS)**, which regulates blood pressure through hormone-mediated pathways.

Pathophysiology of Hypertension

1. **Renin release from the kidneys** in response to low blood pressure activates the **RAAS cascade**.
2. Renin converts **angiotensinogen to angiotensin I**, which is then converted to **angiotensin II** by **angiotensin-converting enzyme (ACE)**.
3. Angiotensin II causes **vasoconstriction**, leading to increased peripheral resistance and **elevated blood pressure**.
4. Angiotensin II also stimulates the release of **aldosterone**, leading to **sodium and water retention**, further increasing blood volume.

Pharmacotherapeutic Approach

- **ACE Inhibitors (e.g., Enalapril, Lisinopril)**: These drugs **inhibit the conversion of angiotensin I to angiotensin II**, reducing vasoconstriction and lowering blood pressure.
- **Angiotensin Receptor Blockers (ARBs) (e.g., Losartan, Valsartan)**: These drugs **block angiotensin II receptors**, preventing vasoconstriction and sodium retention.
- **Diuretics (e.g., Hydrochlorothiazide, Furosemide)**: These drugs **reduce blood volume** by promoting sodium and water excretion.
- **Calcium Channel Blockers (e.g., Amlodipine, Nifedipine)**: These drugs prevent calcium influx into smooth muscle cells, causing **vasodilation and reduced vascular resistance**.

- **Beta-Blockers (e.g., Metoprolol, Atenolol):** These drugs **reduce heart rate and cardiac output,** decreasing blood pressure.

The choice of antihypertensive therapy depends on **patient-specific factors,** including age, co-existing conditions (e.g., diabetes, kidney disease), and tolerance to medications.

Depression: Neurotransmitter Dysfunction and Targeted Treatment

Depression is a **psychiatric disorder** characterized by **low mood, anhedonia, fatigue, and cognitive dysfunction.** The primary cause is believed to be an **imbalance in neurotransmitters,** particularly **serotonin, norepinephrine, and dopamine.**

Pathophysiology of Depression

1. **Reduced serotonin levels** in the brain are associated with feelings of sadness and emotional instability.
2. **Deficiency in norepinephrine** contributes to fatigue, low energy, and reduced motivation.
3. **Dopamine dysfunction** leads to decreased pleasure and reward-seeking behavior.

Pharmacotherapeutic Approach

- **Selective Serotonin Reuptake Inhibitors (SSRIs) (e.g., Fluoxetine, Sertraline):** These drugs **block serotonin reuptake** in the synapse, increasing its availability for neurotransmission.
- **Serotonin-Norepinephrine Reuptake Inhibitors (SNRIs) (e.g., Venlafaxine, Duloxetine):** These drugs **increase serotonin and norepinephrine levels,** improving mood and energy levels.
- **Tricyclic Antidepressants (TCAs) (e.g., Amitriptyline, Imipramine):** These drugs **block the reuptake of both serotonin and norepinephrine,** though they have more side effects.
- **Monoamine Oxidase Inhibitors (MAOIs) (e.g., Phenelzine, Tranylcypromine):** These drugs **inhibit the enzyme monoamine oxidase,** preventing the breakdown of serotonin, norepinephrine, and dopamine.

By **correcting neurotransmitter imbalances,** these medications help alleviate the symptoms of depression and improve cognitive function.

Case Study: Role of ACE Inhibitors in Heart Failure

A sixty-year-old male with **chronic heart failure** presented with **shortness of breath, fluid retention, and reduced exercise tolerance.** Echocardiography revealed **reduced ejection fraction (35%),** indicating **systolic heart failure.**

Pathophysiology of Heart Failure

1. **Reduced cardiac output** leads to **compensatory activation of the RAAS,** causing vasoconstriction and sodium retention.
2. **Increased afterload and preload** further weaken the failing heart.

Pharmacotherapeutic Intervention

- The patient was started on **Enalapril (5 mg twice daily)** to inhibit the RAAS system.
- Within **six weeks**, ejection fraction improved to **45%**, and symptoms significantly reduced.
- Combination therapy with a **beta-blocker (Metoprolol 50 mg daily)** provided additional **heart rate control and reduced myocardial oxygen demand.**

This case highlights how **identifying the key pathophysiological mechanism of heart failure** allows for targeted pharmacological treatment, improving long-term patient outcomes.

1.1.3 Goals of Pharmacotherapy: Cure, Symptom Management, and Prevention

Pharmacotherapy plays a crucial role in disease management, and its goals can be broadly classified into three categories: cure, symptom management, and prevention. The objective of drug therapy depends on the nature of the disease, its progression, and patient-specific factors. While some drugs aim to completely eradicate the disease, others focus on relieving symptoms or preventing disease occurrence in high-risk individuals. Understanding these goals helps clinicians tailor treatment strategies for optimal patient outcomes.

Curing a disease is the ideal goal of pharmacotherapy and is typically achieved using antimicrobial agents, antiviral drugs, and chemotherapy. This approach involves eliminating the underlying cause of the disease, leading to complete recovery. A classic example is the use of antibiotics for bacterial infections such as tuberculosis, pneumonia, and urinary tract infections. The success of antimicrobial therapy depends on factors such as proper drug selection, adherence to the prescribed regimen, and resistance patterns. For example, the standard triple therapy for peptic ulcer disease caused by Helicobacter pylori includes a proton pump inhibitor, clarithromycin, and amoxicillin or metronidazole. This regimen has been shown to achieve a cure rate of approximately ninety-five percent, significantly reducing ulcer recurrence. Similarly, antimalarial drugs such as artemisinin-based combination therapies have been highly effective, with a cure rate exceeding ninety-eight percent in uncomplicated Plasmodium falciparum infections. Advances in antiviral therapy have also led to the near-complete eradication of hepatitis C, with direct-acting antivirals achieving cure rates above ninety-five percent.

Symptom management is a primary goal of pharmacotherapy for many chronic conditions where a complete cure is not possible. This approach focuses on alleviating pain, inflammation, and other distressing symptoms to improve the patient's quality of life. Analgesics such as paracetamol and nonsteroidal anti-inflammatory drugs are commonly used for pain relief in conditions like arthritis, migraines, and post-surgical recovery. In more severe cases, opioids such as morphine and fentanyl are prescribed for pain management, particularly in cancer patients and those with terminal illnesses. Symptom control is also crucial in chronic diseases such as asthma and diabetes, where inhaled corticosteroids and insulin therapy help maintain stable disease conditions. Effective symptom management reduces hospitalizations and complications, ensuring better long-term health outcomes. For example, inhaled corticosteroids combined with long-acting beta-agonists reduce asthma exacerbations by over fifty percent, while the use of disease-modifying antirheumatic drugs in rheumatoid arthritis significantly slows disease progression and joint damage.

Prevention is a key component of pharmacotherapy, aiming to reduce the risk of developing diseases, especially in high-risk individuals. This is achieved through vaccination, chemoprevention, and chronic disease management. Statins are widely used for the prevention of cardiovascular diseases by lowering cholesterol levels and stabilizing atherosclerotic plaques. Studies have shown that statins reduce low-density lipoprotein cholesterol levels by up to fifty percent and lower the risk of major cardiovascular events by approximately twenty-five to thirty percent. Antiplatelet agents such as aspirin are prescribed for patients with a history of myocardial infarction or stroke to prevent recurrence. Similarly, anticoagulants such as warfarin and direct oral anticoagulants are used for stroke prevention in patients with atrial fibrillation. The role of vaccination in preventing infectious diseases is well-established, with vaccines for hepatitis B, human papillomavirus, and influenza reducing disease incidence by over eighty percent in vaccinated populations.

A strong pharmacotherapeutic approach integrates all three goals to provide comprehensive disease management. For example, in diabetes, metformin is used for both treatment and prevention in high-risk individuals, while insulin therapy manages symptoms of hyperglycemia. In cancer care, chemotherapy aims to cure early-stage malignancies, while palliative care focuses on symptom relief in advanced disease. Pharmacotherapy also plays a preventive role in oncology, with drugs such as tamoxifen reducing the risk of breast cancer recurrence.

1.2 Evidence-Based Medicine

1.2.1 Definition and Principles

Evidence-based medicine is a structured approach to medical decision-making that integrates the best available research evidence with clinical expertise and patient values. It ensures that healthcare professionals rely on scientifically validated data rather than anecdotal experience or outdated practices. This methodology enhances treatment efficacy, minimizes harm, and improves overall patient outcomes. In pharmacotherapeutics, evidence-based medicine is essential for selecting appropriate drug therapies, optimizing dosing regimens, and minimizing adverse drug reactions.

The core framework of evidence-based medicine consists of three essential components. The first is the best available evidence, which refers to the highest-quality research data obtained from systematic reviews, randomized controlled trials, and well-conducted observational studies. For instance, systematic reviews have confirmed the efficacy of sodium-glucose cotransporter two inhibitors in reducing cardiovascular risks in patients with type two diabetes. The second component is clinical expertise, which involves the judgment and experience of healthcare professionals in applying evidence to individual patient scenarios. Pharmacists and clinicians interpret research findings, assess risks versus benefits, and tailor therapy based on comorbidities and medication history. The third component is patient preferences, which emphasizes the importance of involving patients in treatment decisions. Shared decision-making considers patient-specific concerns, lifestyle choices, and financial constraints, ensuring that the therapy aligns with their values and expectations.

A structured workflow is followed in evidence-based medicine, beginning with formulating a clinical question using the problem, intervention, comparison, and outcome framework. The next step is acquiring relevant evidence by searching medical literature databases such as PubMed, Cochrane Library, and clinical guideline repositories. This is followed by critical appraisal, where the quality and validity of the study are assessed, ensuring that findings are applicable to clinical practice. Once the evidence is deemed reliable, it is integrated with clinical expertise and patient preferences to make an informed decision. Finally, the effectiveness of the chosen intervention is evaluated through patient monitoring and follow-up to ensure optimal outcomes.

1.2.2 Hierarchy of Evidence

The hierarchy of evidence is a structured ranking system that categorizes research studies based on their methodological strength and reliability. At the top of the hierarchy are systematic reviews and meta-analyses, which combine data from multiple high-quality studies to provide the most comprehensive assessment of treatment efficacy. Randomized controlled trials follow, offering robust evidence by comparing interventions under controlled conditions. These trials eliminate bias by randomizing participants into different treatment groups and ensuring blinding where neither patients nor researchers know which treatment is administered.

Observational studies, including cohort and case-control studies, are ranked lower in the hierarchy because they lack randomization, making them more susceptible to confounding variables. However, they are valuable for studying long-term drug effects and rare adverse reactions that may not be captured in clinical trials. At the bottom of the hierarchy are case reports and expert opinions, which provide anecdotal evidence based on individual cases but lack statistical rigor.

For example, systematic reviews have demonstrated the effectiveness of sodium-glucose cotransporter two inhibitors in managing diabetes and reducing cardiovascular mortality. Randomized controlled trials have compared the efficacy of newer antidepressants such as vortioxetine to selective serotonin reuptake inhibitors, demonstrating superior cognitive benefits in major depressive disorder. Data from these trials indicate that drugs tested in randomized controlled trials show approximately twenty percent higher efficacy than those evaluated solely through observational studies, underscoring the importance of rigorous research methodologies in clinical decision-making.

1.2.3 Pharmacist's Role in Evidence-Based Medicine

Pharmacists play a crucial role in the implementation of evidence-based medicine by evaluating research findings, optimizing medication regimens, and ensuring patient safety. Their primary responsibility is to critically assess clinical studies and guidelines to determine the most appropriate drug therapy. Pharmacists rely on medical databases such as PubMed, Cochrane Library, and clinical guideline resources from organizations like the American Diabetes Association and the European Society of Cardiology. By systematically reviewing high-quality evidence, they can make data-driven recommendations to physicians and patients.

The application of evidence-based medicine extends beyond literature review to practical implementation in patient care. Pharmacists optimize drug regimens based on clinical guidelines, ensuring that patients receive the most effective and safe medications. For example, in anticoagulation therapy for atrial fibrillation, pharmacists use the CHA2DS2-VASc scoring system to assess stroke risk and determine the necessity of anticoagulation. A patient with a score of two or higher is typically prescribed a direct oral anticoagulant such as apixaban or rivaroxaban to prevent thromboembolic events. Additionally, pharmacists monitor international normalized ratio levels in patients on warfarin, adjusting dosages to maintain therapeutic anticoagulation and prevent bleeding complications.

In real-world scenarios, pharmacists contribute to medication reconciliation, ensuring that prescribed drugs do not interact adversely with existing therapies. For example, if a patient receiving a selective serotonin reuptake inhibitor requires an analgesic, the pharmacist may recommend acetaminophen instead of a nonsteroidal anti-inflammatory drug to minimize the risk of gastrointestinal bleeding. By actively participating in patient counseling, pharmacists educate individuals about drug adherence, potential side effects, and lifestyle modifications, enhancing treatment effectiveness.

1.3 Patient-Centric Pharmacotherapy

1.3.1 Individualized Therapeutic Plans

Individualized therapy is an approach in pharmacotherapy that tailors drug selection, dosing, and monitoring based on patient-specific factors such as age, weight, renal function, genetic makeup, and comorbidities. Unlike standardized treatment regimens, individualized pharmacotherapy ensures that medications are optimized for maximum efficacy while minimizing adverse effects. This is particularly important in patients with multiple comorbidities, where drug interactions and organ function must be carefully considered.

For example, in anticoagulation therapy, warfarin requires careful dose adjustments based on international normalized ratio (INR) values to maintain therapeutic anticoagulation and prevent excessive bleeding. Similarly, in patients with renal impairment, antibiotic dosing must be adjusted to prevent drug accumulation and toxicity. The Cockcroft-Gault equation is commonly used to estimate creatinine clearance, which helps in determining the appropriate dose of renally excreted drugs.

$$\text{Creatinine Clearance (CrCl)} = \frac{(140 - \text{age}) \times \text{weight (kg)}}{72 \times \text{serum creatinine (mg/dL)}}$$

For females, the estimated creatinine clearance is multiplied by **0.85** to account for lower muscle mass. This calculation is essential for adjusting doses of nephrotoxic drugs such as aminoglycosides and vancomycin, ensuring that drug levels remain within the therapeutic range without causing renal toxicity.

Example 1: Warfarin Dose Adjustment Based on INR

Warfarin is a commonly used oral anticoagulant with a **narrow therapeutic index**, meaning that small dose variations can lead to significant clinical consequences. Its dosing is guided by INR levels, where an INR of **2.0–3.0** is the typical target for conditions such as atrial fibrillation and deep vein thrombosis. A subtherapeutic INR (below 2.0) increases the risk of thromboembolism, while a supratherapeutic INR (above 3.0) raises the risk of bleeding.

For instance, if a patient is prescribed **5 mg of warfarin daily** but has an INR of **1.5** after three days, the dose may be increased to **7.5 mg daily** under careful monitoring. Conversely, if an INR of **3.8** is recorded, the dose might be reduced to **2.5 mg daily**, or a dose may be skipped to avoid hemorrhagic complications. The **genetic polymorphisms in CYP2C9 and VKORC1**, which influence warfarin metabolism, also necessitate individualized dosing, as certain genetic variants require lower starting doses.

Example 2: Antibiotic Dose Adjustments in Renal Impairment

Patients with chronic kidney disease often require **dose adjustments for renally excreted antibiotics** to prevent toxicity. For example, **gentamicin**, an aminoglycoside antibiotic, is primarily eliminated via the kidneys. If a patient has an estimated creatinine clearance of **30 mL/min**, the standard **once-daily dosing regimen (5 mg/kg)** may be adjusted to **every 48 hours** to prevent drug accumulation and nephrotoxicity.

Consider a **65-year-old male weighing 70 kg with a serum creatinine of 1.8 mg/dL**. Using the Cockcroft-Gault equation:

$$\mathrm{CrCl} = \frac{(140 - 65) \times 70}{72 \times 1.8} = \frac{75 \times 70}{129.6} = 40.5\,\mathrm{mL/min}$$

Since the creatinine clearance is reduced, dose adjustments must be made for renally excreted drugs such as cefepime and levofloxacin to prevent drug accumulation.

Case Study: Individualized Therapy in a Patient with Multiple Comorbidities

A **72-year-old female with chronic kidney disease (CrCl = 28 mL/min), atrial fibrillation, and diabetes** was admitted for an acute infection. Her prescribed medications included metformin for diabetes, rivaroxaban for anticoagulation, and ceftriaxone for bacterial pneumonia. Due to her **reduced renal function**, modifications were made as follows:

- **Metformin** was discontinued to prevent the risk of **lactic acidosis**, a known complication in renal impairment.
- **Rivaroxaban** dose was reduced from **20 mg once daily to 15 mg once daily**, as per dosing guidelines for CrCl below 30 mL/min.
- **Ceftriaxone** was adjusted from **2 g once daily to 1 g once daily** to avoid excessive drug accumulation.

After five days of treatment with adjusted doses, the patient's infection resolved, her renal function remained stable, and she did not experience any bleeding complications. This case highlights the importance of **individualized therapy**, demonstrating how patient-specific dose adjustments prevent drug toxicity while ensuring therapeutic efficacy.

1.3.2 Patient-Specific Parameters

Patient-specific parameters play a crucial role in pharmacotherapy, ensuring that drug selection, dosing, and monitoring are tailored to an individual's unique physiological and biochemical profile. These parameters help clinicians optimize treatment efficacy while minimizing adverse effects and drug toxicity. Several factors must be considered when prescribing medications, including **clinical parameters** such as age, weight, comorbidities, and genetic factors, as well as **laboratory parameters** such as liver and renal function.

Clinical Parameters

Age and Drug Metabolism

Age is a key determinant of drug absorption, distribution, metabolism, and excretion. In neonates and elderly patients, altered physiological functions require dose adjustments for many drugs.

- **Neonates and Infants**

  - Immature liver enzymes result in **reduced drug metabolism**, prolonging the half-life of medications such as theophylline and aminoglycosides.
  - **Renal clearance is lower**, necessitating careful dosing of renally excreted drugs like aminoglycosides and vancomycin.
  - Example: **Gentamicin** is dosed at **4 mg/kg once every 24 hours** in neonates, compared to every 8 hours in adults.

- **Elderly Patients**

  - **Reduced hepatic metabolism** due to decreased liver enzyme activity affects drugs metabolized by the liver, such as benzodiazepines and opioids.

- ◦ **Renal function declines**, requiring dose adjustments for drugs such as digoxin and enoxaparin.
- ◦ Example: **Diazepam**, which has a long half-life, is avoided in elderly patients due to the risk of sedation and falls.

Weight and Body Composition

Body weight and fat distribution influence drug dosing, especially for **lipophilic drugs** such as propofol and diazepam, which accumulate in adipose tissue.

- **Dosing Based on Weight**

  - ◦ Many medications, such as **aminoglycosides and chemotherapy drugs**, require weight-based dosing to ensure appropriate therapeutic levels.
  - ◦ Example: **Gentamicin is dosed at 5–7 mg/kg body weight per day in adults.**
  - ◦ In **obese patients**, adjusted body weight is often used for dosing, especially for drugs with **high volume of distribution**.

Comorbidities and Polypharmacy

Patients with multiple chronic diseases require special attention to **drug-drug interactions** and **organ function limitations**.

- **Hypertension with Chronic Kidney Disease**

  - ◦ **ACE inhibitors** are preferred but require monitoring of serum potassium and renal function.
  - ◦ **Metformin is avoided if creatinine clearance is below 30 mL/min** due to the risk of lactic acidosis.

- **Liver Cirrhosis and Drug Dosing**

  - ◦ **Hepatic metabolism is impaired,** leading to prolonged drug half-life for **warfarin, benzodiazepines, and opioids.**
  - ◦ **Propranolol and carvedilol require dose adjustments** to prevent hypotension.

Laboratory Parameters

Renal Function and Drug Clearance

Renal function is a critical factor in adjusting drug doses, particularly for medications that are primarily eliminated by the kidneys. The **Cockcroft-Gault equation** is commonly used to estimate creatinine clearance and determine appropriate drug dosing.

$$\text{Creatinine Clearance (CrCl)} = \frac{(140 - \text{age}) \times \text{weight (kg)}}{72 \times \text{serum creatinine (mg/dL)}}$$

For females, the value is multiplied by **0.85** due to lower muscle mass.

- **Example of Drug Adjustments in Renal Impairment**

  - Enoxaparin dose is reduced from 1 mg/kg twice daily to 1 mg/kg once daily when CrCl < 30 mL/min.
  - Metformin is discontinued if CrCl < 30 mL/min to avoid lactic acidosis.
  - Digoxin dose is reduced as it is primarily excreted by the kidneys, preventing toxicity.

Liver Function and Drug Metabolism

The liver is the primary site of drug metabolism, and hepatic impairment can **alter drug clearance**, leading to accumulation and toxicity. Liver function is assessed using **alanine aminotransferase (ALT), aspartate aminotransferase (AST), and bilirubin levels.**

- **Drugs requiring dose reduction in hepatic impairment**

  - Opioids such as morphine and fentanyl
  - Warfarin, which has an increased anticoagulant effect due to reduced clotting factor synthesis

- ◦ Benzodiazepines, which may accumulate and cause excessive sedation

- Drugs that are contraindicated in severe liver disease

  - ◦ Paracetamol in high doses due to hepatotoxicity
  - ◦ Methotrexate, which can cause hepatic fibrosis

Case Study: Impact of Patient-Specific Parameters on Drug Therapy

A **68-year-old male with chronic kidney disease (CrCl = 25 mL/min), hypertension, and atrial fibrillation** was prescribed **warfarin, metoprolol, and amoxicillin for a respiratory infection**. After reviewing his **renal function and drug interactions**, the following modifications were made:

- **Warfarin dose was reduced and INR was closely monitored** to avoid excessive anticoagulation due to altered metabolism in chronic kidney disease.
- **Metoprolol dose was adjusted** to prevent bradycardia, as beta-blockers are eliminated more slowly in renal impairment.
- **Amoxicillin dose was reduced from 500 mg every 8 hours to 250 mg every 12 hours** to prevent accumulation and toxicity.

After implementing these adjustments, the patient's infection resolved without complications, and he did not experience bleeding or drug toxicity. This case highlights the importance of **tailoring pharmacotherapy based on renal function, drug metabolism, and comorbidities** to ensure safe and effective treatment.

1.3.3 Monitoring Therapeutic Outcomes

Monitoring therapeutic outcomes is an essential aspect of pharmacotherapy that ensures medications are achieving their intended effects while minimizing adverse reactions. Regular assessment helps determine whether a drug is providing clinical benefits, whether dose adjustments are necessary, and whether alternative treatments should be considered. Therapeutic monitoring involves evaluating clinical efficacy and identifying adverse effects, both of which contribute to optimizing patient care and improving long-term health outcomes.

Clinical Efficacy

Assessing the efficacy of a drug requires objective measurements that reflect the intended therapeutic effect. This evaluation varies depending on the disease being treated and the pharmacological mechanism of the drug. Clinical efficacy can be determined through laboratory markers, physiological parameters, and patient-reported outcomes.

Methods to Assess Drug Efficacy

1. **Hypertension Management**

- The effectiveness of antihypertensive medications is monitored by measuring blood pressure regularly.
- The target blood pressure for patients with hypertension is less than 130 over 80 millimeters of mercury.
- Home blood pressure monitoring is recommended to avoid white coat hypertension.

1. **Diabetes Control**

  - The primary marker for assessing diabetes management is glycated hemoglobin, which reflects average blood glucose levels over three months.
  - The target glycated hemoglobin level for most patients is less than seven percent.
  - Fasting blood glucose should be maintained between seventy to one hundred thirty milligrams per deciliter, while postprandial glucose should be less than one hundred eighty milligrams per deciliter.

2. **Hyperlipidemia Management**

  - Lipid-lowering therapy, such as statins, is evaluated by measuring low-density lipoprotein cholesterol levels.
  - The target for patients at high cardiovascular risk is less than seventy milligrams per deciliter.

3. **Anticoagulation Therapy**

- The efficacy of warfarin and other anticoagulants is assessed by monitoring the international normalized ratio.
- The therapeutic range for most indications, such as atrial fibrillation, is between two and three.
- If the international normalized ratio exceeds three, there is an increased risk of bleeding, while a value below two increases the risk of thromboembolism.

4. **Asthma Control**

- The efficacy of inhaled corticosteroids and bronchodilators is monitored using peak expiratory flow rate measurements.
- A peak expiratory flow greater than eighty percent of the patient's predicted value indicates good asthma control.

5. **Heart Failure Management**

- The effectiveness of heart failure medications is monitored by assessing ejection fraction using echocardiography.
- A left ventricular ejection fraction above fifty percent is considered normal, while values below forty percent indicate systolic dysfunction.

6. **Infectious Disease Treatment**

- Antibiotic therapy is monitored using clinical improvement parameters, such as resolution of fever and normalization of white blood cell count.
- In bacterial infections such as tuberculosis, treatment efficacy is confirmed by sputum culture conversion to negative after two months of therapy.

7. **Psychiatric Medication Monitoring**

- The response to antidepressants and antipsychotics is assessed using clinical rating scales.
- In schizophrenia, the positive and negative syndrome scale is used to measure symptom reduction.

Numerical Targets for Therapeutic Monitoring

- Blood pressure should be maintained below one hundred thirty over eighty millimeters of mercury in hypertensive patients.
- Glycated hemoglobin should be less than seven percent in diabetes management.
- Low-density lipoprotein cholesterol should be reduced to below seventy milligrams per deciliter in high-risk cardiovascular patients.
- The international normalized ratio should be maintained between two and three for most anticoagulated patients.
- Peak expiratory flow should be greater than eighty percent of the predicted value for optimal asthma control.
- Left ventricular ejection fraction should be maintained above forty percent in patients with heart failure.

Adverse Effect Profiles

While assessing therapeutic efficacy is crucial, monitoring for adverse drug effects is equally important to ensure patient safety. Certain medications carry predictable risks that require close observation, dose adjustments, or alternative therapies. Adverse drug reactions may be mild and self-limiting or severe enough to necessitate discontinuation of therapy.

Common Adverse Effects and Their Monitoring

1. **ACE Inhibitor-Induced Cough**

   - Up to thirty percent of patients on angiotensin-converting enzyme inhibitors experience a persistent dry cough.
   - The cough is attributed to bradykinin accumulation in the lungs.
   - If the cough becomes bothersome, switching to an angiotensin receptor blocker is recommended.

2. **Statin-Induced Myopathy**

   - Patients on statins should be monitored for muscle pain and weakness.
   - If creatine kinase levels exceed five times the upper normal limit, the statin should be discontinued.

- ◦ Lower doses or alternative lipid-lowering therapies may be considered.

3. **Metformin and Lactic Acidosis**

   - ◦ Patients with impaired renal function should be monitored for signs of lactic acidosis, such as fatigue and abdominal pain.
   - ◦ Metformin should be avoided if creatinine clearance is less than thirty milliliters per minute.

4. **Warfarin and Bleeding Risk**

   - ◦ Patients on warfarin require regular international normalized ratio monitoring to prevent excessive anticoagulation.
   - ◦ If the international normalized ratio exceeds four, the risk of major bleeding increases significantly.
   - ◦ In cases of life-threatening bleeding, vitamin k and fresh frozen plasma should be administered.

5. **Beta-Blockers and Bradycardia**

   - ◦ Beta-blockers can reduce heart rate excessively, leading to dizziness and fatigue.
   - ◦ If resting heart rate falls below fifty beats per minute, dose reduction or discontinuation should be considered.

6. **Aminoglycosides and Nephrotoxicity**

   - ◦ Renal function should be closely monitored in patients receiving aminoglycoside antibiotics.
   - ◦ If serum creatinine levels rise significantly, the drug should be discontinued or dosing intervals extended.

7. **Proton Pump Inhibitors and Hypomagnesemia**

   - ◦ Long-term proton pump inhibitor use can lead to hypomagnesemia, resulting in muscle cramps and arrhythmias.

◦ Magnesium levels should be checked in patients on prolonged therapy.

8. Antipsychotic-Induced Tardive Dyskinesia

◦ Chronic use of dopamine-blocking antipsychotics can lead to involuntary movements of the face and extremities.
◦ Discontinuation or switching to a second-generation antipsychotic may be necessary.

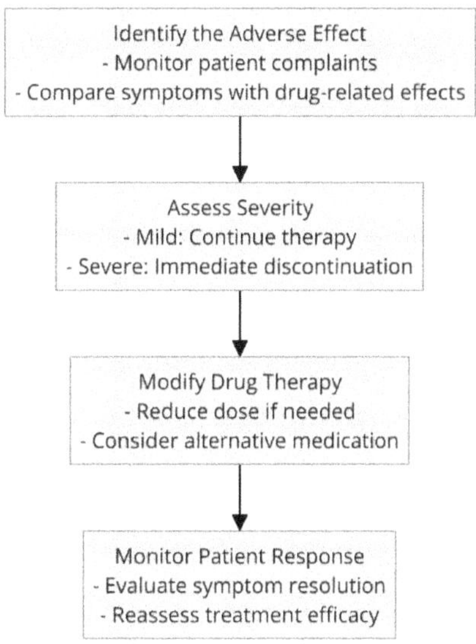

Flowchart for Adverse Effect Management

REVIEW QUESTIONS

1. Discuss the scope and objectives of pharmacotherapeutics in clinical practice.
2. Explain the importance of pharmacotherapeutics in improving clinical outcomes.
3. How does pharmacotherapeutics bridge the gap between pathophysiology and treatment?
4. Outline the primary goals of pharmacotherapy.
5. Describe the concept of evidence-based medicine (EBM) and its relevance in pharmacotherapeutics.
6. What are the fundamental principles of evidence-based medicine?
7. Explain the hierarchy of evidence in evidence-based medicine.
8. Discuss the role of pharmacists in promoting evidence-based medicine.
9. What does patient-centric pharmacotherapy mean, and why is it important?
10. How does tailored dosing contribute to effective pharmacotherapy?
11. Explain the role of clinical parameters such as age, weight, and comorbidities in designing an individualized therapeutic plan.
12. Discuss how laboratory parameters, such as liver and renal function, affect pharmacotherapy decisions.
13. What strategies can be employed to monitor therapeutic outcomes in patient-centric pharmacotherapy?
14. How can a clinician balance the goals of cure, symptom management, and prevention when selecting pharmacotherapy?
15. Discuss the challenges of integrating evidence-based medicine into everyday clinical practice.
16. How do clinical guidelines and systematic reviews support pharmacotherapeutic decision-making?
17. Explain the significance of randomized controlled trials (RCTs) in the hierarchy of evidence.
18. What role does meta-analysis play in evidence-based pharmacotherapy?
19. How do patient preferences and values influence the application of evidence-based medicine in pharmacotherapy?
20. In what ways can pharmacists help to mitigate adverse drug reactions through evidence-based practices?

21. Discuss how personalized medicine is related to patient-centric pharmacotherapy.
22. What are some common challenges in tailoring drug therapy to individual patients?
23. How can the use of electronic health records (EHRs) facilitate evidence-based and patient-centric pharmacotherapy?
24. Describe how ongoing monitoring of therapeutic outcomes can inform adjustments in a patient's pharmacotherapy plan.
25. Reflect on the future directions of pharmacotherapeutics.

MCQS

1. **Pharmacotherapeutics primarily deals with:**
   A) The economic aspects of drug production
   B) The clinical use of drugs to treat diseases
   C) The chemical synthesis of medications
   D) The distribution of pharmaceuticals
   Correct Answer: B

2. **Which of the following best defines evidence-based medicine (EBM)?**
   A) Medicine based solely on expert opinions
   B) Integrating clinical expertise with the best available research evidence and patient values
   C) Relying on traditional practices without scientific support
   D) Using anecdotal experiences for treatment decisions
   Correct Answer: B

3. **The hierarchy of evidence places randomized controlled trials (RCTs) at the:**
   A) Bottom
   B) Middle
   C) Top
   D) Lowest level
   Correct Answer: C

4. **Patient-centric pharmacotherapy emphasizes:**
   A) Standardized treatment for all patients
   B) Tailoring therapeutic plans based on individual patient characteristics
   C) Reducing the role of patient input in treatment decisions
   D) Focusing only on cost-effective medications
   Correct Answer: B

5. **One of the primary goals of pharmacotherapy is to:**
   A) Increase the cost of treatment
   B) Cure, manage symptoms, and prevent disease progression
   C) Replace surgical interventions entirely
   D) Focus solely on experimental therapies
   Correct Answer: B

6. **The pharmacist's role in evidence-based medicine includes:**
   A) Solely dispensing medications
   B) Evaluating and applying clinical evidence to optimize drug therapy
   C) Designing drug manufacturing processes
   D) Overseeing hospital administrative functions
   Correct Answer: B

7. **Tailored dosing is important because it helps to:**
   A) Standardize treatment regardless of patient differences
   B) Optimize drug efficacy and minimize adverse effects based on patient-specific factors
   C) Increase the overall dosage for all patients
   D) Eliminate the need for therapeutic monitoring
   Correct Answer: B

8. **Which parameter is critical when adjusting a drug dose for a patient with renal impairment?**
   A) Blood pressure
   B) Renal function (e.g., creatinine clearance)
   C) Skin tone
   D) Height
   Correct Answer: B

9. **Evidence-based medicine requires clinicians to consider:**
   A) Only the cost of treatment
   B) The best available research, clinical expertise, and patient preferences
   C) Historical treatment methods exclusively
   D) Only laboratory test results
   Correct Answer: B

10. **Which of the following is an example of a clinical parameter important for individualized pharmacotherapy?**
    A) Age
    B) Blood type
    C) Shoe size
    D) Hair color
    Correct Answer: A

11. **Pharmacotherapeutics helps to bridge pathophysiology with treatment by:**
    A) Ignoring the disease mechanism
    B) Using knowledge of disease processes to select appropriate drugs
    C) Focusing only on drug side effects

D) Limiting treatment options to one drug class

Correct Answer: B

12. **Which of the following best describes symptom management in pharmacotherapy?**

    A) Completely curing the disease

    B) Reducing or alleviating the symptoms without necessarily curing the disease

    C) Ignoring patient discomfort

    D) Increasing the duration of symptoms

    Correct Answer: B

13. **Preventive pharmacotherapy primarily aims to:**

    A) Treat diseases only after they occur

    B) Prevent the onset or recurrence of disease

    C) Increase hospitalization rates

    D) Replace lifestyle modifications

    Correct Answer: B

14. **The term "hierarchy of evidence" refers to:**

    A) A ranking of diseases based on severity

    B) The systematic arrangement of research evidence according to its quality and reliability

    C) A list of medications arranged by cost

    D) A ranking of hospitals based on patient outcomes

    Correct Answer: B

15. **Which type of study is considered the highest level of evidence?**

    A) Case reports

    B) Randomized controlled trials (RCTs)

    C) Expert opinion

    D) In vitro studies

    Correct Answer: B

16. **The concept of "bridging pathophysiology with treatment" involves:**

    A) Ignoring the underlying disease mechanism

    B) Understanding how a drug's mechanism of action targets the biological basis of a disease

    C) Focusing solely on patient symptoms

    D) Relying exclusively on diagnostic tests

    Correct Answer: B

17. **Patient-specific laboratory parameters, such as liver function tests, are used to:**

A) Predict hair color changes

B) Guide dosage adjustments and monitor potential drug toxicity

C) Determine a patient's blood type

D) Assess mental health status

Correct Answer: B

18. **In evidence-based medicine, clinical expertise refers to:**

A) The personal opinions of a clinician without any scientific support

B) The skill and experience of a clinician in diagnosing and treating patients

C) The financial background of a clinician

D) The educational qualifications of a pharmacist only

Correct Answer: B

19. **Which of the following best describes a patient-centric therapeutic plan?**

A) A one-size-fits-all approach

B) An individualized treatment strategy based on the patient's unique clinical and laboratory parameters

C) A plan that ignores patient preferences

D) A treatment regimen chosen solely based on cost considerations

Correct Answer: B

20. **Monitoring therapeutic outcomes in pharmacotherapy involves assessing:**

A) Only the economic cost of the drug

B) Clinical efficacy and adverse effect profiles

C) The color and shape of the medication

D) The geographic location of the patient

Correct Answer: B

21. **Which of the following is an example of an adverse effect that must be monitored during pharmacotherapy?**

A) Improved vision

B) Drug-induced liver injury

C) Weight gain that is beneficial

D) Enhanced cognitive function

Correct Answer: B

22. **The goals of pharmacotherapy include all of the following EXCEPT:**

A) Cure

B) Symptom management

C) Prevention

D) Increasing treatment costs

Correct Answer: D

23. **Which role does the pharmacist play in evidence-based medicine?**

    A) Solely dispensing medications without further involvement

    B) Evaluating research, assisting in medication therapy management, and educating patients

    C) Only handling administrative tasks

    D) Designing pharmaceutical manufacturing processes

    Correct Answer: B

24. **Individualized therapeutic plans often require consideration of a patient's comorbidities because:**

    A) Comorbidities have no effect on drug choice

    B) They can affect drug metabolism, efficacy, and safety

    C) They simplify the selection of a single treatment for all conditions

    D) They are irrelevant to pharmacotherapy decisions

    Correct Answer: B

25. **Which aspect of evidence-based medicine ensures that clinical decisions remain patient-focused?**

    A) Ignoring the latest research findings

    B) Integrating patient values and preferences into treatment decisions

    C) Relying solely on laboratory data

    D) Following a fixed protocol regardless of patient differences

    Correct Answer: B

26. **Pharmacotherapeutics is essential in clinical practice because it:**

    A) Promotes the use of untested treatments

    B) Guides clinicians in selecting the most appropriate therapy based on scientific evidence

    C) Focuses exclusively on cost reduction

    D) Limits therapeutic options to one medication

    Correct Answer: B

27. **A key benefit of using evidence-based medicine is that it:**

    A) Replaces clinical judgment entirely

    B) Provides a systematic approach to decision-making that improves patient outcomes

    C) Disregards patient feedback

    D) Focuses solely on historical data

    Correct Answer: B

28. **When adjusting drug doses, why is patient weight an important parameter?**

A) It determines the color of the medication

B) It helps calculate the appropriate dose to achieve therapeutic efficacy without toxicity

C) It is used to schedule patient appointments

D) It solely determines the drug's cost

Correct Answer: B

29. **The process of monitoring therapeutic outcomes includes:**

A) Only checking if the patient feels better

B) Systematically assessing both the clinical benefits and potential adverse effects of the treatment

C) Discontinuing treatment immediately after symptom resolution

D) Relying solely on patient self-report without clinical evaluation

Correct Answer: B

30. **In patient-centric pharmacotherapy, which factor is least likely to influence drug dosing?**

A) Age

B) Weight

C) Comorbidities

D) Patient's favorite color

Correct Answer: D

31. **The integration of pathophysiology with pharmacotherapy helps clinicians to:**

A) Randomly select medications

B) Target the underlying disease mechanisms for more effective treatment

C) Avoid using any diagnostic tests

D) Focus only on symptomatic relief

Correct Answer: B

32. **Which level of evidence is considered the strongest in the hierarchy?**

A) Expert opinion

B) Case series

C) Randomized controlled trials (RCTs)

D) Observational studies

Correct Answer: C

33. **A major challenge in implementing evidence-based medicine is:**

A) A surplus of high-quality evidence

B) The rapid evolution of clinical research and its integration into practice

C) A complete lack of patient diversity

D) An overreliance on anecdotal evidence

Correct Answer: B

34. **The pharmacist's role in evidence-based medicine often includes:**

A) Solely focusing on drug manufacturing

B) Reviewing clinical studies to inform medication therapy management

C) Ignoring recent research findings

D) Only managing inventory

Correct Answer: B

35. **In developing individualized therapeutic plans, why are liver function tests important?**

A) They determine the patient's blood type

B) They help assess the patient's ability to metabolize drugs

C) They predict a patient's response to dietary changes

D) They are used to measure bone density

Correct Answer: B

36. **Which of the following best illustrates the concept of symptom management in pharmacotherapy?**

A) Administering antibiotics to cure an infection

B) Using analgesics to relieve pain while the underlying condition is treated

C) Performing surgery to remove a tumor

D) Ignoring patient symptoms in favor of long-term prevention

Correct Answer: B

37. **Preventive pharmacotherapy primarily aims to:**

A) Treat symptoms after they occur

B) Prevent the onset or recurrence of disease

C) Increase the dosage of medication unnecessarily

D) Focus solely on cost reduction

Correct Answer: B

38. **Which of the following is NOT a principle of evidence-based medicine?**

A) Integration of the best research evidence

B) Clinical expertise

C) Patient values and preferences

D) Ignoring high-quality research

Correct Answer: D

39. **Individualized therapeutic plans often rely on which type of data to determine the proper dose?**
    A) Patient-specific clinical and laboratory parameters
    B) General population averages without adjustment
    C) The clinician's personal preference only
    D) The cheapest available medication
    Correct Answer: A

40. **Which of the following is a key outcome monitored in patient-centric pharmacotherapy?**
    A) Clinical efficacy and adverse effect profiles
    B) The number of pills dispensed
    C) The brand popularity of the drug
    D) Only the cost of the medication
    Correct Answer: A

41. **Evidence-based medicine improves patient care by:**
    A) Relying exclusively on traditional practices
    B) Guiding treatment decisions with current best evidence
    C) Ignoring patient-specific factors
    D) Utilizing outdated research findings
    Correct Answer: B

42. **Pharmacotherapeutics is important in clinical practice because it:**
    A) Focuses solely on the biochemical properties of drugs
    B) Integrates drug therapy with clinical outcomes to improve patient health
    C) Neglects the disease mechanism
    D) Only considers the economic impact of drugs
    Correct Answer: B

43. **Which of the following best describes a randomized controlled trial (RCT)?**
    A) A study design where participants are randomly assigned to treatment or control groups
    B) A study based on observational data
    C) A trial that only includes historical data
    D) An expert opinion forum
    Correct Answer: A

44. **Patient-specific factors such as comorbidities are critical in pharmacotherapy because they:**

A) Have no impact on drug therapy decisions

B) Influence drug selection, dosing, and potential interactions

C) Are only considered in surgical treatments

D) Are irrelevant to clinical outcomes

Correct Answer: B

45. **The term "pharmacotherapy" refers to:**

A) The study of drug manufacturing processes

B) The therapeutic use of drugs to treat disease

C) The distribution of medications to pharmacies

D) The economic evaluation of healthcare

Correct Answer: B

46. **A key component of bridging pathophysiology with treatment is understanding:**

A) The chemical structure of a drug only

B) How a drug's mechanism of action targets the underlying disease process

C) The administrative procedures in a hospital

D) Patient scheduling protocols

Correct Answer: B

47. **Which of the following is an example of a laboratory parameter used in patient-specific pharmacotherapy?**

A) Height measurement

B) Renal function tests (e.g., serum creatinine)

C) Hair color analysis

D) Body temperature

Correct Answer: B

48. **Clinical efficacy in monitoring therapeutic outcomes is measured by:**

A) The cost of the drug

B) The degree to which a treatment achieves its intended health benefits

C) The number of medications prescribed

D) The duration of the prescription

Correct Answer: B

49. **Adverse effect profiles are monitored to:**

A) Increase drug dosages regardless of side effects

B) Identify, manage, and minimize harmful side effects of a drug

C) Ignore patient complaints

D) Ensure that all patients experience the same side effects

Correct Answer: B

50. **Which aspect of patient-centric pharmacotherapy is essential for ensuring long-term treatment success?**
    A) Ignoring patient feedback
    B) Regular monitoring and adjustment of therapy based on outcomes
    C) Using a fixed treatment protocol for everyone
    D) Focusing solely on initial treatment without follow-up
    Correct Answer: B

51. **In evidence-based medicine, the "best available evidence" is typically derived from:**
    A) Anecdotal reports
    B) High-quality clinical research studies such as RCTs and meta-analyses
    C) Unverified internet sources
    D) Historical texts only
    Correct Answer: B

52. **A pharmacist contributes to patient-centric pharmacotherapy by:**
    A) Dispensing drugs without counseling
    B) Collaborating with the healthcare team to individualize and optimize medication therapy
    C) Focusing exclusively on drug pricing
    D) Avoiding patient interactions
    Correct Answer: B

53. **Which of the following best exemplifies symptom management?**
    A) Using an antihypertensive to reduce blood pressure
    B) Using an analgesic to relieve pain while underlying inflammation is treated
    C) Administering a vaccine
    D) Performing a surgical procedure
    Correct Answer: B

54. **The process of "bridging pathophysiology with treatment" involves:**
    A) Treating the patient's symptoms without addressing the disease mechanism
    B) Using an understanding of the disease's underlying mechanisms to guide therapy selection
    C) Choosing treatment based solely on cost
    D) Ignoring laboratory findings
    Correct Answer: B

55. **Which of the following is an example of preventive pharmacotherapy?**
    A) Prescribing statins to reduce the risk of cardiovascular events

B) Using pain relievers to treat headaches

C) Administering antibiotics to treat an infection

D) Prescribing antipyretics for fever management

Correct Answer: A

56. **In evidence-based medicine, a systematic review is designed to:**

A) Provide a narrative of personal opinions

B) Summarize and critically evaluate all relevant studies on a particular topic

C) Report only one case study

D) Offer unverified recommendations

Correct Answer: B

57. **Which factor is most likely to influence tailored dosing in pharmacotherapy?**

A) The patient's eye color

B) The patient's weight and age

C) The brand name of the drug

D) The clinician's personal preferences

Correct Answer: B

58. **Patient-centric pharmacotherapy is best achieved when:**

A) All patients receive the same standardized treatment

B) Therapy is individualized based on clinical, laboratory, and patient-specific parameters

C) Treatment decisions are made solely by insurance companies

D) Pharmacotherapy ignores patient history

Correct Answer: B

59. **Which of the following best describes the term "adverse effect profile"?**

A) A list of all the benefits of a drug

B) A summary of the side effects and potential risks associated with a drug

C) The cost analysis of a drug

D) A measure of a drug's efficacy only

Correct Answer: B

60. **The ultimate goal of integrating evidence-based and patient-centric approaches in pharmacotherapy is to:**

A) Standardize treatment without regard to individual differences

B) Optimize patient outcomes by using the best available evidence and tailoring therapy to individual needs

C) Increase the complexity of treatment without improving outcomes
D) Rely solely on cost-effectiveness analysis
Correct Answer: B

CHAPTER TWO

Gastrointestinal System

2.1 Peptic Ulcer Disease (PUD)

2.1.1 Pathophysiology

Peptic ulcer disease is characterized by the formation of open sores in the gastric or duodenal mucosa due to an imbalance between aggressive and protective factors in the stomach. The primary aggressive factors include excessive acid secretion, Helicobacter pylori infection, and chronic nonsteroidal anti-inflammatory drug use, while protective factors include mucus secretion, bicarbonate production, and mucosal blood flow. Disruption of this balance leads to mucosal damage and ulcer formation.

Balance Between Acid Secretion and Mucosal Protective Mechanisms

The stomach maintains a delicate balance between **acid secretion** by parietal cells and protective mechanisms that prevent mucosal damage.

1. **Acid Secretion by Parietal Cells**

   - Parietal cells in the gastric mucosa secrete **hydrochloric acid** through the action of the **H+/K+ ATPase proton pump**.
   - Acid secretion is stimulated by three key pathways:

     - **Gastrin:** Secreted by G cells in response to food intake, stimulating histamine release from enterochromaffin-like cells.
     - **Histamine:** Binds to H2 receptors on parietal cells, activating cyclic adenosine monophosphate and increasing acid secretion.
     - **Acetylcholine:** Released by the vagus nerve, stimulating muscarinic M3 receptors and enhancing acid output.

2. Protective Mechanisms Against Acid Damage

- **Mucus Layer:** Goblet cells secrete a thick mucus barrier that prevents direct contact of acid with the gastric lining.
- **Bicarbonate Secretion:** Neutralizes acid at the epithelial surface, maintaining a pH gradient.
- **Prostaglandins:** Stimulate mucus and bicarbonate production while promoting mucosal blood flow, aiding in tissue repair.

When aggressive factors overpower protective mechanisms, mucosal damage occurs, leading to the formation of ulcers.

Role of Helicobacter pylori in Peptic Ulcer Disease

Helicobacter pylori is a gram-negative, spiral-shaped bacterium that colonizes the gastric mucosa and plays a significant role in ulcer formation.

1. Mechanisms of Mucosal Damage

- **Urease Activity:** H. pylori produces urease, an enzyme that hydrolyzes urea into ammonia, neutralizing stomach acid and creating an alkaline environment that allows bacterial survival.
- **Inflammatory Response:** The bacterium induces an immune response, leading to **chronic gastritis** and mucosal injury.
- **Toxins:** Cytotoxin-associated gene A (CagA) and vacuolating cytotoxin A (VacA) disrupt tight junctions in epithelial cells, increasing mucosal permeability and ulcer susceptibility.

2. Prevalence of H. pylori in Peptic Ulcer Disease

- Helicobacter pylori infection is found in **seventy to ninety percent of duodenal ulcer cases** and **fifty to seventy percent of gastric ulcers.**
- Eradication therapy significantly reduces ulcer recurrence rates, with triple therapy achieving a **ninety-five percent eradication rate.**

Impact of Nonsteroidal Anti-Inflammatory Drugs on Peptic Ulcer Disease

Nonsteroidal anti-inflammatory drugs (NSAIDs) are another major cause of peptic ulcer disease, particularly in **chronic users.** These medications contribute to ulcer formation through multiple mechanisms.

1. **Mechanism of NSAID-Induced Ulcers**

    - NSAIDs inhibit **cyclooxygenase-1 (COX-1)**, an enzyme responsible for **prostaglandin synthesis.**
    - Reduced prostaglandin levels lead to:

      - **Decreased mucus and bicarbonate secretion**, weakening the protective barrier.
      - **Reduced mucosal blood flow**, impairing repair mechanisms.
      - **Increased gastric acid secretion**, further contributing to mucosal injury.

2. **Prevalence of NSAID-Induced Ulcers**

    - **Twenty-five percent of chronic NSAID users develop ulcers**, with many remaining asymptomatic until complications such as bleeding or perforation occur.
    - The risk of ulcer development increases with higher doses and longer duration of NSAID therapy.
    - **Elderly patients are at a higher risk** due to decreased mucosal defense and concurrent use of multiple medications.

Patients on long-term NSAIDs, particularly those with a history of ulcers, are often prescribed **proton pump inhibitors or misoprostol** to prevent gastric mucosal damage.

Diagram of Acid Secretion Pathways

A diagram illustrating **acid secretion regulation** can be helpful in understanding the pathophysiology of peptic ulcer disease. The image should include:

1. **Parietal cells and H+/K+ ATPase pump** responsible for acid secretion.
2. **Gastrin, histamine, and acetylcholine pathways** stimulating acid production.
3. **Mucosal protective factors, including mucus and bicarbonate secretion.**

This visual representation will clarify the **interplay between acid secretion and mucosal defense**, highlighting the mechanisms targeted by anti-ulcer therapies such as proton pump inhibitors, H2 receptor antagonists, and prostaglandin analogs.

2.1.2 Diagnosis

The diagnosis of peptic ulcer disease involves a combination of **clinical assessment, non-invasive tests, and invasive procedures such as endoscopy and biopsy**. The choice of diagnostic method depends on the severity of symptoms, patient history, and the need for detecting **Helicobacter pylori infection**, which is a major contributor to ulcer formation. **Non-invasive tests** are preferred for initial screening, while **endoscopy and biopsy** are used in cases where complications or malignancy are suspected.

Non-Invasive Tests

Non-invasive tests are commonly used to detect Helicobacter pylori infection, which is present in the majority of patients with peptic ulcers. These tests are easy to perform, cost-effective, and suitable for both initial diagnosis and post-treatment monitoring.

Urea Breath Test

The urea breath test is one of the most accurate non-invasive methods for detecting Helicobacter pylori infection.

1. **Principle**

   - Helicobacter pylori produces **urease**, an enzyme that breaks down **urea** into **carbon dioxide and ammonia**.
   - In the test, the patient ingests **radioactive or non-radioactive urea labeled with carbon-13 or carbon-14**.
   - If Helicobacter pylori is present, the urease enzyme metabolizes urea, releasing labeled carbon dioxide, which is detected in the patient's breath.

2. **Sensitivity and Specificity**

   - The urea breath test has a **sensitivity and specificity greater than ninety percent**, making it highly reliable for detecting active infections.
   - It is particularly useful in confirming eradication after treatment.

3. **Advantages and Limitations**

   - **Advantages:**

     - Non-invasive and convenient.
     - Detects only active infections, reducing the risk of false positives.

   - **Limitations:**

     - False negatives may occur if the patient has recently taken **proton pump inhibitors, antibiotics, or bismuth-containing compounds**, as these can suppress Helicobacter pylori.
     - Requires specialized equipment for breath sample analysis.

Stool Antigen Test
The stool antigen test detects **Helicobacter pylori antigens in feces** and is widely used for initial diagnosis and post-treatment monitoring.

1. **Principle**

   - The test uses **enzyme-linked immunosorbent assay (ELISA) or immunochromatographic methods** to detect Helicobacter pylori antigens in stoo
     l samples.

2. **Sensitivity and Specificity**

   - The stool antigen test has a **sensitivity and specificity of eighty-eight to ninety-eight percent**, making it a reliable diagnostic tool.

3. **Advantages and Limitations**

   - **Advantages:**

     - Non-invasive and does not require fasting.
     - Suitable for both diagnosis and monitoring eradication.

   - **Limitations:**

- False negatives can occur if the patient is on **proton pump inhibitors, antibiotics, or bismuth therapy.**
- Some patients may find sample collection inconvenient.

Both the urea breath test and the stool antigen test are recommended by guidelines for diagnosing Helicobacter pylori infection and confirming eradication after treatment.

Test	Sensitivity (%)	Specificity (%)	Best Used For	Limitations
Urea Breath Test	95-98	95-98	Detecting active Helicobacter pylori infection, confirming eradication	False negatives with recent proton pump inhibitor or antibiotic use
Stool Antigen Test	88-98	88-98	Initial diagnosis, post-treatment monitoring	Affected by recent antibiotic or proton pump inhibitor use
Endoscopy with Biopsy	90-95	100	Diagnosis of ulcers, malignancy, and Helicobacter pylori	Invasive, expensive, requires sedation
Rapid Urease Test	90-95	90-100	Fast Helicobacter pylori detection	False negatives in atrophic gastritis

Comparison of Diagnostic Methods

Endoscopy and Biopsy

Endoscopy is the **gold standard** for diagnosing peptic ulcer disease, particularly in cases of **complicated ulcers, persistent symptoms, or suspected malignancy.** This invasive procedure allows direct visualization of the gastric and duodenal mucosa, facilitating **biopsy collection and histological examination.**

Indications for Endoscopy

- **Patients with alarm symptoms**, including weight loss, gastrointestinal bleeding, anemia, or persistent vomiting.
- **Patients over forty-five to fifty years of age** with new-onset dyspepsia.
- **Recurrent or refractory ulcers** despite medical therapy.
- **Suspicion of gastric malignancy**, especially in patients with chronic Helicobacter pylori infection.

Endoscopic Findings

- **Gastric ulcers:** Appear as **well-defined mucosal breaks** with surrounding inflammation, often located in the antrum or body of the stomach.
- **Duodenal ulcers:** Typically **smaller and located in the proximal duodenum**, commonly on the anterior wall.
- **Complications:** Endoscopy can identify **bleeding ulcers, perforation, or pyloric obstruction.**

Biopsy and Histological Examination

Biopsy specimens collected during endoscopy are examined for:

1. **Helicobacter pylori Detection**

   - Histological staining methods such as **hematoxylin and eosin (H&E), Giemsa stain, and immunohistochemistry** allow visualization of the bacteria in the gastric mucosa.
   - The **rapid urease test (CLO test)** is commonly performed on biopsy specimens. If Helicobacter pylori is present, urease converts urea into ammonia, leading to a **color change in the test medium** within

minutes to hours.

2. **Gastric Mucosal Changes**

- In **Helicobacter pylori-associated gastritis**, histology shows **lymphocytic infiltration, neutrophilic activity, and glandular atrophy**.
- **Intestinal metaplasia and dysplasia** suggest a higher risk of gastric cancer.

3. **Ruling Out Malignancy**

- **Young patients with mild symptoms** and no alarm features can be diagnosed using a **non-invasive test such as the urea breath test or stool antigen test**.
- **Patients with persistent or severe symptoms, gastrointestinal bleeding, or weight loss require endoscopy with biopsy** to confirm ulcer presence and exclude malignancy.
- **Post-treatment monitoring is best done using the stool antigen test or urea breath test**, typically four weeks after completion of therapy.

2.1.3 Pharmacological Management

Pharmacological management of peptic ulcer disease aims to promote **ulcer healing, relieve symptoms, eradicate Helicobacter pylori infection, and prevent recurrence**. The primary drug classes used include **proton pump inhibitors, H2 receptor antagonists, antibiotics, and cytoprotective agents**. Among these, **proton pump inhibitors (PPIs)** are the most effective in suppressing gastric acid production, facilitating ulcer healing, and preventing complications.

2.1.3.1 Proton Pump Inhibitors (PPIs)

Proton pump inhibitors are the first-line therapy for **peptic ulcer disease**, providing superior acid suppression compared to H2 receptor antagonists. They are widely used for **treating active ulcers, preventing ulcer recurrence, and as part of Helicobacter pylori eradication therapy**.

Mechanism of Action

Proton pump inhibitors work by **irreversibly inhibiting the H+/K+ ATPase enzyme (proton pump) in the parietal cells of the stomach,** which is responsible for the final step in gastric acid secretion.

- **Under normal conditions:**

  - Parietal cells secrete gastric acid by actively transporting **hydrogen ions into the stomach lumen** through the proton pump.
  - Acid secretion is stimulated by **gastrin, histamine, and acetylcholine.**

- **Effect of proton pump inhibitors:**

  - The drugs bind covalently to the proton pump, **blocking acid secretion for 24 to 48 hours.**
  - Since the enzyme needs to be resynthesized for acid secretion to resume, proton pump inhibitors provide **prolonged acid suppression** even after a single dose.
  - The gastric pH increases, creating an environment favorable for **ulcer healing** and reducing the risk of complications such as bleeding.

Drug	Usual Dose for Peptic Ulcer Disease
Omeprazole	20–40 mg once daily
Pantoprazole	40 mg once daily
Esomeprazole	20–40 mg once daily
Lansoprazole	30 mg once daily
Rabeprazole	20 mg once daily

-

In cases of **severe peptic ulcer disease or upper gastrointestinal** bleeding, higher doses or **intravenous formulations (e.g., pantoprazole 80 mg IV bolus followed by continuous infusion of 8 mg/hour for 72**

hours) may be required.

For **Helicobacter pylori eradication,** proton pump inhibitors are given twice daily as part of **triple or quadruple therapy.**
Indications for Proton Pump Inhibitors

- **Peptic ulcer disease treatment**

    - Proton pump inhibitors **accelerate ulcer healing** by maintaining an intragastric pH above four, preventing further mucosal injury.
    - Healing rates exceed **90% within 4–8 weeks of therapy.**

    Side Effects of Proton Pump Inhibitors
    While proton pump inhibitors are **well-tolerated,** prolonged use has been associated with **several adverse effects.**

- **Hypomagnesemia**

    - Long-term use (>1 year) can lead to **low magnesium levels,** causing symptoms such as muscle cramps, weakness, and cardiac arrhythmias.
    - Mechanism: **Reduced intestinal magnesium absorption** due to altered transport mechanisms.
    - Monitoring: Serum magnesium levels should be checked periodically in long-term users.

- **Bone Fractures**

    - Chronic proton pump inhibitor use is linked to **an increased risk of hip, spine, and wrist fractures,** especially in elderly patients.
    - Mechanism: **Reduced calcium absorption** due to impaired gastric acid production, leading to decreased **bone mineral density.**
    - Preventive Measures: Adequate calcium and vitamin D intake is recommended in long-term users.

- **Clostridium difficile Infection**

- Prolonged suppression of gastric acid can alter gut microbiota, **increasing susceptibility to Clostridium difficile infection**, which causes **severe diarrhea and colitis.**

- **Vitamin B12 Deficiency**

  - Acid is required for **cleaving vitamin B12 from dietary proteins.** Chronic proton pump inhibitor use can lead to **impaired absorption and deficiency**, resulting in **neurological symptoms and anemia.**

- **Rebound Acid Hypersecretion**

  - Discontinuation of proton pump inhibitors may cause a **temporary increase in gastric acid secretion**, leading to worsening dyspepsia.

Gradual tapering is recommended in long-term users to minimize this effect.

Aspect	Details
Mechanism	Irreversible inhibition of H+/K+ ATPase, reducing acid secretion
Common Drugs	Omeprazole (20–40 mg/day), Pantoprazole (40 mg/day)
Indications	Peptic ulcer healing, Helicobacter pylori eradication, NSAID-associated ulcers, GERD, Zollinger-Ellison syndrome
Adverse Effects	Hypomagnesemia, bone fractures, Clostridium difficile infection, vitamin B12 deficiency
Monitoring	Serum magnesium levels in long-term users, bone density screening in high-risk patients

Summary and Clinical Considerations

2.1.3.2 H2 Receptor Antagonists

H2 receptor antagonists reduce gastric acid secretion by **blocking histamine H2 receptors on the parietal cells of the stomach**, leading to decreased stimulation of the proton pump. Histamine normally binds to these receptors and triggers acid release, but H2 receptor antagonists prevent this process, resulting in **lower gastric acid production.**

The two most commonly used drugs in this class are **ranitidine and famotidine.** Ranitidine was widely prescribed but has been withdrawn in many countries due to concerns about contamination with **N-nitrosodimethylamine (NDMA), a potential carcinogen.** Famotidine remains available and is often used in patients who require **alternative acid suppression therapy** due to proton pump inhibitor intolerance.

H2 receptor antagonists are particularly effective for **night-time acid suppression**, as histamine-mediated acid release is most prominent during the night. Unlike proton pump inhibitors, which require several doses before full acid suppression is achieved, H2 receptor antagonists act **rapidly**, making them useful for **on-demand symptom relief.**

Common dosing regimens include **famotidine 20–40 mg once daily at bedtime.** While they are generally well tolerated, long-term use may be associated with **tachyphylaxis**, where the drug's effectiveness diminishes over time due to receptor upregulation.

2.1.3.3 Antibiotics for Helicobacter pylori Eradication

The eradication of Helicobacter pylori is essential for **long-term ulcer healing and prevention of recurrence.** Antibiotic therapy is combined with acid suppression therapy to enhance bacterial clearance.

The two most commonly used **standard regimens** are:

- **Triple Therapy (14 Days)**

    - Proton pump inhibitor (twice daily).
    - Amoxicillin 1 gram twice daily.
    - Clarithromycin 500 milligrams twice daily.
    - This regimen achieves an **eradication rate of 80 to 85 percent** when properly adhered to.

- **Bismuth-Based Quadruple Therapy (10–14 Days)**

    - Proton pump inhibitor (twice daily).
    - Bismuth subsalicylate 300 milligrams four times daily.
    - Tetracycline 500 milligrams four times daily.

- ◦ Metronidazole 500 milligrams three times daily.
- ◦ This regimen achieves **eradication rates of 85 to 90 percent**, making it preferable in areas with **high clarithromycin resistance.**

The choice of regimen depends on **antibiotic resistance patterns, patient allergies, and previous treatment history.** In patients allergic to **penicillin,** metronidazole can be substituted for amoxicillin. **Adherence to the full regimen** is crucial for success, as incomplete therapy contributes to antibiotic resistance and treatment failure.

2.1.3.4 Cytoprotective Agents

Cytoprotective agents help **enhance gastric mucosal defense mechanisms** and support ulcer healing by **forming protective barriers over ulcerated areas or increasing mucus production.**

- ◦ **Sucralfate**

  - ◦ Sucralfate is a **complex of aluminum hydroxide and sulfated sucrose** that binds to ulcerated mucosa, forming a **physical protective layer** that shields the ulcer from acid and pepsin.
  - ◦ It **stimulates prostaglandin release**, enhancing mucus and bicarbonate secretion.
  - ◦ Standard dosage is **one gram four times daily** on an empty stomach.
  - ◦ Side effects are minimal but include **constipation and interference with the absorption of other medications,** particularly fluoroquinolones and tetracyclines.

- ◦ **Bismuth Subsalicylate**

  - ◦ Bismuth subsalicylate has **antibacterial, anti-inflammatory, and gastroprotective properties.** It helps in Helicobacter pylori eradication and also **coats the gastric mucosa,** preventing further damage.
  - ◦ It is commonly used as part of **quadruple therapy for Helicobacter pylori eradication.**
  - ◦ Side effects include **black stools and constipation,** which are benign and caused by bismuth oxidation in the gastrointestinal tract.

2.1.4 Lifestyle Modifications

- Lifestyle modifications play a **supportive role** in the management of peptic ulcer disease, complementing pharmacotherapy by reducing risk factors that contribute to ulcer formation and recurrence.
- **Smoking Cessation**

  - Smoking **impairs gastric mucosal blood flow, reduces bicarbonate secretion,** and **delays ulcer healing.**
  - It is associated with **a twofold increase in ulcer recurrence rates,** particularly in patients with Helicobacter pylori infection.
  - Stopping smoking **enhances treatment efficacy and reduces the risk of complications such as perforation and bleeding.**

- **Avoidance of Dietary Triggers**

  - While **dietary factors do not directly cause ulcers,** certain foods can exacerbate symptoms by **increasing acid production or irritating the gastric lining.**
  - Patients are advised to avoid:

    - **Spicy foods, acidic foods, and caffeinated beverages,** which can worsen symptoms.
    - **Excessive alcohol consumption,** as it **weakens the mucosal barrier** and promotes acid secretion.

- **Role of Stress Management**

  - Chronic psychological stress has been associated with **increased gastric acid secretion and impaired mucosal defense,** potentially exacerbating ulcer symptoms.
  - Relaxation techniques such as **meditation, deep breathing exercises, and physical activity** have been shown to **reduce dyspeptic symptoms** and improve overall gastrointestinal health.

- **Avoidance of NSAIDs When Possible**

- ◦ If NSAID use is unavoidable, **co-prescription of a proton pump inhibitor or misoprostol is recommended** to reduce the risk of NSAID-induced ulcers.
- ◦ Selective **COX-2 inhibitors** may be preferred over non-selective NSAIDs in high-risk individuals.

Cytoprotective agents are particularly useful in **patients who cannot tolerate proton pump inhibitors or require additional mucosal protection**, such as **patients on chronic NSAID therapy**.

2.2 Gastroesophageal Reflux Disease (GERD)

2.2.1 Pathophysiology

Gastroesophageal reflux disease occurs due to the **retrograde flow of gastric contents into the esophagus**, leading to **esophageal mucosal injury and symptoms such as heartburn, regurgitation, and chest discomfort.** This condition results from **lower esophageal sphincter dysfunction**, which fails to prevent acid reflux. Chronic and uncontrolled reflux can lead to **esophageal inflammation, structural changes, and severe complications**.

Lower Esophageal Sphincter Dysfunction and Acid Reflux

The **lower esophageal sphincter** is a **circular band of muscle at the junction between the esophagus and stomach.** Under normal conditions, it **remains contracted** to prevent the backflow of gastric acid. During swallowing, the sphincter **relaxes transiently** to allow food passage into the stomach and then **closes immediately** to prevent reflux.

In GERD, the lower esophageal sphincter exhibits **inappropriate relaxation, low resting pressure, or structural weakness**, allowing acidic gastric contents to enter the esophagus. The **pH of gastric acid is between 1.5 and 3.5**, while the esophageal mucosa is not adapted to withstand such acidity, resulting in **mucosal irritation, inflammation, and erosion**.

Contributing Factors to GERD

Several physiological and lifestyle factors contribute to the development and worsening of GERD by either **reducing lower esophageal sphincter tone, increasing intra-abdominal pressure, or delaying gastric emptying.**

- Obesity

  - Increased **intra-abdominal pressure** due to excess visceral fat compresses the stomach, forcing gastric contents into the esophagus.
  - Studies show that **a body mass index above 30 is associated with a threefold increase in GERD risk.**

- Hiatal Hernia

  - A **hiatal hernia** occurs when the upper part of the stomach moves above the diaphragm, weakening the **anti-reflux barrier.**
  - The diaphragm normally reinforces the lower esophageal sphincter, and its dysfunction increases acid reflux frequency.
  - **Hiatal hernia is present in nearly 70 percent of GERD patients** with severe symptoms.

- Chronic GERD, if left untreated, can lead to severe complications that significantly impact esophageal function and increase the risk of malignancy.
- **Erosive Esophagitis**

  - Persistent acid exposure damages the **esophageal epithelium**, leading to **inflammation, erosions, and ulceration.**
  - Symptoms include **dysphagia (difficulty swallowing), odynophagia (painful swallowing), and bleeding.**

- **Strictures and Esophageal Narrowing**

  - Recurrent esophageal inflammation results in **fibrosis and scar tissue formation,** leading to **esophageal stricture.**
  - Patients may develop **progressive dysphagia,** initially with solid foods and later with liquids.

- **Barrett's Esophagus**

  - Chronic acid exposure induces **metaplastic changes,** where normal **squamous epithelium of the esophagus is replaced by columnar epithelium with goblet cells.**

- Barrett's esophagus is a precancerous condition, found in **5 to 15 percent of GERD patients.**

○ **Esophageal Adenocarcinoma**

- Patients with **long-standing GERD and Barrett's esophagus** are at **increased risk of developing esophageal adenocarcinoma.**
- The **risk of esophageal cancer is nearly 30 times higher in Barrett's esophagus patients compared to the general population.**
- **Regular endoscopic surveillance and biopsy are recommended** for patients with Barrett's esophagus to detect early malignant transformation.

○ **Dietary and Lifestyle Factors**

- **Caffeine, alcohol, and nicotine** relax the lower esophageal sphincter, exacerbating reflux.
- **Carbonated beverages and spicy foods** irritate the esophageal mucosa.
- **Large, high-fat meals** delay gastric emptying, promoting acid exposure.

○ **Pregnancy**

- Increased **abdominal pressure and hormonal changes** lead to lower esophageal sphincter relaxation, increasing GERD risk.

○ **Medications That Reduce Lower Esophageal Sphincter Tone**

- **Calcium channel blockers, nitrates, and anticholinergics** can relax the lower esophageal sphincter and contribute to GERD symptoms.

2.2.2 Pharmacological Management

The pharmacological management of **gastroesophageal reflux disease (GERD)** aims to **reduce acid secretion, enhance lower esophageal sphincter function, and promote gastric emptying.** The primary drug classes used in treatment include **proton pump inhibitors, H2 receptor antagonists, and prokinetics.**

Proton Pump Inhibitors (PPIs) and H2 Receptor Antagonists

Proton Pump Inhibitors (PPIs)

Proton pump inhibitors are the **first-line treatment for moderate to severe GERD** due to their **potent and long-lasting acid suppression.**

- Mechanism of Action

  - Proton pump inhibitors **irreversibly inhibit the H+/K+ ATPase enzyme** in the parietal cells of the stomach, blocking the final step of acid secretion.
  - This leads to **a sustained increase in gastric pH**, reducing acid reflux and promoting esophageal healing.

- Recommended Therapy

  - **Standard treatment duration is 8 weeks**, with once-daily dosing.
  - In **severe or erosive GERD**, proton pump inhibitors may be used **twice daily** for improved symptom control.
  - **Common proton pump inhibitors and dosing:**

Drug	Usual Dose
Omeprazole	20–40 mg once daily
Pantoprazole	40 mg once daily
Esomeprazole	20–40 mg once daily
Lansoprazole	30 mg once daily
Rabeprazole	20 mg once daily

Common proton pump inhibitors and dosing

Indications for Proton Pump Inhibitors

- Mild to severe GERD with frequent symptoms.
- Erosive esophagitis confirmed by endoscopy.
- GERD symptoms not relieved by lifestyle modifications or H2 receptor antagonists.
- **Patients with Barrett's esophagus** to reduce the risk of progression to esophageal adenocarcinoma.

1. **Adverse Effects of Proton Pump Inhibitors**

   - **Long-term use (>1 year) is associated with:**

     - **Hypomagnesemia**, leading to muscle cramps and cardiac arrhythmias.
     - **Osteoporosis and increased fracture risk**, particularly in elderly patients.
     - **Vitamin B12 deficiency** due to reduced gastric acid required for vitamin absorption.
     - **Increased risk of Clostridium difficile infection** due to altered gut microbiota.

H2 Receptor Antagonists (H2 Blockers)

H2 receptor antagonists provide **moderate acid suppression** and serve as an **alternative to proton pump inhibitors (PPIs)** for mild cases of **gastroesophageal reflux disease (GERD)**. They can also be used as **adjunctive therapy in patients experiencing incomplete symptom relief** with PPIs. These drugs are particularly useful for **on-demand symptom relief** due to their **faster onset of action**, although their **acid suppression is less potent compared to PPIs.**

Mechanism of Action

H2 receptor antagonists **block histamine H2 receptors on parietal cells** in the stomach. By inhibiting histamine stimulation, these drugs **reduce the activation of the proton pump**, thereby decreasing **gastric acid secretion.**

Commonly Used H2 Blockers and Dosages

Famotidine is the most commonly used H2 receptor antagonist, given at **20–40 mg once daily at bedtime. Ranitidine was widely used but has been withdrawn in many countries due to safety concerns regarding** contamination with N-nitrosodimethylamine (NDMA), a potential **carcinogen.**

Indications for H2 Receptor Antagonists

- **Mild GERD with occasional symptoms** where continuous PPI use is unnecessary.
- **Adjunct therapy** in patients requiring **additional night-time symptom control** despite PPI therapy.
- **Alternative therapy** in patients who **cannot tolerate PPIs** due to side effects such as headache or gastrointestinal discomfort.

Limitations and Side Effects

Despite their effectiveness, H2 receptor antagonists have **certain limitations and adverse effects**, including:

- **Tolerance (Tachyphylaxis):Prolonged use leads to decreased efficacy** as the body compensates by **upregulating histamine receptors.**
- **Drug Interactions:** Cimetidine, an older H2 blocker that is rarely used today, **inhibits cytochrome P450 enzymes**, leading to increased levels of **warfarin, theophylline, and phenytoin**, which can cause toxicity.
- **Central Nervous System Effects:Confusion, dizziness, and hallucinations** may occur, particularly in **elderly patients** or those with **renal impairment.**

Prokinetics

Prokinetic agents are **adjunctive therapies for GERD** in patients with **delayed gastric emptying** or **lower esophageal sphincter (LES) dysfunction.** These drugs **enhance gastric motility**, improve **LES tone**, and **reduce acid reflux episodes.**

Mechanism of Action

Prokinetics work by two primary mechanisms:

1. **Increasing Lower Esophageal Sphincter Tone**

   - Metoclopramide and domperidone **increase acetylcholine release**, stimulating smooth muscle contraction in the esophagus and stomach.
   - This strengthens the **lower esophageal sphincter**, preventing reflux of gastric contents into the esophagus.

2. Enhancing Gastric Emptying

- By **blocking dopamine receptors**, prokinetics **reduce dopamine-mediated inhibition of gastrointestinal motility.**
- This accelerates **gastric emptying**, minimizing the **retention of acidic contents**, which can trigger reflux symptoms.

Commonly Used Prokinetic Drugs and Their Dosages

- **Metoclopramide** is administered at **10 mg three times daily before meals.**
- **Domperidone** is also dosed at **10 mg three times daily.**

Safety Concerns with Prokinetics

While prokinetic agents are **effective for GERD management**, their use is often **limited due to safety concerns**, particularly with **long-term therapy.**

Metoclopramide and Tardive Dyskinesia

- Metoclopramide **crosses the blood-brain barrier** and **blocks dopamine receptors in the central nervous system.**
- Chronic use **beyond 12 weeks** increases the risk of **tardive dyskinesia**, a serious movement disorder characterized by **involuntary facial and limb movements.**
- Due to its effects on dopamine, metoclopramide is **contraindicated in Parkinson's disease**, as it **worsens dopaminergic dysfunction.**

Domperidone and Cardiac Arrhythmias

- Domperidone **does not cross the blood-brain barrier significantly**, reducing the risk of **tardive dyskinesia.**
- However, **it prolongs the QT interval**, increasing the risk of **ventricular arrhythmias and sudden cardiac death**, especially when doses **exceed 30 mg per day.**
- Patients with **pre-existing heart disease or electrolyte imbalances** require **careful monitoring** when using domperidone.

Summary of GERD Pharmacological Management

1. Proton Pump Inhibitors (PPIs)

- **Mechanism:** Irreversibly inhibit the **H+/K+ ATPase pump** in parietal cells, leading to **profound and long-lasting acid suppression.**
- **Indications:**First-line treatment for **GERD, erosive esophagitis, and Barrett's esophagus.**
- **Common Side Effects:** Hypomagnesemia, osteoporosis with long-term use, and **increased risk of Clostridium difficile infection.**

2. H2 Receptor Antagonists (H2 Blockers)

- **Mechanism:** Block **H2 receptors**, reducing gastric acid secretion.
- **Indications:**Mild GERD, adjunct therapy for night-time symptoms.
- **Limitations:**Tachyphylaxis (tolerance with prolonged use), CNS effects in elderly.

3. Prokinetics

- **Mechanism:**Increase LES tone and **enhance gastric motility.**
- **Indications:** Used as **adjunct therapy in GERD patients with delayed gastric emptying.**
- **Common Side Effects:**Tardive dyskinesia (metoclopramide), QT prolongation (domperidone).

2.2.3 Surgical Interventions

Surgical interventions for **gastroesophageal reflux disease (GERD)** are considered in **patients with severe, refractory symptoms** despite optimal medical therapy or in those with **complications such as Barrett's esophagus, recurrent strictures, or aspiration pneumonia.** Surgery aims to **strengthen the lower esophageal sphincter (LES)** and prevent acid reflux while preserving normal esophageal function.

Indications for Surgery

Surgical management is recommended in the following situations:

1. **Severe Reflux Unresponsive to Medical Therapy**

- Patients who **continue to have GERD symptoms despite an 8–12 week trial of proton pump inhibitors at maximum doses.**
- Persistent regurgitation and **chronic aspiration leading to respiratory complications** such as chronic cough, asthma, or recurrent pneumonia.

2. **Complications of GERD**

- **Barrett's Esophagus:** Metaplastic changes in the esophageal lining due to chronic acid exposure, which increase the risk of **esophageal adenocarcinoma.**
- **Recurrent Peptic Strictures:** Persistent **esophageal narrowing** leading to **dysphagia**, requiring frequent **endoscopic dilation.**
- **Hiatal Hernia (>5 cm):** Large hernias compromise **lower esophageal sphincter function**, worsening reflux and symptoms.

3. **Young Patients with Long-Term GERD**

- Patients who **wish to avoid lifelong proton pump inhibitor therapy** due to concerns about **side effects such as osteoporosis, vitamin B12 deficiency, and Clostridium difficile infection.**

4. **Severe Volume Regurgitation or Extra-Esophageal Symptoms**

- Patients with **chronic nocturnal regurgitation, aspiration pneumonia, or laryngopharyngeal reflux (hoarseness, chronic cough, or sinusitis)** that does not respond to medical treatment.

Surgical Procedures for GERD
The most commonly performed **anti-reflux surgery** is **Nissen Fundoplication**, which restores **lower esophageal sphincter competence** and reduces acid reflux.
Nissen Fundoplication

1. **Procedure Overview**

- The **fundus of the stomach is wrapped 360 degrees around the lower esophagus**, creating a **valve-like mechanism** that prevents acid reflux.

- The wrap **reinforces lower esophageal sphincter pressure**, preventing gastric contents from flowing back into the esophagus.

2. **Types of Fundoplication**

- **Complete (360-degree) Fundoplication:** Standard Nissen procedure, fully wrapping the fundus around the esophagus.
- **Partial Fundoplication (Toupet or Dor procedure):** In cases with esophageal motility disorders, a **270-degree (Toupet) or anterior (Dor) wrap** is performed to reduce the risk of dysphagia.

3. **Surgical Approach**

- **Laparoscopic Nissen Fundoplication** is the preferred method due to **faster recovery, lower complication rates, and minimal post-operative pain.**
- Open surgery is rarely performed unless **severe adhesions or large hiatal hernias** are present.

Post-Surgical Outcomes and Complications

1. **Success Rates**

- Nissen fundoplication achieves **excellent symptom control in 85–90% of patients**, significantly reducing **reflux and regurgitation.**
- Many patients **discontinue proton pump inhibitor therapy after surgery.**

2. **Potential Complications**

- **Dysphagia:** Occurs in **10–20% of cases** due to excessive tightening of the wrap. Most cases resolve within a few weeks, but some require **dilation or revision surgery.**
- **Gas Bloat Syndrome:** Since belching is limited, patients may experience **bloating and increased flatulence.**
- **Wrap Failure or Slippage:** Over time, **5–10% of patients may experience recurrence of reflux** due to wrap loosening.

- ○ **Esophageal Injury or Vagus Nerve Damage:** Rare but serious complications can lead to **gastric emptying disorders or persistent dyspepsia.**

Alternative Surgical and Endoscopic Options

1. **LINX Reflux Management System**

   - ○ A **magnetic bead ring** is placed around the **lower esophageal sphincter**, reinforcing it while allowing swallowing.
   - ○ **Minimally invasive procedure**, but long-term durability remains under study.

2. **Stretta Procedure (Endoscopic Therapy)**

   - ○ Delivers **radiofrequency energy to the lower esophageal sphincter**, causing muscle tightening and improved reflux control.

Non-surgical option but has **lower efficacy compared to fundoplication**

2.3 Inflammatory Bowel Disease (IBD)

Inflammatory bowel disease is a **chronic, immune-mediated disorder** that primarily affects the **gastrointestinal tract**, leading to **relapsing and remitting episodes of inflammation.** The two main subtypes of inflammatory bowel disease are **ulcerative colitis and Crohn's disease.** These conditions differ in their **pathogenesis, distribution of inflammation, and treatment approaches.**

2.3.1 Ulcerative Colitis

Ulcerative colitis is characterized by **chronic inflammation of the colon and rectum.** Unlike Crohn's disease, which can affect any part of the gastrointestinal tract, ulcerative colitis is **limited to the large intestine** and only involves the **mucosal and submucosal layers.** The disease typically presents with **bloody diarrhea, abdominal pain, urgency, and weight loss.**
   Pathogenesis

1. **Localized to the Colon and Rectum**

   - The inflammation in ulcerative colitis **begins in the rectum** and extends proximally in a **continuous** fashion, unlike Crohn's disease, which occurs in **patchy segments.**
   - The disease **never involves the small intestine** or other parts of the gastrointestinal tract.

2. **Mucosal and Submucosal Inflammation**

   - The inflammatory process in ulcerative colitis **is limited to the mucosa and submucosa**, sparing the deeper layers of the intestinal wall.
   - This leads to **crypt abscess formation, epithelial damage, and ulcerations.**

3. **Dysregulated Immune Response**

   - The immune system mistakenly attacks the **colonic epithelium,** leading to excessive **inflammatory cytokine release.**
   - Key immune mediators include **tumor necrosis factor-alpha, interleukin-12, and interleukin-23.**

4. **Role of Environmental and Genetic Factors**

   - Genetic predisposition plays a role, with **mutations in genes related to immune function** increasing susceptibility.
   - **Dietary factors, smoking, and gut microbiota alterations** also contribute to disease progression.

Aminosalicylates for Ulcerative Colitis

Aminosalicylates are **first-line agents** for the treatment of mild to moderate ulcerative colitis. They work by **reducing inflammation in the colonic mucosa** and are effective in both **inducing and maintaining remission.**

1. **Common Drugs and Dosing**

- Sulfasalazine: **500 milligrams four times daily**
- Mesalamine (Oral and Rectal Formulations): **1.5–4.8 grams per day**
- Balsalazide and Olsalazine: Used in cases where patients cannot tolerate sulfasalazine.

2. Mechanism of Action

- Aminosalicylates **inhibit prostaglandin and leukotriene synthesis,** reducing inflammation in the colonic mucosa.
- They also **decrease cytokine release** and modulate the **immune response.**

3. Efficacy and Role in Treatment

- In **mild to moderate ulcerative colitis,** aminosalicylates achieve clinical remission in **40–60 percent of patients.**
- **Topical mesalamine suppositories** are particularly effective for **proctitis and left-sided colitis.**

4. Adverse Effects

- Sulfasalazine may cause **nausea, headache, rash, and reversible male infertility** due to its sulfapyridine component.
- Mesalamine has **fewer side effects** but can still cause **diarrhea and nephrotoxicity** in rare cases.

Biologic Therapy in Ulcerative Colitis

Biologics are used in patients with **moderate to severe ulcerative colitis** who do not respond adequately to aminosalicylates or corticosteroids. These drugs **target specific immune pathways,** reducing systemic inflammation.

1. Common Biologic Agents and Dosing

- Infliximab: **5 milligrams per kilogram intravenously every 8 weeks**
- Adalimumab: **160 milligrams subcutaneously on day 1, followed by 80 milligrams at week 2, then 40 milligrams every 2 weeks**
- Golimumab: Used for **patients with refractory ulcerative colitis**

2. **Mechanism of Action**

- Biologics such as infliximab and adalimumab are **tumor necrosis factor-alpha inhibitors**, blocking the **pro-inflammatory effects of TNF-alpha.**
- This reduces **intestinal inflammation, ulceration, and disease progression.**

3. **Efficacy and Clinical Use**

- **Induction of remission occurs in approximately 60–70 percent of patients** receiving infliximab.
- Long-term maintenance therapy significantly **reduces hospitalization rates and the need for colectomy.**

4. **Adverse Effects**

- Biologic therapy increases the risk of **opportunistic infections, tuberculosis, and malignancies.**
- Before starting infliximab, **patients must be screened for tuberculosis and hepatitis B.**

2.3.2 Crohn's Disease

Crohn's disease is a chronic inflammatory bowel disease that can affect any part of the gastrointestinal tract, from the mouth to the anus. Unlike ulcerative colitis, which is limited to the colon and rectum, Crohn's disease is characterized by patchy, transmural inflammation that can lead to complications such as strictures, fistulas, and malabsorption.

Differences Between Crohn's Disease and Ulcerative Colitis

One of the key distinguishing features of Crohn's disease is transmural inflammation, which affects the entire thickness of the intestinal wall. This is in contrast to ulcerative colitis, where inflammation is limited to the mucosal and submucosal layers. Another major difference is the distribution of the disease. Crohn's disease can affect any segment of the gastrointestinal tract, but it most commonly involves the terminal ileum and proximal colon. The inflammation occurs in a discontinuous pattern, with areas of inflamed bowel interspersed with normal mucosa, a phenomenon known as skip lesions.

Due to its deeper involvement, Crohn's disease is associated with complications such as strictures, which result from fibrosis and narrowing of the bowel lumen, and fistulas, which occur when the inflammation extends to adjacent structures, forming abnormal connections between the bowel and other organs.

Corticosteroids for Acute Flares

Corticosteroids are the first-line treatment for moderate to severe Crohn's disease during acute exacerbations. They rapidly reduce inflammation and control symptoms such as abdominal pain, diarrhea, and weight loss.

Prednisolone is the most commonly used corticosteroid for inducing remission in Crohn's disease. The typical dose for moderate flares is 40 to 60 milligrams per day, tapered gradually over six to eight weeks to minimize adrenal suppression and steroid dependence. In severe cases, intravenous hydrocortisone or methylprednisolone may be required.

While corticosteroids are effective for short-term control of inflammation, they do not prevent disease recurrence and are not suitable for long-term maintenance therapy. Chronic steroid use is associated with significant adverse effects, including osteoporosis, hyperglycemia, hypertension, and increased susceptibility to infections.

Immunomodulators for Maintenance Therapy

Since corticosteroids are not suitable for long-term use, immunomodulators play a crucial role in maintaining remission and reducing the need for repeated steroid courses.

Azathioprine is one of the most commonly used immunomodulators in Crohn's disease. It works by inhibiting purine synthesis, thereby suppressing the proliferation of lymphocytes and reducing inflammation. The usual dose is 1.5 to 2.5 milligrams per kilogram per day, adjusted based on thiopurine methyltransferase enzyme activity to minimize toxicity. Azathioprine is particularly useful in patients who are steroid-dependent or those who require an alternative to biologic therapy.

Methotrexate is another immunosuppressant used in Crohn's disease, especially for patients intolerant to azathioprine. It is given as a weekly intramuscular or subcutaneous injection at a dose of 15 to 25 milligrams. Methotrexate is effective in maintaining remission but requires close monitoring for hepatotoxicity and bone marrow suppression.

2.3.3 Role of Nutrition

Nutritional management is a crucial component of treatment in inflammatory bowel disease, particularly in Crohn's disease, where malabsorption and nutrient deficiencies are common. Patients with active disease often experience **weight loss, malnutrition, and deficiencies of essential vitamins and minerals** due to chronic inflammation, reduced dietary intake, and impaired absorption. Optimizing nutrition helps in **reducing disease complications, improving treatment response, and enhancing overall quality of life.**

Addressing Malnutrition and Nutrient Deficiencies

Malnutrition is a common concern in inflammatory bowel disease, especially in patients with **extensive small intestinal involvement, chronic diarrhea, and frequent disease flares.** The most commonly observed deficiencies include **iron, vitamin B12, folate, and fat-soluble vitamins (A, D, E, and K).**

1. **Iron Deficiency**

    - Chronic blood loss from inflamed intestinal mucosa and impaired iron absorption contribute to iron deficiency anemia.
    - Patients with low hemoglobin levels or ferritin below 30 nanograms per milliliter should receive iron supplementation.
    - Oral iron supplements such as ferrous sulfate at a dose of 200 milligrams per day can be used in mild cases. However, intravenous iron (iron sucrose or ferric carboxymaltose) is preferred in patients with **severe anemia or intolerance to oral iron** due to gastrointestinal side effects.

2. **Vitamin B12 Deficiency**

    - The terminal ileum is the primary site of vitamin B12 absorption, and **patients with ileal disease or those who have undergone ileal resection** are at high risk of developing deficiency.
    - Low vitamin B12 levels can cause **megaloblastic anemia, fatigue, and neurological symptoms** such as tingling and numbness.

- Intramuscular vitamin B12 injections (1000 micrograms once monthly) are recommended for patients with **confirmed deficiency or after ileal resection**.

3. **Folate Deficiency**

- Folate absorption occurs in the **jejunum**, and patients with extensive disease or those on long-term sulfasalazine therapy may develop deficiency.
- Folate deficiency can lead to **anemia and impaired DNA synthesis,** worsening disease-related complications.
- Daily folic acid supplementation of 1 to 5 milligrams is recommended in at-risk patients.

4. **Fat-Soluble Vitamin Deficiencies (A, D, E, and K)**

- Chronic diarrhea and bile salt malabsorption can result in **deficiencies of fat-soluble vitamins**, particularly in Crohn's disease.
- Vitamin D deficiency is common and **increases the risk of osteoporosis**, particularly in patients on long-term corticosteroid therapy.
- Regular vitamin level monitoring and **supplementation of vitamin D (1000–2000 IU per day) and calcium (1000 milligrams per day) are recommended to prevent bone loss.**

Role of Enteral Feeding During Flares
During acute flares of inflammatory bowel disease, patients often experience **severe diarrhea, abdominal pain, and reduced oral intake,** leading to further nutritional depletion. In such cases, **enteral nutrition is preferred over parenteral nutrition**, as it **preserves gut function and reduces intestinal inflammation.**

1. **Exclusive Enteral Nutrition in Crohn's Disease**

- Exclusive enteral nutrition with a **liquid formula diet for 6 to 8 weeks** has been shown to induce remission in Crohn's disease, particularly in children and adolescents.

- ◦ It works by **reducing gut inflammation, restoring intestinal barrier function, and modifying gut microbiota.**
- ◦ Standard polymeric formulas are usually well-tolerated, but in patients with **severe disease, elemental or semi-elemental formulas** may be required for better absorption.

2. **Enteral Nutrition as an Adjunct Therapy**

- ◦ In ulcerative colitis, enteral feeding is **not a primary treatment** but can be **used to prevent malnutrition** and improve energy intake.
- ◦ In hospitalized patients who are unable to eat adequately, **nasogastric or nasojejunal tube feeding may be necessary.**

3. **Parenteral Nutrition in Severe Cases**

- ◦ Total parenteral nutrition is reserved for **patients with intestinal failure, severe malabsorption, or those recovering from surgery.**
- ◦ Long-term parenteral nutrition is associated with complications such as **infections, electrolyte imbalances, and liver dysfunction,** and should only be used when enteral nutrition is not feasible.

2.4.1 Alcoholic Liver Disease

Alcoholic liver disease is a progressive liver disorder caused by **chronic alcohol consumption,** leading to **fat accumulation, inflammation, and fibrosis.** The disease progresses through **three main stages,** each with increasing severity and potential for irreversible liver damage. Early intervention is crucial to prevent long-term complications such as **cirrhosis and liver failure.**

Stages of Alcoholic Liver Disease

The progression of alcoholic liver disease occurs in the following stages:

- ◦ **Steatosis (Fatty Liver)**

  - ◦ **Pathophysiology:** Excessive alcohol consumption disrupts lipid metabolism in hepatocytes, leading to **triglyceride accumulation in the liver.** This causes **hepatic steatosis,** which is **reversible with** abstinence.

- **Clinical Features:** Often asymptomatic but may present with **hepatomegaly, mild elevation of liver enzymes, and fatigue.**
- **Reversibility:** With complete alcohol cessation, steatosis resolves within **two to four weeks.**

- **Alcoholic Hepatitis**

  - **Pathophysiology:** Continued alcohol intake induces **inflammatory damage** through increased production of **reactive oxygen species, cytokines, and neutrophil infiltration.**
  - **Clinical Features:** Symptoms include **jaundice, fever, right upper quadrant pain, hepatomegaly, and significant elevation of aspartate aminotransferase and alanine aminotransferase levels.**
  - **Prognosis:** Severe alcoholic hepatitis has a **30–50% mortality rate within six months**, requiring aggressive medical intervention.

- **Cirrhosis**

  - **Pathophysiology:** Chronic inflammation leads to **fibrosis and nodule formation**, causing **irreversible liver damage** and loss of hepatocellular function.
  - **Clinical Features:** Patients develop **portal hypertension, ascites, hepatic encephalopathy, and coagulopathy.**
  - **Prognosis:** Once cirrhosis develops, the risk of **hepatic decompensation and hepatocellular carcinoma** increases significantly.

Pharmacotherapy for Alcoholic Liver Disease

Although the cornerstone of treatment remains **alcohol abstinence and supportive care**, specific pharmacological agents help **prevent complications and improve survival.**

- **Thiamine Supplementation**

  - **Indication:** Chronic alcohol use leads to **thiamine (vitamin B1) deficiency**, increasing the risk of **Wernicke's encephalopathy and Korsakoff syndrome.**

- **Mechanism of Action**: Thiamine is essential for **glucose metabolism** and **nerve function**, preventing **neurological complications** in patients with chronic alcohol dependence.
- **Dosage:**

  - **Mild Deficiency**: 100 milligrams orally once daily.
  - **Severe Deficiency/Wernicke's Encephalopathy**: 500 milligrams intravenously three times daily for two days, followed by 250 milligrams once daily for five days.

- **N-Acetylcysteine (NAC)**

  - **Indication**: Used as an adjunct therapy to **reduce oxidative stress and liver injury** in patients with **alcoholic hepatitis.**
  - **Mechanism of Action**: N-acetylcysteine replenishes **glutathione stores**, neutralizing **reactive oxygen species** and reducing oxidative damage to hepatocytes.
  - **Dosage**: Typically administered intravenously in **severe cases of alcoholic hepatitis**, though its use remains under investigation.

- **Corticosteroids (Prednisolone)**

  - **Indication**: Patients with **severe alcoholic hepatitis (Maddrey's Discriminant Function > 32)** benefit from corticosteroid therapy, which **reduces inflammation and improves short-term survival.**
  - **Mechanism of Action**: Suppresses **immune activation and cytokine release**, decreasing liver injury.
  - **Dosage**: 40 milligrams of **prednisolone orally once daily for four weeks**, followed by gradual tapering.

- **Pentoxifylline**

  - **Indication**: Used as an alternative to corticosteroids in patients at **high risk of infection or gastrointestinal bleeding.**
  - **Mechanism of Action**: Reduces **tumor necrosis factor-alpha levels**, improving hepatic microcirculation.
  - **Efficacy**: Studies suggest it is **less effective than corticosteroids but still beneficial in certain patients.**

- ◦ **Liver Transplantation**

  - ◦ **Indication:** Patients with **end-stage liver disease and severe hepatic decompensation** despite abstinence and medical therapy.
  - ◦ **Eligibility Criteria:** Many centers require **at least six months of documented alcohol abstinence** before considering transplantation.

2.4.2 Viral Hepatitis

Viral hepatitis refers to **inflammation of the liver caused by hepatotropic viruses,** primarily **hepatitis B and hepatitis C,** both of which can lead to **chronic liver disease, cirrhosis, and hepatocellular carcinoma** if left untreated. The goal of treatment is to **reduce viral replication, prevent liver damage, and improve long-term survival.**

Hepatitis B

Hepatitis B is a **DNA virus** that integrates into the hepatocyte genome, making complete viral eradication difficult. The primary aim of treatment is to **suppress viral replication and prevent progression to cirrhosis and liver cancer.**

Pharmacological Management

1. **Nucleotide and Nucleoside Analogues**

   - ◦ These antiviral agents inhibit **hepatitis B viral polymerase,** reducing viral replication and **decreasing liver inflammation.**
   - ◦ **Tenofovir disoproxil fumarate (300 milligrams once daily)** is a first-line treatment due to its **high potency and low resistance rates.**
   - ◦ **Entecavir (0.5–1 milligram once daily)** is another potent antiviral used for treatment-naïve patients and those with **lamivudine-resistant hepatitis B virus infections.**
   - ◦ These medications require **long-term use,** often for life, to maintain viral suppression and prevent liver complications.

2. **Goals of Therapy**

   - ◦ Reduce **hepatitis B viral DNA to undetectable levels.**
   - ◦ Prevent **progression to cirrhosis and hepatocellular carcinoma.**

○ Improve **hepatic function and prevent decompensation in patients with existing liver disease.**

Hepatitis C

Hepatitis C is a **RNA virus** that, unlike hepatitis B, does not integrate into the host genome, making it **curable with antiviral therapy.** Advances in treatment with **direct-acting antivirals (DAAs)** have transformed the management of hepatitis C, achieving **cure rates exceeding 95 percent.**

Direct-Acting Antivirals (DAAs)

1. **Mechanism of Action**

   ○ Direct-acting antivirals target **specific viral enzymes** involved in hepatitis C replication, including **NS5A inhibitors, NS5B polymerase inhibitors, and protease inhibitors.**
   ○ Unlike older interferon-based therapies, DAAs **offer higher efficacy with fewer side effects.**

2. **Common Treatment Regimens**

   ○ **Sofosbuvir + Velpatasvir (one tablet once daily for 12 weeks):** A pan-genotypic regimen effective against all hepatitis C genotypes.
   ○ **Glecaprevir + Pibrentasvir (three tablets once daily for 8–12 weeks):** Used for shorter-duration treatment in **non-cirrhotic patients.**
   ○ **Ledipasvir + Sofosbuvir (one tablet daily for 12 weeks):** Effective against **genotype 1 hepatitis C.**

3. **Cure Rates and Benefits**

   ○ Direct-acting antivirals achieve **sustained virologic response in over 95 percent of patients,** meaning the virus is **undetectable in the blood six months after therapy completion.**
   ○ Successful treatment reduces the risk of **cirrhosis, liver failure, and hepatocellular carcinoma.**

4. **Monitoring and Follow-Up**

- Liver function tests, hepatitis C viral RNA, and fibrosis markers are assessed **before, during, and after treatment.**
- Patients with advanced fibrosis or cirrhosis **require continued surveillance for hepatocellular carcinoma** even after viral clearance.

2.4.3 Drug-Induced Liver Disorders

Drug-induced liver disorders occur when certain medications cause **direct hepatotoxicity or immune-mediated liver injury**, leading to **hepatocellular damage, cholestasis, or liver failure.** Some drugs cause **dose-dependent toxicity,** while others trigger **idiosyncratic reactions.**
Common Drug Offenders and Mechanisms of Hepatotoxicity

1. **Acetaminophen (Paracetamol) – Dose-Dependent Hepatotoxicity**

- Acetaminophen overdose is a **leading cause of acute liver failure,** primarily due to **toxic metabolite (NAPQI) accumulation.**
- At therapeutic doses, NAPQI is detoxified by **glutathione,** but in overdose, **glutathione stores deplete,** leading to hepatocyte necrosis.
- **Toxic dose threshold:**

  - More than **4 grams per day** in adults increases the risk of hepatotoxicity.
  - Single doses above **7.5 grams in adults** or **150 milligrams per kilogram in children** can cause severe liver damage.

- **Antidote:** N-acetylcysteine replenishes **glutathione levels** and prevents liver cell injury when administered **within 8 hours of overdose.**

2. **Amiodarone – Chronic Liver Injury**

- Amiodarone is an **antiarrhythmic agent** that can cause **chronic hepatotoxicity,** presenting as **elevated liver enzymes and fibrosis** with long-term use.
- The drug **accumulates in hepatocytes,** leading to mitochondrial dysfunction and oxidative stress.

- ○ **Monitoring:** Liver function tests should be **checked every 6 months** in patients on long-term therapy.

Other Notable Hepatotoxic Drugs

Several commonly used medications have **hepatotoxic potential**, leading to **various forms of liver injury**. These drugs can cause **acute, chronic, or idiosyncratic liver damage**, requiring careful monitoring of **liver function tests (LFTs)** in patients receiving long-term therapy.
Methotrexate – Chronic Hepatotoxicity

- Methotrexate is an **immunosuppressive and chemotherapeutic agent** used to treat **rheumatoid arthritis, psoriasis, and certain cancers.**
- **Mechanism of Hepatotoxicity:**

  - ○ **Chronic exposure** leads to **hepatic fibrosis and cirrhosis,** primarily due to **oxidative stress and folate depletion.**
  - ○ Methotrexate accumulates in hepatocytes, generating **reactive oxygen species (ROS)** that promote **inflammation and fibrosis.**

- **Monitoring Recommendations:**

  - ○ Baseline liver function tests (ALT, AST, ALP, bilirubin) before starting therapy.
  - ○ Periodic monitoring (every 8-12 weeks) to assess hepatotoxicity risk.
  - ○ Liver biopsy in long-term users (≥5 years) or patients with persistent transaminase elevation.

  Isoniazid – Acute Hepatocellular Injury

- Isoniazid is an **antitubercular drug** that may cause **severe hepatotoxicity, particularly in elderly patients and those with genetic susceptibility.**
- **Mechanism of Hepatotoxicity:**

- ○ Direct mitochondrial toxicity due to **metabolite accumulation (hydrazine derivatives)**.
- ○ Leads to **oxidative damage, mitochondrial dysfunction, and hepatocyte necrosis**.
- ○ **Risk factors** include **age >35 years**, alcohol use, and genetic polymorphisms in NAT2 (slow acetylators).

- **Clinical Presentation:**

  - ○ **Acute liver injury** occurs within **weeks to months of therapy**.
  - ○ **Symptoms include jaundice, fatigue, nausea, and elevated ALT/ AST (>5× upper normal limit).**

- **Monitoring and Prevention:**

  - ○ **LFTs before treatment initiation and monthly during therapy.**
  - ○ **Avoid alcohol and other hepatotoxic drugs** during isoniazid therapy.
  - ○ **Discontinue if ALT/AST exceed three times the upper normal limit with symptoms.**

Statins – Mild Liver Enzyme Elevation

- Statins are **lipid-lowering agents** that can cause **mild, transient** elevations in liver enzymes, though **severe liver damage is rare**.
- **Mechanism of Hepatotoxicity:**

  - ○ **Hepatocellular inflammation** due to **mitochondrial dysfunction and lipid peroxidation**.
  - ○ Primarily affects **hepatic cytochrome P450 metabolism**.

- **Clinical Considerations:**

  - ○ **1-3% of statin users develop mild ALT/AST elevations** (<3× upper normal limit), which **resolve spontaneously**.
  - ○ **Severe hepatotoxicity is rare**, with an incidence of **1 in 100,000 cases**.

- **Monitoring Recommendations:**

- Baseline liver function tests before initiating statin therapy.
- Routine monitoring not required unless symptoms of liver injury appear.
- Statin discontinuation is unnecessary for mild LFT elevations, but alternative lipid-lowering therapy may be considered if levels exceed three times the normal range.

Herbal Supplements – Idiosyncratic Liver Injury

- **Certain herbal and dietary supplements** can cause **unpredictable liver toxicity,** often through unknown mechanisms.
- Common hepatotoxic herbal products:

  - **Green tea extract:** Reported cases of **acute hepatitis due to catechin-induced oxidative stress.**
  - **Kava (Piper methysticum):** Associated with **fulminant hepatic failure requiring liver transplantation.**
  - **Black cohosh, Aloe vera, and Garcinia cambogia** have been implicated in **liver toxicity cases.**

- **Mechanism of Hepatotoxicity:**

  - Largely **idiosyncratic,** with variable onset and severity.
  - Some components may **inhibit hepatic enzymes or trigger immune-mediated liver injury.**

- **Monitoring and Prevention:**

  - Educate patients on the **potential risks of unregulated herbal products.**
  - Avoid herbal supplements in patients with **pre-existing liver disease.**
  - Liver function monitoring for individuals using hepatotoxic herbal remedies.

Monitoring and Diagnosis of Drug-Induced Liver Injury

1. Liver Enzyme Elevations

- Alanine aminotransferase (ALT) and aspartate aminotransferase (AST) are markers of **hepatocyte injury.**
- A significant **increase in ALT (>3 times upper normal limit) or bilirubin (>2 times upper limit) suggests hepatotoxicity.**

2. **Pattern of Liver Injury**

- **Hepatocellular injury** (elevated ALT, normal alkaline phosphatase): Acetaminophen, isoniazid.
- **Cholestatic injury** (elevated alkaline phosphatase, normal ALT): Amoxicillin-clavulanate, chlorpromazine.
- **Mixed liver injury** (both ALT and alkaline phosphatase elevated): Phenytoin, methimazole.

3. **Management of Drug-Induced Liver Injury**

- **Discontinuation of the offending drug is the most important step.**
- **Supportive care** for mild cases; liver transplantation may be required in **severe acute liver failure.**
- **Regular liver function monitoring** in patients on known hepatotoxic drugs helps in early detection.

REVIEW QUESTIONS

1. Explain the pathophysiology of peptic ulcer disease (PUD), emphasizing the balance between acid secretion and protective mucosal mechanisms.

2. Discuss how Helicobacter pylori infection contributes to the development of PUD.

3. Describe the role of non-steroidal anti-inflammatory drugs (NSAIDs) in disrupting mucosal defenses and causing ulcers.

4. What non-invasive diagnostic tests are used for detecting H. pylori in PUD, and how do they work?

5. How does endoscopy, along with biopsy, assist in the diagnosis and assessment of peptic ulcers?

6. Explain the mechanism of action of proton pump inhibitors (PPIs) in the treatment of PUD.

7. Compare standard-dose and high-dose PPI regimens in terms of their clinical indications and outcomes.

8. Identify common side effects associated with long-term PPI therapy and their clinical significance.

9. What is the role of H2 receptor antagonists in managing peptic ulcer disease, particularly for nocturnal acid control?

10. Outline the components of triple and quadruple therapy for H. pylori eradication and discuss the rationale behind combination antibiotic regimens.

11. Describe how cytoprotective agents (such as sucralfate and bismuth subsalicylate) contribute to mucosal defense in PUD.

12. Discuss the importance of lifestyle modifications (e.g., smoking cessation, avoiding dietary triggers) in managing and preventing PUD.

13. Explain the pathophysiological mechanisms underlying gastroesophageal reflux disease (GERD), focusing on lower esophageal sphincter (LES) dysfunction and delayed gastric emptying.

14. Compare the pharmacological management of GERD with that of PUD, including the use of PPIs, H2 blockers, and prokinetic agents.

15. What are the safety concerns associated with prokinetic drugs like metoclopramide and domperidone when used in GERD management?

16. Under what clinical circumstances is surgical intervention (such as fundoplication) indicated in patients with GERD?

17. Differentiate between ulcerative colitis and Crohn's disease in terms of their pathogenesis, distribution in the gastrointestinal tract, and typical histological findings.

18. Discuss the pharmacological options for managing ulcerative colitis, including the roles of aminosalicylates and anti-TNF biologic agents.

19. Outline the treatment strategies for Crohn's disease, focusing on the use of corticosteroids and immunomodulators.

20. Explain the role of nutrition in inflammatory bowel disease (IBD) management and how nutritional deficiencies are addressed.

21. Describe the progression of alcoholic liver disease from steatosis to hepatitis and eventually cirrhosis, including the role of thiamine and antioxidant therapy.

22. What are the current antiviral treatment options for hepatitis B and hepatitis C, and how do they differ?

23. Identify common drugs known to cause drug-induced liver disorders and explain the importance of monitoring liver enzymes during therapy.

24. How does disruption of the gastric mucosal barrier lead to the formation of ulcers in PUD?

25. Discuss the implications of H. pylori eradication on the long-term recurrence of peptic ulcer disease.

26. Compare the mechanisms of acid suppression between proton pump inhibitors and H2 receptor antagonists.

27. Explain why combination antibiotic therapy is preferred for H. pylori eradication over monotherapy.

28. What factors determine whether a patient with GERD is managed medically versus surgically?

29. How do corticosteroids differ from immunomodulators in the long-term management of Crohn's disease?

30. Evaluate the impact of early nutritional intervention on the outcomes of patients with inflammatory bowel disease.

MCQS

75 Multiple-Choice Questions (MCQs)

1. **Which of the following best describes the role of acid secretion in PUD pathophysiology?**
   A) It promotes mucosal regeneration.
   B) Excess acid damages the protective mucosal barrier.
   C) It neutralizes bacterial toxins.
   D) It is irrelevant to ulcer formation.
   Correct Answer: B

2. **Which organism is most commonly associated with peptic ulcer disease?**
   A) Escherichia coli
   B) Staphylococcus aureus
   C) Helicobacter pylori
   D) Streptococcus pneumoniae
   Correct Answer: C

3. **NSAIDs contribute to peptic ulcer disease primarily by:**
   A) Increasing mucus production.
   B) Enhancing acid secretion.
   C) Inhibiting prostaglandin synthesis.
   D) Stimulating mucosal blood flow.
   Correct Answer: C

4. **The urea breath test is used to detect:**
   A) Gastric cancer
   B) H. pylori infection
   C) Acid secretion levels
   D) Gastric motility
   Correct Answer: B

5. **Which of the following is a non-invasive test for PUD diagnosis?**
   A) Endoscopy
   B) Biopsy
   C) Stool antigen test
   D) Laparoscopy

Correct Answer: C

6. **Endoscopy in the diagnosis of PUD primarily allows clinicians to:**
   A) Assess gastric emptying
   B) Visualize ulcers and obtain biopsies
   C) Measure acid secretion quantitatively
   D) Diagnose irritable bowel syndrome
   Correct Answer: B

7. **Proton pump inhibitors (PPIs) act by inhibiting:**
   A) H+/K+ ATPase in parietal cells
   B) Cyclooxygenase enzymes
   C) H2 receptors
   D) Gastrin secretion
   Correct Answer: A

8. **Which of the following is an example of a PPI?**
   A) Ranitidine
   B) Omeprazole
   C) Metoclopramide
   D) Sucralfate
   Correct Answer: B

9. **High-dose PPI regimens are typically used for:**
   A) Mild acid reflux
   B) Severe or refractory peptic ulcers
   C) NSAID-induced ulcers only
   D) Constipation treatment
   Correct Answer: B

10. **A known side effect of long-term PPI use is:**
    A) Hypomagnesemia
    B) Hyperkalemia
    C) Hypocalcemia
    D) Hypernatremia
    Correct Answer: A

11. **H2 receptor antagonists work by:**
    A) Inhibiting the H+/K+ ATPase pump
    B) Blocking histamine-induced acid secretion
    C) Increasing mucus production
    D) Eradicating H. pylori infection
    Correct Answer: B

12. **An example of an H2 receptor antagonist is:**
    A) Pantoprazole
    B) Cimetidine
    C) Omeprazole
    D) Clarithromycin
    Correct Answer: B

13. **Triple therapy for H. pylori typically consists of a PPI plus:**
    A) Two H2 blockers
    B) Two antibiotics
    C) An antibiotic and a cytoprotective agent
    D) A prokinetic and an antiemetic
    Correct Answer: B

14. **A common antibiotic combination in triple therapy for H. pylori includes:**
    A) Amoxicillin and clarithromycin
    B) Ciprofloxacin and metronidazole
    C) Erythromycin and amoxicillin
    D) Tetracycline and doxycycline
    Correct Answer: A

15. **Cytoprotective agents, such as sucralfate, act by:**
    A) Inhibiting acid secretion
    B) Forming a protective barrier over ulcers
    C) Directly eradicating H. pylori
    D) Increasing acid secretion
    Correct Answer: B

16. **Bismuth subsalicylate is used in PUD management for its:**
    A) Cytoprotective properties
    B) Acid suppression effects
    C) Prokinetic effects
    D) H2 receptor blocking properties
    Correct Answer: A

17. **A key lifestyle modification in the management of PUD is:**
    A) Smoking cessation
    B) Increased alcohol consumption
    C) High-fat diets
    D) Sedentary lifestyle
    Correct Answer: A

18. **GERD is primarily caused by dysfunction of the:**
    A) Pyloric sphincter
    B) Lower esophageal sphincter (LES)
    C) Ileocecal valve
    D) Cardiac muscle
    Correct Answer: B

19. **Delayed gastric emptying contributes to:**
    A) GERD
    B) Ulcerative colitis
    C) Hepatitis
    D) Pancreatitis
    Correct Answer: A

20. **The first-line pharmacological treatment for GERD is typically:**
    A) Proton pump inhibitors
    B) Antibiotics
    C) Corticosteroids
    D) Immunomodulators
    Correct Answer: A

21. **Prokinetic agents like metoclopramide are used in GERD to:**
    A) Increase LES tone directly
    B) Enhance gastric emptying
    C) Inhibit acid secretion
    D) Eradicate H. pylori
    Correct Answer: B

22. **Domperidone is a prokinetic used because it:**
    A) Acts centrally to enhance motility
    B) Enhances gastric emptying with fewer central side effects
    C) Blocks H2 receptors
    D) Functions as a PPI
    Correct Answer: B

23. **Surgical intervention for GERD, such as fundoplication, is indicated when:**
    A) Lifestyle modifications suffice
    B) Medical therapy fails to control symptoms
    C) The patient has only mild symptoms
    D) There is no evidence of reflux
    Correct Answer: B

24. **Fundoplication surgery works by:**
    A) Removing the esophagus
    B) Strengthening the lower esophageal sphincter
    C) Increasing acid production
    D) Dilating the esophagus
    Correct Answer: B

25. **Ulcerative colitis is characterized by:**
    A) Transmural inflammation
    B) Continuous colonic involvement limited to the mucosa and submucosa
    C) Skip lesions
    D) Predominant small intestine involvement
    Correct Answer: B

26. **Aminosalicylates such as sulfasalazine are used in the treatment of:**
    A) Peptic ulcer disease
    B) Ulcerative colitis
    C) GERD
    D) Hepatitis
    Correct Answer: B

27. **Mesalamine is classified as a/an:**
    A) Corticosteroid
    B) Aminosalicylate
    C) Immunomodulator
    D) Biologic agent
    Correct Answer: B

28. **Anti-TNF therapy in IBD is an example of:**
    A) A biologic agent
    B) An antibiotic regimen
    C) A prokinetic
    D) A cytoprotective drug
    Correct Answer: A

29. **Crohn's disease is distinguished from ulcerative colitis by its:**
    A) Continuous colonic involvement
    B) Transmural inflammation and skip lesions
    C) Superficial mucosal involvement only
    D) Exclusive left-sided colonic disease
    Correct Answer: B

30. **Corticosteroids in IBD are primarily used for:**
    A) Long-term maintenance therapy
    B) Inducing remission during acute flares
    C) Preventing nutritional deficiencies
    D) Enhancing gut motility
    Correct Answer: B

31. **Immunomodulators in Crohn's disease are used mainly for:**
    A) Short-term symptom relief
    B) Long-term maintenance of remission
    C) Immediate pain relief
    D) Eradicating bacterial infections
    Correct Answer: B

32. **Nutritional deficiencies in IBD often include:**
    A) Vitamin C deficiency
    B) Iron deficiency
    C) Hypercalcemia
    D) Excess vitamin A
    Correct Answer: B

33. **Nutritional supplementation in IBD aims to:**
    A) Correct deficiencies and support overall health
    B) Replace all pharmacologic treatments
    C) Increase caloric restriction
    D) Induce remission solely through diet
    Correct Answer: A

34. **Alcoholic liver disease typically progresses through which stages?**
    A) Steatosis, hepatitis, cirrhosis
    B) Fibrosis, hepatitis, cancer
    C) Inflammation, ulceration, necrosis
    D) Steatosis, pancreatitis, cirrhosis
    Correct Answer: A

35. **Thiamine supplementation in alcoholic liver disease is recommended to:**
    A) Prevent Wernicke-Korsakoff syndrome
    B) Lower cholesterol levels
    C) Reduce liver enzyme production
    D) Enhance alcohol metabolism
    Correct Answer: A

36. **Antioxidant therapy in alcoholic liver disease is used to:**
    A) Increase oxidative stress
    B) Reduce oxidative damage to liver cells
    C) Increase liver enzyme production
    D) Stimulate fibrosis
    Correct Answer: B

37. **For hepatitis B treatment, which antiviral is commonly used?**
    A) Tenofovir
    B) Metronidazole
    C) Omeprazole
    D) Sucralfate
    Correct Answer: A

38. **Entecavir is used primarily in the treatment of:**
    A) Hepatitis C
    B) Hepatitis B
    C) Peptic ulcer disease
    D) GERD
    Correct Answer: B

39. **Direct-acting antivirals (DAAs) are used for treating:**
    A) Hepatitis B
    B) Hepatitis C
    C) Alcoholic liver disease
    D) Drug-induced liver disorders
    Correct Answer: B

40. **Drug-induced liver disorders are commonly associated with:**
    A) Antibiotics
    B) Acetaminophen
    C) Proton pump inhibitors
    D) H2 receptor antagonists
    Correct Answer: B

41. **Amiodarone is known to cause:**
    A) Gastrointestinal bleeding
    B) Liver toxicity
    C) Renal failure
    D) Pulmonary fibrosis
    Correct Answer: B

42. **Monitoring liver enzymes is critical in patients taking medications that can cause:**

A) Cardiac arrhythmias

B) Drug-induced liver injury

C) Skin rashes

D) Neurological disorders

Correct Answer: B

43. **In PUD, the use of NSAIDs contributes to ulcer formation by:**

A) Increasing mucus secretion

B) Reducing prostaglandin synthesis

C) Enhancing gastric motility

D) Improving mucosal blood flow

Correct Answer: B

44. **H. pylori infection in PUD is most commonly detected using:**

A) Urea breath test

B) Complete blood count

C) Electrocardiogram

D) Ultrasound

Correct Answer: A

45. **Endoscopic biopsy in PUD is performed to:**

A) Measure acid production

B) Detect H. pylori and assess ulcer histology

C) Evaluate renal function

D) Monitor liver enzymes

Correct Answer: B

46. **Which class of drugs directly inhibits the H+/K+ ATPase pump?**

A) H2 receptor antagonists

B) Proton pump inhibitors

C) Antibiotics

D) Cytoprotective agents

Correct Answer: B

47. **Omeprazole and pantoprazole are examples of:**

A) H2 receptor antagonists

B) Proton pump inhibitors

C) Prokinetic agents

D) Biologics

Correct Answer: B

48. **Clarithromycin is used in PUD primarily as part of:**

A) GERD treatment

B) H. pylori eradication regimens

C) Crohn's disease management

D) Liver disorder therapy

Correct Answer: B

49. **Sucralfate provides cytoprotection by:**

A) Neutralizing stomach acid

B) Forming a protective barrier over the ulcer

C) Increasing acid secretion

D) Directly eradicating H. pylori

Correct Answer: B

50. **Bismuth subsalicylate is used in PUD for its:**

A) Acid suppression

B) Cytoprotective and antibacterial properties against H. pylori

C) H2 receptor blocking effects

D) Prokinetic actions

Correct Answer: B

51. **A primary lifestyle modification recommended for PUD patients is:**

A) Smoking cessation

B) Increasing alcohol intake

C) High-fat diet consumption

D) Sedentary behavior

Correct Answer: A

52. **GERD is primarily associated with dysfunction of the:**

A) Lower esophageal sphincter

B) Pyloric sphincter

C) Ileocecal valve

D) Cardiac muscle

Correct Answer: A

53. **Delayed gastric emptying can exacerbate:**

A) Ulcerative colitis

B) GERD

C) Hepatitis

D) Pancreatitis

Correct Answer: B

54. **In GERD management, PPIs are used to:**

A) Increase LES tone

B) Reduce gastric acid secretion

C) Enhance gastric motility

D) Eradicate H. pylori

Correct Answer: B

55. **Prokinetic agents such as metoclopramide function by:**
    A) Inhibiting acid secretion
    B) Accelerating gastric emptying
    C) Strengthening the LES
    D) Reducing bile production
    Correct Answer: B

56. **Fundoplication is a surgical procedure used in GERD to:**
    A) Remove the esophagus
    B) Reinforce the lower esophageal sphincter
    C) Increase acid production
    D) Dilate the esophagus
    Correct Answer: B

57. **Ulcerative colitis primarily affects the:**
    A) Entire GI tract
    B) Colon and rectum
    C) Small intestine
    D) Stomach exclusively
    Correct Answer: B

58. **Sulfasalazine is used in ulcerative colitis due to its:**
    A) Antiviral properties
    B) Anti-inflammatory effects
    C) Prokinetic effects
    D) Cytoprotective properties
    Correct Answer: B

59. **Mesalamine is a type of:**
    A) Corticosteroid
    B) Aminosalicylate
    C) Immunomodulator
    D) Biologic
    Correct Answer: B

60. **Anti-TNF therapy in IBD is classified as a:**
    A) Biologic agent
    B) Antibiotic regimen
    C) Prokinetic
    D) Cytoprotective drug
    Correct Answer: A

61. **Crohn's disease is characterized by:**
    A) Continuous colonic involvement
    B) Transmural inflammation and skip lesions
    C) Only superficial mucosal involvement
    D) Exclusively left-sided colonic disease
    Correct Answer: B

62. **Corticosteroids in IBD are primarily used for:**
    A) Long-term maintenance therapy
    B) Induction of remission during acute flares
    C) Preventing nutritional deficiencies
    D) Enhancing gut motility
    Correct Answer: B

63. **Immunomodulators in Crohn's disease are used for:**
    A) Short-term symptom control
    B) Long-term maintenance of remission
    C) Immediate pain relief
    D) Eradicating bacterial infections
    Correct Answer: B

64. **A common nutritional deficiency seen in IBD patients is:**
    A) Vitamin D deficiency
    B) Excess vitamin C
    C) Hypercalcemia
    D) Overconsumption of calories
    Correct Answer: A

65. **Nutritional supplementation in IBD aims to:**
    A) Worsen the disease
    B) Correct deficiencies and support overall health
    C) Replace all pharmacological treatments
    D) Eliminate the need for surgical intervention
    Correct Answer: B

66. **Alcoholic liver disease typically progresses through which sequence?**
    A) Steatosis, hepatitis, cirrhosis
    B) Fibrosis, hepatitis, cancer
    C) Inflammation, ulceration, necrosis
    D) Steatosis, pancreatitis, cirrhosis
    Correct Answer: A

67. **Thiamine supplementation in alcoholic liver disease is recommended to:**

A) Prevent Wernicke-Korsakoff syndrome

B) Lower cholesterol levels

C) Reduce liver enzyme production

D) Enhance alcohol metabolism

Correct Answer: A

68. **Antioxidant therapy in alcoholic liver disease is used to:**

A) Increase oxidative stress

B) Reduce oxidative damage to liver cells

C) Increase liver enzyme production

D) Stimulate liver fibrosis

Correct Answer: B

69. **For hepatitis B, which antiviral is commonly used?**

A) Tenofovir

B) Metronidazole

C) Omeprazole

D) Sucralfate

Correct Answer: A

70. **Entecavir is used primarily in the treatment of:**

A) Hepatitis C

B) Hepatitis B

C) Peptic ulcer disease

D) GERD

Correct Answer: B

71. **Direct-acting antivirals (DAAs) are indicated for treating:**

A) Hepatitis B

B) Hepatitis C

C) Alcoholic liver disease

D) Drug-induced liver injury

Correct Answer: B

72. **Acetaminophen overdose is a common cause of:**

A) Alcoholic liver disease

B) Viral hepatitis

C) Drug-induced liver disorders

D) Autoimmune hepatitis

Correct Answer: C

73. **Amiodarone-induced liver toxicity is an example of a:**

A) Viral hepatitis

B) Drug-induced liver disorder

C) Alcoholic liver disease

D) Non-alcoholic fatty liver disease

Correct Answer: B

74. **Monitoring liver enzymes is important in patients receiving medications that may cause:**

A) Cardiac arrhythmias

B) Drug-induced liver injury

C) Skin rashes

D) Neurological disorders

Correct Answer: B

CHAPTER THREE

Hematological System

3.1.1 Iron Deficiency Anemia

Iron deficiency anemia is the most common type of anemia worldwide, occurring due to **insufficient iron availability for hemoglobin synthesis**, leading to the production of **microcytic hypochromic red blood cells**. The condition results in **reduced oxygen-carrying capacity**, leading to symptoms such as **fatigue, pallor, dizziness, and shortness of breath**. Early diagnosis and appropriate iron supplementation are critical to restoring normal hematopoiesis.

Pathophysiology

Iron is an essential component of **hemoglobin, myoglobin, and various enzymatic systems**. When iron levels are insufficient, **hemoglobin synthesis is impaired**, resulting in small, pale red blood cells (microcytosis and hypochromia).

1. **Reduced Iron Availability**

   - **Iron is stored in the body as ferritin**, mainly in the liver, spleen, and bone marrow.
   - When iron intake is inadequate or iron loss exceeds absorption, **ferritin stores deplete**, leading to iron-deficient erythropoiesis.

2. **Common Causes of Iron Deficiency**

- **Blood loss**: Chronic gastrointestinal bleeding (peptic ulcers, colorectal cancer, inflammatory bowel disease), **heavy menstrual bleeding (menorrhagia)**, frequent blood donation.
- **Inadequate dietary intake**: Common in vegetarians or individuals with poor nutrition.
- **Malabsorption syndromes**: Celiac disease, gastrectomy, Helicobacter pylori infection.
- **Increased demand**: Pregnancy, infancy, and rapid growth phases.

Oral Iron Therapy

Oral iron supplementation is the **first-line treatment** for most cases of iron deficiency anemia. It is effective, inexpensive, and generally well tolerated.

Common Oral Iron Preparations and Dosage

Several oral iron formulations are available, each differing in **elemental iron content and absorption efficiency**. The selection of an appropriate preparation depends on **patient tolerance, iron deficiency severity, and gastrointestinal side effects.**

- **Ferrous sulfate** is one of the most commonly prescribed iron supplements. A standard dose of **325 mg once daily** provides **65 mg of elemental iron**.
- **Ferrous fumarate** has a higher elemental iron content compared to ferrous sulfate. A typical dose of **300 mg once daily** delivers **99 mg of elemental iron**, making it suitable for patients requiring higher iron replenishment.
- **Ferrous gluconate** is often preferred in patients who experience gastrointestinal discomfort with other iron salts. A **325 mg once-daily dose** supplies **35 mg of elemental iron**, which is lower than other formulations but may have **better tolerability**.
- **Ferric carboxymaltose** is a parenteral iron preparation that offers **high bioavailability** and is used in patients with **severe iron deficiency anemia or intolerance to oral iron supplements**. It is administered at doses ranging from **500 mg to 1000 mg once weekly**, depending on the severity of deficiency.

Choosing the **right iron supplement** depends on factors such as **absorption, side effects, and patient compliance**, with **ferrous sulfate** being the most commonly used due to its affordability and effectiveness.

Mechanism of Action

Oral iron supplements **replenish body iron stores,** allowing the bone marrow to restore normal red blood cell production. The absorbed iron binds to **transferrin,** which transports it to **developing erythrocytes in the bone marrow.**

Side Effects of Oral Iron Therapy

- Gastrointestinal side effects are common and include **nausea, constipation, diarrhea, epigastric discomfort, and black stools.**
- **Managing side effects:**

  - Start with a **lower dose** and gradually increase.
  - Take iron **with food** to reduce gastric irritation (though this may slightly reduce absorption).
  - Switch to **ferric formulations,** which cause **less gastrointestinal discomfort.**

Parenteral Iron Therapy

Intravenous iron is reserved for patients who cannot tolerate or **do not respond to oral iron supplementation.** It provides **rapid iron repletion** and is useful in patients with severe anemia or chronic blood loss.

Indications for Parenteral Iron Therapy

- **Severe iron deficiency anemia,** particularly in patients with hemoglobin **below 7 g/dL.**
- **Intolerance to oral iron** due to **persistent gastrointestinal side effects.**
- **Malabsorption syndromes,** such as **celiac disease, inflammatory bowel disease, or after bariatric surgery.**
- **Chronic kidney disease (CKD)** patients on hemodialysis, who often require iron supplementation due to **erythropoiesis-stimulating agents.**

Common Parenteral Iron Preparations and Dosage

Parenteral iron therapy is used in **patients with severe iron deficiency anemia,** those who **cannot tolerate oral iron supplements,** or in cases of **chronic blood loss requiring rapid iron replenishment.** Different formulations vary in **dosing schedules and administration methods,** influencing **treatment convenience and patient compliance.**

- **Ferric gluconate** is typically administered as **125 mg intravenously (IV) once per week** through a **slow IV infusion.** Since the total iron requirement is often higher, multiple infusions are necessary to achieve full iron repletion.
- **Iron sucrose** is given at **200 mg IV every 2 to 3 days,** requiring **multiple doses** to correct iron deficiency effectively. This formulation is commonly used in **chronic kidney disease (CKD) patients on dialysis** due to its **lower risk of hypersensitivity reactions.**
- **Ferric carboxymaltose** offers the advantage of **high single-dose administration,** allowing doses of **500 to 1000 mg IV once every week.** This reduces the **number of hospital visits,** making it a preferred choice for **patients requiring rapid iron restoration.**

While **ferric gluconate and iron sucrose require multiple infusions** for complete iron repletion, **ferric carboxymaltose provides a more convenient single-dose therapy,** minimizing patient discomfort and healthcare visits. The selection of a **parenteral iron formulation** should be based on **efficacy, safety, patient tolerance, and healthcare setting availability**

Drug	Dose	Administration
Ferric gluconate	125 mg IV weekly	Slow IV infusion
Iron sucrose	200 mg IV every 2-3 days	Multiple doses
Ferric carboxymaltose	500–1000 mg IV once every week	Single-dose therapy

Common Parenteral Iron Preparations and Dosage

Monitoring and Safety Concerns

- **Hypersensitivity reactions** can occur, including **anaphylaxis with iron dextran,** requiring a **test dose before full administration.**

- Patients receiving IV iron should be **monitored for hypotension, allergic reactions, and iron overload.**

Monitoring Response to Iron Therapy

Regular monitoring ensures that iron therapy is **effective and well tolerated.**

1. **Expected Hemoglobin Response**

   - Hemoglobin should rise by **1 gram per deciliter within two to four weeks** of starting therapy.
   - Full correction of anemia usually takes **two to three months,** but therapy should continue **for at least six months** to replenish iron stores.

2. **Serum Ferritin and Transferrin Saturation**

   - **Ferritin levels below 15 nanograms per milliliter confirm iron deficiency.**
   - **Transferrin saturation below 20 percent** suggests iron depletion.
   - These parameters should be re-evaluated **every three months** to assess iron repletion and prevent recurrence.

3. **Reticulocyte Count**

   - A **rise in reticulocyte count within one week** indicates an early response to therapy.

3.1.2 Megaloblastic Anemia

Megaloblastic anemia is a **macrocytic anemia** caused by **impaired DNA synthesis** due to deficiencies in **vitamin B12 or folate.** This results in the production of **large, immature red blood cells (megaloblasts)** with **defective nuclear maturation.** Unlike iron deficiency anemia, which presents with microcytic hypochromic red blood cells, megaloblastic anemia is characterized by **macrocytosis (high mean corpuscular volume), hypersegmented neutrophils, and ineffective erythropoiesis.**

Pathophysiology

1. **Deficiency of Vitamin B12 or Folate Impairs DNA Synthesis**

   - Vitamin B12 and folate are essential for **thymidine synthesis,** a key component of DNA.
   - When either of these nutrients is deficient, cells cannot divide properly, leading to **large, immature erythrocytes** in the bone marrow.

2. **Causes of Vitamin B12 Deficiency**

   - **Pernicious anemia**: Autoimmune destruction of **gastric parietal cells,** leading to **intrinsic factor deficiency** and impaired vitamin B12 absorption.
   - **Dietary deficiency**: Vitamin B12 is found in animal products, so strict vegans are at risk.
   - **Gastrectomy or intestinal malabsorption**: Conditions such as **celiac disease, Crohn's disease, or ileal resection** reduce B12 absorption.
   - **Long-term use of metformin or proton pump inhibitors** can interfere with vitamin B12 absorption.

3. **Causes of Folate Deficiency**

   - **Poor dietary intake**: Folate is found in **leafy vegetables, legumes, and citrus fruits,** and deficiency is common in **malnourished individuals.**
   - **Alcoholism**: Chronic alcohol use reduces folate absorption and hepatic storage.
   - **Pregnancy**: Increased folate demand for fetal neural tube development.
   - **Hemolytic anemia**: Increased erythropoiesis leads to folate depletion.

Treatment of Vitamin B12 Deficiency

Vitamin B12 therapy is essential for **correcting anemia and preventing neurological complications,** as vitamin B12 deficiency can lead to **subacute combined degeneration of the spinal cord**, which is irreversible if untreated.

1. **Hydroxocobalamin (Preferred over Cyanocobalamin)**

   - **Intramuscular injection** is required for pernicious anemia or severe deficiency.
   - **Dose regimen:**

     - **1 milligram intramuscularly daily for one week** (to replenish stores).
     - **Once weekly for four weeks** (for continued correction).
     - **Once monthly for lifelong maintenance** (in cases of irreversible malabsorption).

   - Oral vitamin B12 (1000–2000 micrograms daily) may be used for dietary deficiency but is **not effective for pernicious anemia.**

2. **Monitoring Response to Therapy**

   - **Serum vitamin B12 levels** should be measured **before treatment and after 8 weeks.**
   - **Reticulocyte count rises within 3–5 days**, indicating early bone marrow response.
   - **Neurological improvement is expected within 6–12 weeks**, but in **severe cases, recovery may be incomplete.**

   Treatment of Folate Deficiency
   Folate therapy is essential for **correcting macrocytic anemia and preventing complications during pregnancy.**

1. **Folic Acid Supplementation**

   - **Dose:** 5 milligrams orally once daily.
   - **Duration:** At least 4 months to **fully restore folate stores.**

2. **Special Considerations**

- ○ **Pregnancy**: Women should take **400 micrograms daily** to prevent **neural tube defects.**
- ○ **Patients with hemolytic anemia** require **long-term folate supplementation** due to increased erythropoiesis.

Clinical Monitoring of Treatment Response

1. **Mean Corpuscular Volume (MCV) Monitoring**

- ○ Macrocytosis starts correcting **within 6–8 weeks of therapy.**
- ○ **Complete normalization of MCV may take 2–3 months.**

2. **Reticulocyte Response**

- ○ Reticulocytosis (increased reticulocyte count) occurs within **7–10 days**, indicating effective erythropoiesis.

3. **Neurological Symptom Resolution**

- ○ Improvement in **paresthesia, ataxia, and cognitive dysfunction** begins within **6–12 weeks** in vitamin B12 deficiency.
- ○ If treatment is delayed, **neurological deficits may become irreversible.**

3.1.3 Hemolytic Anemia

Hemolytic anemia is a condition characterized by **premature destruction of red blood cells,** leading to **anemia, jaundice, and an increased reticulocyte count** as the bone marrow attempts to compensate for the loss. Hemolysis can occur due to **immune-mediated or non-immune mechanisms,** with varying treatment approaches depending on the underlying cause.

Pathophysiology

1. **Increased Red Blood Cell Destruction**

- ○ In hemolytic anemia, red blood cells are destroyed **before their normal lifespan of 120 days,** resulting in **excess hemoglobin**

breakdown and release of **unconjugated bilirubin**, leading to **jaundice**.

- **Reticulocyte count rises as bone marrow increases RBC production** to compensate for premature loss.

2. Immune-Mediated Hemolysis (Autoimmune Hemolytic Anemia)

- In **warm autoimmune hemolytic anemia, IgG antibodies bind to RBCs** at body temperature, leading to destruction primarily in the **spleen**.
- In **cold agglutinin disease, IgM antibodies activate complement**, causing **intravascular hemolysis**.

3. Non-Immune Hemolysis

- **Glucose-6-phosphate dehydrogenase (G6PD) deficiency**: RBCs are more vulnerable to oxidative stress, leading to episodic hemolysis after exposure to certain drugs (e.g., primaquine, sulfonamides) or infections.
- **Hereditary spherocytosis**: Defects in **RBC membrane proteins** cause premature splenic destruction.

Immunosuppressants for Autoimmune Hemolytic Anemia
Autoimmune hemolytic anemia requires **immunosuppression to reduce antibody-mediated RBC destruction.**

1. First-Line Therapy: Corticosteroids

- **Prednisolone at 1–2 milligrams per kilogram per day** is the first-line treatment for **warm autoimmune hemolytic anemia.**
- It reduces antibody production and **suppresses macrophage activity in the spleen**, leading to improved RBC survival.
- If hemolysis resolves, steroids are **tapered over weeks to months** to prevent relapse.

2. Second-Line Therapy: Rituximab and Splenectomy

- ◦ **Rituximab (375 milligrams per square meter weekly for 4 weeks)** targets **CD20 on B-cells,** reducing autoantibody production.
- ◦ **Splenectomy is considered in refractory cases,** as the spleen is the primary site of RBC destruction in warm autoimmune hemolytic anemia.

Supportive Therapy

Supportive care plays a crucial role in managing **hemolytic anemia and preventing complications.**

1. **Blood Transfusions for Severe Anemia**

   - ◦ Transfusions are indicated if **hemoglobin drops below 7 grams per deciliter** or if there are **signs of hemodynamic instability.**
   - ◦ In **autoimmune hemolytic anemia,** transfusion must be carefully matched due to **cross-matching difficulties from autoantibodies.**

2. **Folate Supplementation**

   - ◦ Chronic hemolysis increases **erythropoietic activity,** leading to higher folate requirements.
   - ◦ Daily folic acid supplementation of **1 to 5 milligrams** supports **RBC production and prevents megaloblastic changes.**

3.2.1 Risk Stratification for Venous Thromboembolism

Venous thromboembolism includes **deep vein thrombosis (DVT) and pulmonary embolism (PE),** both of which are life-threatening conditions requiring **early diagnosis and treatment. Risk stratification tools,** such as the **Wells Score,** help estimate the probability of venous thromboembolism, guiding further investigations and management.

Wells Score for Venous Thromboembolism

The **Wells Score** is a clinical prediction tool used to stratify patients based on their **risk of deep vein thrombosis (DVT) or pulmonary embolism (PE).** This scoring system helps determine whether **further diagnostic testing, such as D-dimer or imaging, is required.**

Wells Score Criteria for Deep Vein Thrombosis (DVT)

Each criterion is assigned a specific point value, with higher scores indicating greater probability of DVT.

Clinical Criteria	Points
Active cancer (treatment ongoing or within the last 6 months)	+1
Paralysis, paresis, or recent immobilization of lower limb	+1
Bedridden for >3 days or major surgery in the last 4 weeks	+1
Localized tenderness along the deep venous system	+1
Entire leg swollen	+1
Calf swelling >3 cm compared to the other leg (measured 10 cm below the tibial tuberosity)	+1
Pitting edema (greater in symptomatic leg)	+1
Collateral superficial veins (non-varicose)	+1
Alternative diagnosis more likely than DVT	−2

Wells Score Criteria for Deep Vein Thrombosis (DVT)

Total Score	Risk Category	Probability of DVT
≤1	Low risk	<5%
2–6	Moderate risk	17–20%
≥7	High risk	>50%

Interpretation of Wells Score for DVT

For **low-risk patients, D-dimer testing** is recommended to rule out DVT. In **moderate to high-risk patients, imaging (e.g., Doppler ultrasound)** is required for definitive diagnosis.

D-Dimer Testing

D-dimer is a **fibrin degradation product** that is elevated in conditions involving **clot formation and breakdown**. It is used as a **rule-out test** for venous thromboembolism in **low-risk patients**.

1. **Role of D-Dimer Testing**

- ◦ A **negative D-dimer (<500 nanograms per milliliter)** effectively **rules out venous thromboembolism in low-risk patients,** avoiding unnecessary imaging.
- ◦ An **elevated D-dimer (>500 nanograms per milliliter)** requires further imaging, such as **Doppler ultrasound for DVT or CT angiography for PE,** as D-dimer elevation is **not specific for venous thromboembolism.**

2. **Limitations of D-Dimer**

- ◦ **False-positive results** are common in conditions such as **pregnancy, infection, cancer, recent surgery, or trauma.**
- ◦ In **high-risk patients,** D-dimer is not reliable for diagnosis, and **imaging should be performed directly.**

3.2.2 Anticoagulant Therapy

The primary goal of anticoagulant therapy in venous thromboembolism is to **prevent clot propagation, reduce the risk of pulmonary embolism, and lower the recurrence rate.** Treatment options include **parenteral anticoagulants (heparin) and direct oral anticoagulants (DOACs).**

Heparin Therapy

Heparin is used for **initial anticoagulation** due to its **rapid onset of action and reversibility.** It is particularly useful in **hospitalized patients, those with renal impairment, or in cases requiring procedural anticoagulation adjustments.**

Mechanism of Action

- Heparin **binds and activates antithrombin III,** enhancing its ability to **inhibit thrombin (Factor IIa) and Factor Xa,** thereby preventing clot formation and propagation.
- Unfractionated heparin acts **immediately** and is cleared **by the liver,** making it suitable for use in patients with **renal dysfunction.**

Dosing and Administration

1. **Unfractionated Heparin (UFH)**

   - **Loading dose: 80 units per kilogram intravenously.**
   - **Continuous infusion: 18 units per kilogram per hour**, adjusted based on **activated partial thromboplastin time (aPTT)** levels.

2. **Low Molecular Weight Heparin (LMWH) (e.g., Enoxaparin)**

   - Enoxaparin is preferred in **outpatient settings** due to its predictable effect.
   - **Dose: 1 milligram per kilogram subcutaneously every 12 hours**, or **1.5 milligrams per kilogram once daily** for low-risk patients.
   - Unlike unfractionated heparin, LMWH **does not require frequent aPTT monitoring.**

Monitoring and Adjustments

- **Unfractionated heparin therapy requires regular aPTT monitoring,** with the target range set at **1.5–2.5 times the normal value** (typically **60–80 seconds**).
- **LMWH does not require routine monitoring,** but **anti-Xa levels** may be checked in **pregnant women, obese patients, and those with renal impairment.**

Side Effects of Heparin

- **Bleeding:** The most common complication, requiring careful dose adjustments and reversal with **protamine sulfate** if needed.
- **Heparin-induced thrombocytopenia (HIT):**

  - A severe immune-mediated complication where **platelet factor 4 binds heparin,** leading to **platelet activation, thrombosis, and low platelet counts.**
  - Requires immediate **discontinuation of heparin** and switching to a **direct thrombin inhibitor (argatroban or bivalirudin).**

Direct Oral Anticoagulants (DOACs)

DOACs are now **first-line agents** for the treatment of **venous thromboembolism** due to their **predictable pharmacokinetics, ease of administration, and lack of routine monitoring requirements.**

Drug	Loading Dose	Maintenance Dose
Rivaroxaban	15 mg twice daily for 21 days	20 mg once daily
Apixaban	10 mg twice daily for 7 days	5 mg twice daily
Edoxaban	Initial LMWH for 5–10 days	60 mg once daily
Dabigatran	Initial LMWH for 5–10 days	150 mg twice daily

Common DOACs Used in VTE

Rivaroxaban and Apixaban are preferred because they can be **initiated immediately without prior heparin use.**

Edoxaban and Dabigatran require **initial parenteral anticoagulation with LMWH** for 5–10 days before switching to oral therapy.

Mechanism of Action

- **Rivaroxaban, Apixaban, and Edoxaban inhibit Factor Xa,** preventing thrombin formation.
- **Dabigatran directly inhibits thrombin (Factor IIa),** blocking fibrin clot formation.

Advantages of DOACs

- **No need for routine coagulation monitoring**, unlike warfarin and unfractionated heparin.
- **Predictable pharmacokinetics**, allowing for **fixed dosing regimens.**
- **Lower risk of intracranial hemorrhage** compared to vitamin K antagonists.

Limitations and Considerations

- **Renal function adjustments** are required for **creatinine clearance below 30 milliliters per minute**, as these drugs are **partially renally excreted.**
- **Bleeding risk** remains a concern, but **specific reversal agents** are available:

  - **Andexanet alfa** for **rivaroxaban and apixaban reversal.**
  - **Idarucizumab** for **dabigatran reversal.**

3.2.3 Prevention of Venous Thromboembolism

Prevention of venous thromboembolism is crucial in patients at high risk, such as **post-surgical patients, those with prolonged immobility, hospitalized patients, and individuals with a history of venous thromboembolism.** Preventive measures include **mechanical interventions (compression stockings) and pharmacological anticoagulation (low molecular weight heparin or direct oral anticoagulants).**

Compression Stockings

Compression stockings are a **non-pharmacological method** used to **prevent deep vein thrombosis (DVT) by promoting venous circulation.**

1. **Mechanism of Action**

   - Compression stockings **apply graduated pressure** to the legs, with the highest pressure at the ankle, **gradually decreasing towards the thigh.**

- This **reduces venous stasis and promotes blood flow**, lowering the risk of clot formation.

2. **Indications for Use**

- **Post-operative patients**, particularly after orthopedic surgery (hip and knee replacements).
- **Patients with prolonged immobility**, such as those **on bed rest due to stroke, spinal cord injury, or hospitalization.**
- **Long-distance travelers** at risk of **traveler's thrombosis**, especially flights exceeding 4–6 hours.

3. **Effectiveness**

- Studies show that **compression stockings reduce the incidence of DVT by 50–60 percent** in post-operative patients.

4. **Limitations**

- Should be used **in combination with pharmacologic prophylaxis** in high-risk patients.
- Contraindicated in **patients with severe peripheral arterial disease,** as they can worsen ischemia.

Prophylactic Anticoagulation

Pharmacological anticoagulation is essential for **high-risk patients** to prevent clot formation. It is commonly used in settings such as **major surgery, intensive care units, and cancer-associated thrombosis.**
Low Molecular Weight Heparin (LMWH)

1. **Mechanism of Action**

- LMWH **enhances the activity of antithrombin III**, selectively inhibiting **Factor Xa**, leading to reduced thrombin generation and clot formation.

2. Commonly Used LMWH

- **Enoxaparin (40 milligrams subcutaneously once daily)** is the standard dose for **venous thromboembolism prophylaxis in hospitalized patients.**
- In **obese or high-risk patients,** a higher dose of **40 milligrams twice daily** may be required.

3. Indications

- **Orthopedic surgery (hip and knee replacements):** Patients undergoing major joint surgery have a **high risk of thrombosis,** requiring at least **10–14 days of prophylactic LMWH.**
- **Intensive care unit (ICU) patients:** Hospitalized patients with **sepsis, mechanical ventilation, or prolonged immobilization** require LMWH prophylaxis.
- **Cancer patients:** Cancer is a **prothrombotic state,** and **low-dose LMWH reduces the risk of thrombosis by nearly 50 percent** in these patients.

4. Limitations

- **Requires subcutaneous administration,** making long-term use inconvenient.
- **Renal dose adjustment is required in patients with creatinine clearance below 30 milliliters per minute.**

Direct Oral Anticoagulants (DOACs) for Prevention

DOACs provide an **alternative to LMWH for long-term prophylaxis,** particularly in patients undergoing **elective surgeries.**

1. Mechanism of Action

- **Rivaroxaban inhibits Factor Xa,** reducing thrombin formation.

Drug	Prophylactic Dose	Indications
Rivaroxaban	10 mg once daily	After hip or knee replacement
Apixaban	2.5 mg twice daily	Post-surgical thromboprophylaxis
Dabigatran	110 mg on day 1, then 220 mg daily	Post-orthopedic surger

Commonly Used DOACs

Advantages of DOACs over LMWH

- **Oral administration** (easier for patients compared to injections).
- **No need for routine monitoring.**
- **Lower risk of heparin-induced thrombocytopenia.**

· **Limitations**

- **Renal dose adjustment** is needed for creatinine clearance below 30 milliliters per minute.
- **Higher cost compared to LMWH.**

REVIEW QUESTIONS

1. Describe the pathophysiology of iron deficiency anemia and explain how a deficiency of iron affects red blood cell production.
2. Compare and contrast the oral iron preparations Ferrous Sulfate and Ferric Carboxymaltose regarding their indications, dosing, and common side effects.
3. Explain the rationale for using parenteral iron, such as Ferric Gluconate, in certain patients with iron deficiency anemia.
4. Discuss the gastrointestinal side effects associated with oral iron therapy and outline strategies to manage and mitigate these effects.
5. List the laboratory tests used to diagnose iron deficiency anemia and explain the significance of serum ferritin and hemoglobin levels.
6. Define megaloblastic anemia and explain the roles of vitamin B12 and folate in red blood cell maturation.
7. Describe the clinical presentation and laboratory findings typical of megaloblastic anemia.
8. Compare the treatment options for megaloblastic anemia, specifically the use of Hydroxocobalamin for vitamin B12 deficiency versus folic acid for folate deficiency.
9. Explain the mechanism by which Hydroxocobalamin corrects vitamin B12 deficiency in megaloblastic anemia.
10. Discuss the indications for folic acid supplementation in megaloblastic anemia and potential pitfalls if vitamin B12 deficiency is not also addressed.
11. Define hemolytic anemia and differentiate between autoimmune and non-autoimmune causes.
12. Describe the role of immunosuppressants in the management of autoimmune hemolytic anemia.
13. Outline the indications and protocols for supportive therapy, including blood transfusions, in hemolytic anemia.
14. Explain how the reticulocyte count and other laboratory markers help in the evaluation of hemolytic anemia.
15. Describe the Wells score and its components for risk stratification of venous thromboembolism (VTE).

16. Explain how the D-Dimer test is used in conjunction with the Wells score to assess the probability of VTE.

17. Discuss the limitations and benefits of using clinical risk stratification tools (Wells score and D-Dimer) in diagnosing VTE.

18. Outline the mechanism of action of unfractionated heparin in anticoagulant therapy and describe how it is monitored using aPTT.

19. Compare unfractionated heparin with direct oral anticoagulants (DOACs) such as Rivaroxaban and Apixaban, highlighting their mechanisms, administration routes, and monitoring requirements.

20. Discuss the advantages and potential risks of using DOACs in the management of VTE.

21. Explain the rationale for prophylactic anticoagulation in high-risk patients and describe common clinical scenarios where it is indicated.

22. Describe the role of compression stockings in the prevention of VTE and how they complement pharmacological prophylaxis.

23. Discuss the importance of patient-specific factors (such as renal function and bleeding risk) when selecting an anticoagulant regimen.

24. Explain how regular monitoring (using tests like aPTT) ensures the safety and efficacy of heparin therapy.

25. Discuss the impact of patient adherence on the success of oral iron therapy and the management of anemia.

26. Explain how individualized therapeutic plans are developed in hematology based on clinical and laboratory parameters.

27. Discuss the challenges in managing hemolytic anemia and the role of blood transfusions as supportive care.

28. Describe how advances in risk stratification have improved the management and outcomes of venous thromboembolism.

29. Explain the importance of integrating clinical evidence and patient-specific factors in making therapeutic decisions for anemia and VTE.

30. Reflect on how emerging anticoagulant therapies are influencing current clinical practice in the management of VTE.

31. Summarize the key takeaways from the hematological system chapter and discuss how these principles guide the clinical management of anemia and thromboembolic disorders.

MCQS

1. **Which of the following is the most common cause of iron deficiency anemia?**
   A) Chronic gastrointestinal bleeding
   B) Overconsumption of iron
   C) Genetic disorders
   D) Vitamin B12 deficiency
   Correct Answer: A

2. **Which oral iron supplement is most commonly used for iron deficiency anemia?**
   A) Ferrous sulfate
   B) Ferric gluconate
   C) Hydroxocobalamin
   D) Folic acid
   Correct Answer: A

3. **According to the chapter outline, Ferric Carboxymaltose is classified as which type of iron formulation?**
   A) Oral iron
   B) Parenteral iron
   C) Vitamin supplement
   D) Anticoagulant
   Correct Answer: A

4. **Which of the following is a parenteral iron formulation?**
   A) Ferrous sulfate
   B) Ferric gluconate
   C) Ferric carboxymaltose
   D) Folic acid
   Correct Answer: B

5. **A common gastrointestinal side effect of oral iron therapy is:**
   A) Nausea and abdominal discomfort
   B) Hypertension
   C) Constipation
   D) Both A and C
   Correct Answer: D

6. **A recommended strategy to manage GI side effects of oral iron is:**
   A) Taking iron with food
   B) Increasing the dose abruptly
   C) Taking the supplement on an empty stomach only
   D) Skipping doses frequently
   Correct Answer: A

7. **Which laboratory test is most indicative of iron deficiency anemia?**
   A) Elevated hemoglobin
   B) Low serum ferritin
   C) High serum vitamin B12
   D) Increased mean corpuscular volume
   Correct Answer: B

8. **Megaloblastic anemia is primarily due to deficiencies in which nutrients?**
   A) Iron and vitamin C
   B) Vitamin B12 and folate
   C) Calcium and vitamin D
   D) Vitamin K and magnesium
   Correct Answer: B

9. **Hydroxocobalamin is used in the treatment of megaloblastic anemia caused by:**
   A) Iron deficiency
   B) Vitamin B12 deficiency
   C) Folate deficiency
   D) Hemolytic anemia
   Correct Answer: B

10. **Folic acid supplementation is indicated in the treatment of megaloblastic anemia due to:**
    A) Iron deficiency
    B) Folate deficiency
    C) Vitamin B12 deficiency
    D) Hemolytic anemia
    Correct Answer: B

11. **Megaloblastic anemia is characterized by which of the following red blood cell features?**
    A) Microcytic, hypochromic cells
    B) Normocytic, normochromic cells
    C) Macrocytic cells with hypersegmented neutrophils

D) Spherocytes

Correct Answer: C

12. **In hemolytic anemia of autoimmune origin, immunosuppressants are used to:**

    A) Increase iron absorption

    B) Suppress antibody-mediated red blood cell destruction

    C) Enhance erythropoietin production

    D) Stimulate platelet function

    Correct Answer: B

13. **Supportive therapy in hemolytic anemia may include:**

    A) Iron supplementation

    B) Blood transfusion

    C) Vitamin B12 injections

    D) Corticosteroid therapy alone

    Correct Answer: B

14. **A typical laboratory finding in hemolytic anemia is:**

    A) Low lactate dehydrogenase (LDH)

    B) Elevated haptoglobin

    C) Elevated indirect bilirubin

    D) Decreased reticulocyte count

    Correct Answer: C

15. **The Wells score is used to assess the risk of:**

    A) Iron deficiency anemia

    B) Megaloblastic anemia

    C) Venous thromboembolism (VTE)

    D) Hemolytic anemia

    Correct Answer: C

16. **The D-Dimer test in the context of VTE is primarily used to:**

    A) Confirm VTE diagnosis definitively

    B) Rule out VTE in patients with low clinical probability

    C) Monitor heparin therapy

    D) Assess bleeding risk

    Correct Answer: B

17. **Heparin exerts its anticoagulant effect mainly by:**

    A) Inhibiting vitamin K synthesis

    B) Activating antithrombin III to inhibit thrombin and factor Xa

    C) Directly lysing clots

    D) Inhibiting platelet aggregation

Correct Answer: B

18. **The activated partial thromboplastin time (aPTT) is used to monitor:**
    A) Warfarin therapy
    B) Unfractionated heparin therapy
    C) DOAC therapy
    D) Antiplatelet therapy
    Correct Answer: B

19. **Direct oral anticoagulants (DOACs) such as Rivaroxaban and Apixaban primarily inhibit:**
    A) Thrombin (Factor IIa)
    B) Factor Xa
    C) Vitamin K epoxide reductase
    D) Platelet aggregation
    Correct Answer: B

20. **One of the main advantages of DOACs over unfractionated heparin is that they:**
    A) Require routine aPTT monitoring
    B) Can be given in fixed doses without regular coagulation monitoring
    C) Are administered intravenously
    D) Have a higher bleeding risk
    Correct Answer: B

21. **Compression stockings help prevent VTE by:**
    A) Increasing venous stasis
    B) Enhancing venous return
    C) Inhibiting clot formation directly
    D) Dilating arteries
    Correct Answer: B

22. **Prophylactic anticoagulation is indicated primarily in:**
    A) Low-risk outpatients
    B) Patients at high risk for VTE (e.g., postoperative or immobilized patients)
    C) Patients with bleeding disorders
    D) Healthy young individuals
    Correct Answer: B

23. **In VTE risk stratification, the Wells score is used to:**
    A) Diagnose VTE with absolute certainty
    B) Stratify patients based on clinical factors into low, moderate, or high risk

    C) Replace imaging studies entirely

    D) Monitor the effect of anticoagulant therapy

    Correct Answer: B

24. **Heparin's mechanism of action is best described as:**

    A) Direct inhibition of the H^+ /K^+ ATPase pump

    B) Activation of antithrombin III to inhibit clotting factors

    C) Blocking vitamin K recycling

    D) Direct lysis of blood clots

    Correct Answer: B

25. **Which of the following DOACs is approved for the treatment of VTE?**

    A) Warfarin

    B) Rivaroxaban

    C) Aspirin

    D) Clopidogrel

    Correct Answer: B

26. **Monitoring gastrointestinal side effects is crucial in patients on oral iron therapy because these side effects can:**

    A) Enhance drug absorption

    B) Reduce patient adherence

    C) Increase hemoglobin synthesis

    D) Improve iron bioavailability

    Correct Answer: B

27. **Common gastrointestinal side effects of oral iron therapy include:**

    A) Nausea, vomiting, and constipation

    B) Diarrhea only

    C) Headache and dizziness

    D) Skin rash and pruritus

    Correct Answer: A

28. **The role of vitamin B12 in erythropoiesis is primarily to:**

    A) Increase iron absorption

    B) Aid in DNA synthesis for red blood cell production

    C) Enhance platelet function

    D) Stimulate erythropoietin secretion

    Correct Answer: B

29. **Folate deficiency results in which type of anemia?**

    A) Microcytic anemia

    B) Normocytic anemia

    C) Macrocytic anemia

D) Hemolytic anemia

Correct Answer: C

30. **In the treatment of megaloblastic anemia due to vitamin B12 deficiency, the preferred therapy is:**

    A) Oral iron supplements

    B) Hydroxocobalamin injections

    C) Folic acid supplementation

    D) Blood transfusion

    Correct Answer: B

31. **Folic acid supplementation is used to treat megaloblastic anemia caused by folate deficiency.**

    A) True

    B) False

    Correct Answer: A

32. **A positive direct antiglobulin (Coombs) test is indicative of:**

    A) Iron deficiency anemia

    B) Autoimmune hemolytic anemia

    C) Megaloblastic anemia

    D) Anemia of chronic disease

    Correct Answer: B

33. **In hemolytic anemia, an elevated reticulocyte count typically indicates:**

    A) Decreased bone marrow activity

    B) An appropriate compensatory response to red blood cell destruction

    C) Iron deficiency

    D) Vitamin B12 deficiency

    Correct Answer: B

34. **A contraindication to heparin therapy is:**

    A) A history of heparin-induced thrombocytopenia

    B) Iron deficiency anemia

    C) Folate deficiency

    D) Vitamin B12 deficiency

    Correct Answer: A

35. **Direct oral anticoagulants (DOACs) are characterized by:**

    A) The need for routine coagulation monitoring

    B) Predictable pharmacokinetics and fixed dosing without routine monitoring

C) Intravenous administration

D) A requirement for frequent dose adjustments based on aPTT

Correct Answer: B

36. **The aPTT test is used to monitor which anticoagulant therapy?**

    A) Warfarin

    B) Unfractionated heparin

    C) DOACs

    D) Aspirin

    Correct Answer: B

37. **Which of the following is a primary indication for the use of prophylactic anticoagulation?**

    A) Ambulatory patients with no risk factors

    B) Hospitalized patients with high risk for VTE

    C) Patients with active bleeding

    D) Outpatients with minor injuries

    Correct Answer: B

38. **Ferric gluconate is used in the management of iron deficiency anemia because it is:**

    A) An effective oral iron supplement

    B) Administered parenterally when oral therapy is inadequate

    C) A vitamin supplement

    D) An agent used to treat VTE

    Correct Answer: B

39. **The most important laboratory indicator for diagnosing iron deficiency anemia is:**

    A) Serum ferritin

    B) Serum vitamin B12

    C) aPTT

    D) D-Dimer

    Correct Answer: A

40. **Hydroxocobalamin is administered to treat megaloblastic anemia due to:**

    A) Folate deficiency

    B) Vitamin B12 deficiency

    C) Iron deficiency

    D) Hemolytic anemia

    Correct Answer: B

41. **Folic acid supplementation is indicated for the treatment of megaloblastic anemia due to folate deficiency.**

    A) True

    B) False

    Correct Answer: A

42. **In autoimmune hemolytic anemia, immunosuppressants are used to:**

    A) Increase red blood cell production

    B) Suppress the immune response responsible for red blood cell destruction

    C) Enhance iron absorption

    D) Stimulate erythropoietin secretion

    Correct Answer: B

43. **Blood transfusion is considered supportive therapy in hemolytic anemia when:**

    A) The anemia is mild and asymptomatic

    B) There is severe anemia compromising oxygen delivery

    C) It is used prophylactically in all patients

    D) There is an isolated vitamin deficiency

    Correct Answer: B

44. **The Wells score for VTE includes which of the following factors?**

    A) Recent immobilization

    B) Elevated liver enzymes

    C) Low hemoglobin

    D) High serum ferritin

    Correct Answer: A

45. **A negative D-Dimer test is most useful for:**

    A) Confirming VTE in high-risk patients

    B) Ruling out VTE in patients with low to moderate clinical probability

    C) Monitoring heparin therapy

    D) Diagnosing hemolytic anemia

    Correct Answer: B

46. **Heparin's anticoagulant effect is mediated by its ability to:**

    A) Directly lyse clots

    B) Enhance fibrinolysis

    C) Activate antithrombin III, thereby inhibiting thrombin and factor Xa

    D) Inhibit vitamin K synthesis

    Correct Answer: C

47. **DOACs such as Rivaroxaban and Apixaban primarily function by inhibiting:**

    A) Thrombin (Factor IIa)

    B) Factor Xa

    C) Platelet aggregation

    D) Vitamin K epoxide reductase

    Correct Answer: B

48. **One advantage of DOACs over warfarin is that they:**

    A) Require frequent INR monitoring

    B) Have predictable dosing without routine coagulation monitoring

    C) Are administered intravenously

    D) Have a narrow therapeutic index

    Correct Answer: B

49. **Compression stockings help prevent VTE by:**

    A) Increasing venous stasis

    B) Promoting venous return

    C) Directly dissolving clots

    D) Reducing arterial blood flow

    Correct Answer: B

50. **Prophylactic anticoagulation is most appropriate for:**

    A) Ambulatory patients with low VTE risk

    B) Hospitalized patients at high risk for VTE

    C) Patients with active bleeding disorders

    D) Healthy individuals with no risk factors

    Correct Answer: B

51. **Which of the following is a common indicator of a successful response to oral iron therapy?**

    A) Decrease in serum ferritin

    B) Increase in hemoglobin and serum ferritin levels

    C) Prolonged aPTT

    D) Elevated D-Dimer

    Correct Answer: B

52. **A peripheral blood smear in megaloblastic anemia typically shows:**

    A) Microcytic, hypochromic cells

    B) Normocytic, normochromic cells

    C) Macrocytic cells with hypersegmented neutrophils

    D) Spherocytes

    Correct Answer: C

53. **Which of the following is the preferred treatment for megaloblastic anemia due to folate deficiency?**

    A) Iron supplementation

    B) Folic acid supplementation

    C) Vitamin B12 injections

    D) Corticosteroid therapy

    Correct Answer: B

54. **A positive direct antiglobulin (Coombs) test in a patient with hemolytic anemia suggests:**

    A) Iron deficiency

    B) Autoimmune hemolysis

    C) Megaloblastic anemia

    D) Folate deficiency

    Correct Answer: B

55. **An elevated reticulocyte count in hemolytic anemia indicates:**

    A) Poor bone marrow response

    B) An appropriate compensatory increase in red blood cell production

    C) Iron deficiency

    D) Vitamin B12 deficiency

    Correct Answer: B

56. **A contraindication to heparin therapy is a history of:**

    A) Iron deficiency anemia

    B) Heparin-induced thrombocytopenia

    C) Megaloblastic anemia

    D) Venous stasis

    Correct Answer: B

57. **Which of the following best describes the monitoring requirements for DOACs?**

    A) Routine aPTT monitoring is required

    B) They require regular INR checks

    C) They do not require routine coagulation monitoring

    D) They are monitored by D-Dimer levels

    Correct Answer: C

58. **In the Wells score for VTE, which of the following is NOT a typical factor?**

    A) Recent immobilization

    B) Active cancer

    C) Prior history of DVT

D) Elevated liver enzymes

Correct Answer: D

59. **A negative D-Dimer test is most useful for ruling out VTE in:**

A) High-risk patients

B) Low- to moderate-risk patients

C) Patients with confirmed DVT

D) Patients on anticoagulant therapy

Correct Answer: B

60. **The primary mechanism of action of proton pump inhibitors is to:**

A) Block H2 receptors

B) Inhibit the H^+ /K^+ ATPase pump in gastric parietal cells

C) Form a protective barrier on the gastric mucosa

D) Neutralize gastric acid directly

Correct Answer: B

61. **In the treatment of GERD, prokinetic agents such as metoclopramide are used to:**

A) Inhibit acid secretion

B) Enhance gastric emptying

C) Strengthen the LES directly

D) Eradicate H. pylori

Correct Answer: B

62. **Fundoplication is a surgical procedure performed for GERD when:**

A) Medical therapy is effective

B) Symptoms are refractory to medical management

C) The patient prefers surgery over medication

D) It is used as a diagnostic tool

Correct Answer: B

63. **Aminosalicylates, such as sulfasalazine and mesalamine, are used primarily in the treatment of:**

A) Iron deficiency anemia

B) Ulcerative colitis

C) Hemolytic anemia

D) Venous thromboembolism

Correct Answer: B

64. **Anti-TNF therapy in inflammatory bowel disease is classified as a:**

A) Corticosteroid

B) Aminosalicylate

C) Biologic agent

D) Immunomodulator

Correct Answer: C

65. **Corticosteroids in IBD are primarily used for:**
    A) Long-term maintenance therapy
    B) Inducing remission during acute flares
    C) Preventing nutritional deficiencies
    D) Enhancing gut motility

    Correct Answer: B

66. **Immunomodulators in the management of Crohn's disease are used for:**
    A) Immediate symptom relief
    B) Long-term maintenance of remission
    C) Acute bleeding control
    D) Iron supplementation

    Correct Answer: B

67. **Common nutritional deficiencies in patients with IBD include deficiencies of:**
    A) Vitamin D, iron, and vitamin B12
    B) Vitamin C only
    C) Calcium only
    D) Carbohydrates

    Correct Answer: A

68. **Alcoholic liver disease typically progresses through which sequence?**
    A) Hepatitis, cirrhosis, steatosis
    B) Steatosis, hepatitis, cirrhosis
    C) Cirrhosis, steatosis, hepatitis
    D) Fibrosis, steatosis, cirrhosis

    Correct Answer: B

69. **Thiamine supplementation in alcoholic liver disease is recommended to:**
    A) Lower cholesterol levels
    B) Prevent Wernicke-Korsakoff syndrome
    C) Enhance liver regeneration
    D) Stimulate alcohol metabolism

    Correct Answer: B

70. **Antioxidant therapy in alcoholic liver disease is used to:**
    A) Increase oxidative stress
    B) Reduce oxidative damage to hepatocytes

C) Stimulate fibrosis

D) Enhance viral clearance

Correct Answer: B

71. **For the treatment of hepatitis B, which antiviral agent is commonly used?**

    A) Tenofovir

    B) Metronidazole

    C) Omeprazole

    D) Sulfasalazine

    Correct Answer: A

72. **Direct-acting antivirals (DAAs) are primarily used to treat:**

    A) Hepatitis A

    B) Hepatitis B

    C) Hepatitis C

    D) Alcoholic liver disease

    Correct Answer: C

CHAPTER FOUR

Nervous System

4.1 Epilepsy

4.1.1 Classification of Seizures

Epilepsy is a **neurological disorder characterized by recurrent, unprovoked seizures** due to **abnormal neuronal activity in the brain.** Seizures are classified based on their **origin, clinical presentation, and level of consciousness impairment.** The major classifications include **focal seizures, generalized seizures, and absence seizures.** Understanding these classifications is essential for appropriate **diagnosis and treatment selection.**

Focal Seizures

Focal seizures originate in a **specific area of the brain (unilateral onset)** and can be further divided into **simple focal seizures and complex focal seizures,** depending on **whether consciousness is affected.**

Simple Focal Seizures (Without Impaired Awareness)

- These seizures occur in a **localized region of the brain** without affecting awareness.
- Symptoms depend on the region of the brain involved:

  - **Motor cortex involvement:** Uncontrolled **jerking movements in one limb or one side of the body.**
  - **Sensory cortex involvement:** Tingling **sensations, visual or auditory disturbances.**
  - **Autonomic involvement:** Sweating, flushing, or palpitations.

Complex Focal Seizures (With Impaired Awareness)

- These seizures **affect consciousness**, leading to confusion or **altered awareness.**
- Patients may exhibit **automatisms**, such as **lip-smacking, hand wringing, or repetitive movements.**
- Often originates in the **temporal lobe**, leading to symptoms like **déjà vu, auditory hallucinations, or intense emotions.**

Focal to Bilateral Seizures

- A focal seizure **may spread** to involve both hemispheres, evolving into a **generalized tonic-clonic seizure.**
- The transition is often **preceded by an aura**, which may manifest as a **sudden sense of fear, nausea, or an unusual taste/smell.**

Generalized Seizures

Generalized seizures involve **both hemispheres of the brain simultaneously** and lead to **loss of consciousness** with widespread motor manifestations.

Tonic-Clonic Seizures (Grand Mal Seizures)

- The most recognizable seizure type, involving **sudden, bilateral muscle contractions followed by rhythmic jerking movements.**
- **Tonic phase:** Lasts **10–20 seconds**, characterized by **stiffening of muscles, clenched jaw, and loss of consciousness.**
- **Clonic phase:** Lasts **30–60 seconds**, involving **rhythmic jerking of limbs and face.**
- **Postictal phase:** After the seizure, patients experience **confusion, headache, fatigue, and muscle soreness.**

Myoclonic Seizures

- Involve **brief, shock-like jerks of muscles**, typically in the **arms or legs.**
- Occur **suddenly**, sometimes causing **objects to be dropped.**
- Common in **juvenile myoclonic epilepsy.**

Atonic Seizures (Drop Attacks)

- Characterized by **sudden loss of muscle tone**, leading to **falls and injuries.**
- Patients may **collapse without warning**, requiring **protective headgear** in severe cases.
- Common in **Lennox-Gastaut syndrome.**

Absence Seizures (Petit Mal Seizures)

- **Common in children**, absence seizures are characterized by **brief, sudden lapses in consciousness.**
- Typically **lasts 5–10 seconds**, during which the child appears to **stare blankly**, sometimes with **eyelid fluttering or lip-smacking.**
- **No postictal confusion**; the child resumes activity as if nothing happened.
- Easily provoked by **hyperventilation** or **flashing lights (photosensitive epilepsy).**

Illustration of Brain Regions Involved in Seizures

Diagrams depicting **focal and generalized seizure origins** should highlight:

1. **Frontal Lobe Seizures:** Motor symptoms such as **twitching or abnormal posturing.**
2. **Temporal Lobe Seizures:** Emotional disturbances, **déjà vu, or auditory hallucinations.**
3. **Occipital Lobe Seizures: Visual disturbances or hallucinations.**
4. **Parietal Lobe Seizures:** Sensory symptoms, **tingling or numbness.**
5. **Generalized Seizures:** Originating from the **thalamus and cortex**, involving **bilateral spread.**

4.1.2 Mechanisms of Antiepileptic Drugs (AEDs)

Antiepileptic drugs work by **modulating neuronal excitability and neurotransmission**, primarily through **sodium channel inhibition, enhancement of inhibitory neurotransmitters (GABA), or inhibition of excitatory neurotransmitters (glutamate).** The choice of an AED depends on the **seizure type, patient factors, and drug side effect profile.**

Sodium Channel Blockers

Sodium channel blockers act by **stabilizing neuronal membranes and inhibiting repetitive firing**, making them effective in **focal and generalized tonic-clonic seizures.**

Phenytoin

1. Mechanism of Action

    ◦ Phenytoin **blocks voltage-gated sodium channels**, preventing **sustained high-frequency repetitive neuronal firing.**
    ◦ It **prolongs the inactivation phase** of sodium channels, reducing excessive neuronal excitation.

2. Dosage and Administration

    ◦ **Initial dose**: 300 milligrams per day, adjusted based on **therapeutic plasma levels (10–20 micrograms per milliliter).**
    ◦ IV formulation is used in **status epilepticus** (loading dose **15–20 milligrams per kilogram IV**).

3. Side Effects and Monitoring

    ◦ **Neurological effects**: Nystagmus, ataxia, dizziness.
    ◦ **Gingival hyperplasia**: Occurs in **20–40 percent** of long-term users.
    ◦ **Hirsutism and coarsening of facial features.**
    ◦ **Teratogenicity**: Risk of fetal hydantoin syndrome.

Carbamazepine

1. Mechanism of Action

    ◦ Carbamazepine stabilizes neuronal membranes by **blocking sodium channels**, reducing synaptic transmission.

2. Dosage and Administration

    ◦ **Starting dose: 200–400 milligrams twice daily**, titrated to **800–1200 milligrams per day.**

○ Requires **slow titration over weeks** to minimize side effects.

3. **Side Effects and Risks**

   ○ **Drowsiness, dizziness, diplopia.**
   ○ **Rash and risk of Stevens-Johnson Syndrome**, especially in **HLA-B*1502 positive individuals (common in Asians).**
   ○ **Agranulocytosis and aplastic anemia** (requires regular CBC monitoring).
   ○ **Hepatic enzyme induction** leads to **drug interactions (reduces effectiveness of oral contraceptives, warfarin, and other AEDs).**

GABA Enhancers

GABA is the **primary inhibitory neurotransmitter** in the central nervous system. AEDs that enhance GABAergic activity help **reduce neuronal excitability** and are effective for **generalized seizures, myoclonic seizures, and absence seizures.**

Valproate (Valproic Acid, Sodium Valproate)

1. **Mechanism of Action**

   ○ Increases **GABA levels by inhibiting GABA transaminase,** enhancing inhibitory neurotransmission.
   ○ Also blocks **sodium and calcium channels,** broadening its efficacy.

2. **Dosage and Administration**

   ○ **Starting dose: 15 milligrams per kilogram per day,** increased gradually to **60 milligrams per kilogram per day.**
   ○ Used in **generalized epilepsy syndromes, absence seizures, and myoclonic seizures.**

3. **Side Effects and Precautions**

   ○ **Hepatotoxicity** (requires liver function monitoring, especially in children <2 years).
   ○ **Weight gain, tremor, and hair loss (alopecia).**

- Teratogenicity: Causes **neural tube defects**, requiring **folic acid supplementation** in women of childbearing age.

Clonazepam

1. **Mechanism of Action**

- Clonazepam enhances GABAergic inhibition by **increasing the frequency of chloride channel opening**, reducing excitability.

2. **Indications**

- Primarily used for **myoclonic seizures, absence seizures, and Lennox-Gastaut syndrome.**

3. **Side Effects and Limitations**

- **Sedation, drowsiness, and fatigue.**
- **Tolerance develops with prolonged use**, reducing long-term effectiveness.
- **Withdrawal symptoms and dependence risk** require **gradual dose tapering.**

4.1.3 Drug-Resistant Epilepsy

Drug-resistant epilepsy, also known as **refractory epilepsy**, is defined as the **failure to achieve sustained seizure control despite the appropriate use of two or more antiepileptic drugs (AEDs) at optimal dosages.** It affects **approximately 30–40 percent of epilepsy patients**, significantly impacting **quality of life, cognitive function, and psychosocial well-being.** Alternative treatment options include **surgical interventions, dietary modifications, and neuromodulation therapies.**

Definition and Diagnosis

1. **Criteria for Drug-Resistant Epilepsy**

- ◦ Seizures **persist despite two or more AEDs,** either alone or in combination, at **maximally tolerated doses.**
- ◦ **Inadequate seizure control for more than one year,** leading to increased **risk of injury, cognitive decline, and sudden unexpected death in epilepsy (SUDEP).**
- ◦ Patients should undergo **comprehensive evaluation, including EEG, MRI, and genetic testing,** to determine potential **surgical or alternative treatment options.**

Surgical Interventions

Surgical therapy is considered in **focal epilepsy cases** where a **specific, resectable seizure focus** is identified.

Indications for Epilepsy Surgery

- **Focal seizures originating from a well-defined epileptogenic zone** that does not involve **critical brain areas (speech, motor function, memory).**
- **Patients who fail at least two AEDs** and continue to experience frequent **disabling seizures.**

No significant cognitive impairment or psychiatric contraindications to surgery.

Surgical Procedure	Indications	Mechanism
Temporal Lobectomy	Medically intractable temporal lobe epilepsy (TLE)	Removal of the epileptogenic hippocampus and surrounding structures, eliminating seizure activity
Lesionectomy	Focal seizures due to tumors, cortical dysplasia, or vascular malformations	Resection of the epileptic lesion while preserving healthy brain tissue
Corpus Callosotomy	Drop attacks and atonic seizures, particularly in Lennox-Gastaut syndrome	Severing the corpus callosum to prevent seizure spread between hemispheres
Hemispherectomy	Severe unilateral epileptic syndromes, such as Rasmussen's encephalitis	Removing or disconnecting one cerebral hemisphere to control seizures

Types of Epilepsy Surgery

Outcomes and Success Rates

- Temporal lobectomy has the highest success rate, with seizure freedom achieved in up to 70 percent of cases.
- Lesionectomy results in seizure remission in 50–80 percent of patients, depending on the type of lesion.

- **Corpus callosotomy reduces atonic seizures in 70–80 percent of patients** but rarely achieves complete seizure control.

Neuromodulation Therapy

For patients **not eligible for resective surgery**, neuromodulation therapies provide **alternative treatment options.**
Vagus Nerve Stimulation (VNS)

1. Mechanism of Action

   - Involves **implanting a device** that **delivers intermittent electrical impulses to the left vagus nerve**, which modulates **cortical excitability** and seizure threshold.
   - Reduces seizure **frequency and severity** but rarely achieves complete remission.

2. Indications

   - **Patients with drug-resistant epilepsy who are not candidates for resective surgery.**
   - **Lennox-Gastaut syndrome and refractory focal epilepsy.**

3. Efficacy

   - **Reduces seizure frequency by 30–50 percent in 50 percent of patients.**
   - Improvements in **mood, alertness, and quality of life** have also been reported.

4. Limitations and Side Effects

   - **Hoarseness, throat discomfort, and cough** due to vagus nerve stimulation.
   - **Requires battery replacement every 5–10 years.**

Ketogenic Diet

The **ketogenic diet is a high-fat, low-carbohydrate, and adequate-protein diet** that induces a **state of ketosis,** reducing neuronal excitability. It is particularly effective in **pediatric patients with refractory epilepsy.**

1. Mechanism of Action

    - The diet **induces ketosis,** where the brain uses **ketone bodies (beta-hydroxybutyrate, acetoacetate) instead of glucose,** leading to:

        - Enhanced mitochondrial function and energy efficiency.
        - Inhibition of excitatory neurotransmission (glutamate suppression).
        - Increased production of GABA, enhancing inhibitory neurotransmission.

2. Diet Composition

    - **Fat-to-carbohydrate ratio** of **4:1 or 3:1,** with **80 percent of calories derived from fat.**
    - **Strict monitoring of ketone levels and macronutrient intake** is necessary.

3. Effectiveness

    - **Seizure reduction of ≥50 percent in approximately 50 percent of patients.**
    - **Complete seizure freedom in 10–15 percent of cases.**
    - Most effective in **Lennox-Gastaut syndrome, Dravet syndrome, and GLUT1 deficiency syndrome.**

4. Side Effects and Challenges

    - **Gastrointestinal disturbances** (constipation, vomiting).
    - **Nutritional deficiencies (calcium, vitamin D, folate),** requiring supplementation.
    - **Difficult adherence,** particularly in older children and adults.

Other Dietary Therapies

1. **Modified Atkins Diet (MAD)**

   - More **liberal carbohydrate allowance compared to the ketogenic diet.**
   - **Easier to follow and still effective,** with **seizure reduction of 40–50 percent.**

2. **Low Glycemic Index Diet**

   - Focuses on consuming **low-glycemic foods to maintain stable blood glucose levels.**
   - Suitable for **patients unable to tolerate strict ketogenic diet regimens.**

4.2.1 Levodopa-Carbidopa Therapy in Parkinsonism

Parkinson's disease is a **neurodegenerative disorder** characterized by **progressive loss of dopaminergic neurons in the substantia nigra,** leading to **motor symptoms such as bradykinesia, rigidity, resting tremor, and postural instability. Levodopa-carbidopa remains the most effective treatment,** replenishing dopamine levels in the brain and improving motor function.

Mechanism of Action

1. **Levodopa (L-DOPA)**

   - **Levodopa is a precursor to dopamine** that **crosses the blood-brain barrier,** where it is converted into dopamine by **dopa decarboxylase (DDC)** in the central nervous system.
   - This helps **compensate for the loss of dopamine-producing neurons in the substantia nigra,** alleviating motor symptoms.

2. **Carbidopa**

- ◦ Carbidopa is a **peripheral dopa decarboxylase inhibitor** that prevents **the premature breakdown of levodopa in the bloodstream** before it reaches the brain.
- ◦ This **enhances levodopa's bioavailability**, allowing **lower doses** to be used and reducing peripheral side effects such as **nausea and vomiting**.

Dosage and Administration

Levodopa-carbidopa is administered in **various formulations**, with dosing individualized based on **disease progression, symptom severity, and side effect tolerance**.

Standard Immediate-Release Dosing

- **Initial dose: 100 mg levodopa / 25 mg carbidopa three times daily.**
- **Titration**: Dose adjustments are made **gradually (weekly or biweekly)** to optimize symptom control while minimizing side effects.
- **Maximum dose**: Can be increased up to **800–1000 mg levodopa daily**, divided into **four or more doses** as needed.

Extended-Release and Combination Formulations

- **Controlled-release levodopa-carbidopa (Sinemet CR, Rytary)**: Provides **prolonged dopamine availability**, reducing motor fluctuations.
- **Levodopa-carbidopa-entacapone (Stalevo)**: Includes a **catechol-O-methyltransferase (COMT) inhibitor**, entacapone, which **extends the half-life of levodopa**, improving "**wearing-off**" **symptoms**.

Considerations for Administration

- **Levodopa should be taken on an empty stomach** (30–60 minutes before meals) to enhance absorption.
- **Protein-rich foods can compete with levodopa absorption**, reducing its efficacy.

- **Nighttime dosing may be needed** for patients experiencing **nocturnal akinesia or rigidity.**

Side Effects and Their Management

1. **Dyskinesias (Long-Term Use-Related)**

   - Involuntary **choreiform movements (twitching, writhing)** due to **dopamine fluctuations.**
   - More common with **chronic levodopa use (>5 years).**
   - Managed by:

     - Lowering the levodopa dose.
     - **Adding dopamine agonists (pramipexole, ropinirole)** to reduce levodopa dependency.
     - **Using amantadine,** which has **anti-dyskinetic properties.**

2. **Orthostatic Hypotension**

   - Dopamine affects **vascular tone,** leading to **postural dizziness and falls.**
   - Management:

     - **Increase fluid and salt intake.**
     - **Fludrocortisone or midodrine** may be used if severe.

3. **Nausea and Vomiting**

   - Due to **dopamine stimulation of the chemoreceptor trigger zone (CTZ) in the brainstem.**
   - Management:

     - **Domperidone (10 mg three times daily)** is preferred because it **does not cross the blood-brain barrier** and does not worsen Parkinson's symptoms.

- Carbidopa co-administration reduces nausea by limiting peripheral dopamine conversion.

4. **"Wearing-Off" Effect and Motor Fluctuations**

   - Over time, patients **experience shorter durations of symptom relief** after each dose.
   - Management:

     - Switch to controlled-release formulations.
     - Increase dosing frequency.
     - Add COMT inhibitors (entacapone) or MAO-B inhibitors (rasagiline, selegiline) to prolong levodopa action.

5. **Neuropsychiatric Symptoms**

   - **Hallucinations, confusion, and impulse control disorders** may occur, especially in elderly patients.
   - Management:

     - Dose reduction or switching to dopamine agonists.
     - **Quetiapine or clozapine** may be used if antipsychotic treatment is needed.

4.2.2 Adjunctive Therapies in Parkinson's Disease

While **levodopa-carbidopa remains the primary treatment** for Parkinson's disease, **adjunctive therapies** play a crucial role in **delaying motor complications, reducing levodopa dependence, and managing symptoms in later stages of the disease.** These therapies include **dopamine agonists and catechol-O-methyltransferase (COMT) inhibitors,** which are used to enhance dopamine availability and prolong the effects of levodopa.

Dopamine Agonists

Dopamine agonists are **synthetic compounds that directly stimulate dopamine receptors** in the brain, mimicking the effects of endogenous dopamine. Unlike levodopa, these drugs **do not require enzymatic conversion** and have a **longer half-life**, making them useful for **reducing motor fluctuations and managing early-stage Parkinson's disease.**

Mechanism of Action

Dopamine agonists bind to **dopamine D2 and D3 receptors** in the striatum, activating the dopamine pathways responsible for **motor function and coordination**. These drugs help compensate for the **progressive loss of dopaminergic neurons** and reduce the need for **high-dose levodopa therapy**, thereby **delaying the onset of dyskinesias.**

Drug	Starting Dose	Target Dose	Administration
Ropinirole	0.25 mg three times daily	4–8 mg per day (max 24 mg/day)	Oral
Pramipexole	0.125 mg three times daily	1.5 mg per day (max 4.5 mg/day)	Oral
Rotigotine	2 mg/day	4–8 mg/day	Transdermal patch
Apomorphine	1 mg subcutaneously	Up to 6 mg per dose	Injectable

Commonly Used Dopamine Agonists

Indications for Dopamine Agonists

1. **Early-stage Parkinson's disease:**

   ◦ Used as **monotherapy in younger patients (<65 years)** to delay the need for levodopa.

2. **Advanced Parkinson's disease:**

   - Used as **adjunct therapy** with levodopa to **reduce "off" periods and motor fluctuations.**

3. **Restless Leg Syndrome (RLS):**

   - Low doses of **ropinirole (0.25–2 mg) or pramipexole (0.125–0.75 mg) at bedtime** are effective.

Side Effects and Risk Management

1. **Impulse Control Disorders (ICDs)**

   - **Pathological gambling, hypersexuality, compulsive shopping, and binge eating** can develop in 15–20% of patients.
   - **Higher risk in younger males and those with a history of addictive behaviors.**
   - Management: **Dose reduction or switching to alternative therapies** like amantadine or levodopa.

2. **Somnolence and Sudden Sleep Attacks**

   - **Unpredictable daytime sleep episodes** can impair daily activities.
   - Avoid driving or operating heavy machinery.

3. **Orthostatic Hypotension**

   - Caused by **dopaminergic vasodilation**, leading to dizziness or fainting.
   - Managed by **increasing fluid and salt intake** or using **fludrocortisone if severe.**

4. **Peripheral Edema**

   - **Swelling of the lower limbs** is seen in **10–15% of patients.**
   - Treated with **diuretics or switching to alternative medications.**

Catechol-O-Methyltransferase (COMT) Inhibitors

COMT inhibitors are used to **extend the duration of levodopa's effect** by **blocking the breakdown of dopamine in peripheral tissues.** They are particularly useful in patients **experiencing wearing-off symptoms** or **motor fluctuations** with levodopa therapy.

Mechanism of Action

COMT is an enzyme that **metabolizes levodopa into 3-O-methyldopa,** preventing it from reaching the brain. By inhibiting COMT, these drugs **increase levodopa's half-life,** leading to **more stable dopamine levels** in the brain.

Commonly Used COMT Inhibitors

Drug	Dosage	Administration
Entacapone	200 mg with each levodopa dose	Oral
Tolcapone	100 mg three times daily	Oral (requires liver monitoring)
Opicapone	50 mg once daily	Oral (newer agent)

Commonly Used COMT Inhibitors

Indications for COMT Inhibitors

- Used **only as adjunct therapy with levodopa,** never as monotherapy.
- **Indicated in patients with motor fluctuations** where levodopa effects wear off too quickly.
- **Entacapone is the most commonly used agent** due to **better safety and tolerability compared to tolcapone.**

Side Effects and Risk Management

1. **Diarrhea**

   - **Occurs in 10–20% of patients**, especially with **entacapone**.
   - Managed by **reducing the dose or discontinuing if persistent**.

2. **Hepatotoxicity (Tolcapone-Specific)**

   - Tolcapone has been **linked to fatal liver failure**, requiring **regular liver function tests every two weeks**.
   - **Entacapone and opicapone are preferred due to lower liver toxicity.**

3. **Orange-Colored Urine**

   - Entacapone causes **urine discoloration**, which is **harmless but may alarm patients**.

4. **Exacerbation of Dyskinesias**

   - Increased levodopa bioavailability may worsen **involuntary movements**.
   - Managed by **lowering the levodopa dose when starting COMT inhibitors**.

   Clinical Considerations for Adjunct Therapy

- **Dopamine agonists** are preferred in **younger patients (<65 years)** to delay levodopa initiation and reduce dyskinesias.
- **COMT inhibitors** are used in patients **already on levodopa** experiencing "wearing-off" symptoms.
- Both therapies require **careful monitoring for side effects**, particularly impulse control disorders, orthostatic hypotension, and dyskinesias.

4.3.1 Acute Management of Stroke

Stroke is a **neurological emergency** caused by **sudden disruption of cerebral blood flow**, leading to **ischemic injury or hemorrhage**. Rapid intervention is crucial to **prevent irreversible brain damage and improve functional recovery**. The primary goal of acute stroke management is to restore cerebral perfusion, minimize secondary injury, and reduce the risk of complications.

Thrombolysis for Ischemic Stroke

Thrombolysis with **tissue plasminogen activator (tPA)** is the **gold-standard therapy for acute ischemic stroke** when administered within **4.5 hours of symptom onset.** It works by dissolving the clot responsible for vascular occlusion, thereby **restoring blood flow to the affected brain tissue.**

Mechanism of Action

- **Alteplase (tPA) converts plasminogen into plasmin,** which degrades fibrin and dissolves the thrombus.
- This process **recanalizes occluded cerebral arteries**, improving neurological function.

Dosage and Administration

- Total dose: 0.9 milligrams per kilogram intravenously (maximum 90 milligrams).
- Administration:

  - 10 percent of the total dose as an initial IV bolus over 1 minute.
  - The remaining 90 percent infused over 60 minutes.

- Monitoring:

  - Blood pressure must be **<185/110 mmHg** before starting tPA to minimize hemorrhagic risk.
  - Frequent neurological and blood pressure checks during infusion.

Indications for Thrombolysis

- **Acute ischemic stroke diagnosed within 4.5 hours of symptom onset.**
- **Measurable neurological deficit** (NIH Stroke Scale score ≥4).
- **No evidence of intracranial hemorrhage on CT scan.**

Contraindications to Thrombolysis

Thrombolysis is contraindicated in patients with a **high risk of bleeding or hemorrhagic transformation.**

Effectiveness and Outcomes

- tPA improves functional outcomes by 30-50 percent when given within the golden window (0-4.5 hours).
- Earlier administration (<3 hours) provides the greatest benefit.
- **Risk of symptomatic intracerebral hemorrhage is 6 percent**, requiring careful patient selection.

Aspirin and Anticoagulants

For patients **ineligible for thrombolysis**, aspirin therapy is started **within 24–48 hours** to **prevent clot progression and reduce recurrence.**

Aspirin Therapy

- **Mechanism of action**: Inhibits **cyclooxygenase-1 (COX-1)**, preventing **platelet aggregation** and reducing thrombus formation.
- **Dosage:**

  - **150–300 milligrams orally daily** (initiated within 48 hours of stroke onset).
  - **If thrombolysis is performed, aspirin should be delayed for 24 hours** to minimize bleeding risk.

- **Outcomes**: Reduces **early stroke recurrence by 20 percent** and **mortality by 10 percent.**

Anticoagulants for Cardioembolic Stroke

In strokes caused by **atrial fibrillation or cardiac embolism**, anticoagulation is necessary to **prevent recurrent embolic events.**

- **Indications:**

  - Stroke associated with **atrial fibrillation, prosthetic heart valves, or left atrial thrombus.**
  - Not recommended for **acute non-cardioembolic stroke** due to bleeding risk.

- **Commonly Used Anticoagulants**

Drug	Dosage	Mechanism
Warfarin	Adjusted to INR 2.0–3.0	Vitamin K antagonist, inhibits clotting factors II, VII, IX, X
Rivaroxaban	20 mg once daily	Direct Factor Xa inhibitor
Apixaban	5 mg twice daily	Direct Factor Xa inhibitor
Dabigatran	150 mg twice daily	Direct thrombin inhibitor

Commonly Used Anticoagulants

- **Anticoagulation is usually initiated 7–14 days after an acute stroke** to reduce hemorrhagic transformation risk.
- **DOACs (rivaroxaban, apixaban, dabigatran) are preferred over warfarin** due to their **lower risk of intracranial bleeding and fewer monitoring requirements.**

Supportive Acute Stroke Management

1. **Blood Pressure Control**

- ○ **Target BP in ischemic stroke (without thrombolysis): <220/120 mmHg** to avoid hypoperfusion.
- ○ **If thrombolysis is planned, BP must be <185/110 mmHg** before tPA administration.

2. **Glucose Management**

- ○ **Maintain blood glucose between 140–180 mg/dL** to prevent worsening of ischemic injury.
- ○ **Hyperglycemia increases infarct size and worsens neurological outcomes.**

3. **Oxygen Therapy**

- ○ **Supplemental oxygen if SpO2 <94%** to prevent hypoxia-induced brain damage.

4. **Early Mobilization and Stroke Unit Care**

- ○ **Early physiotherapy and mobilization** reduce the risk of **deep vein thrombosis (DVT), pneumonia, and pressure ulcers.**
- ○ **Multidisciplinary stroke units improve functional outcomes** by 25 percent.

4.4 Alzheimer's Disease

Alzheimer's disease is a **progressive neurodegenerative disorder** that primarily affects memory, cognition, and daily functioning. It is characterized by **accumulation of beta-amyloid plaques and tau neurofibrillary tangles,** leading to **synaptic dysfunction, neuronal loss, and brain atrophy.** Pharmacological treatment aims to **improve cognitive function, slow disease progression, and enhance quality of life.** The two primary drug classes used in Alzheimer's disease are **cholinesterase inhibitors and NMDA antagonists.**

4.4.1 Cholinesterase Inhibitors

Cholinesterase inhibitors are the **first-line therapy for mild to moderate Alzheimer's disease.** They work by **increasing acetylcholine levels in the brain**, thereby enhancing **cholinergic neurotransmission** which is crucial for memory and cognition.

Mechanism of Action

- This leads to **increased acetylcholine availability**, enhancing synaptic transmission and **delaying cognitive decline.**

- **Inhibits acetylcholinesterase**, the enzyme responsible for breaking down **acetylcholine** in synapses.

Indications for Cholinesterase Inhibitors

- **Mild to moderate Alzheimer's disease** (Mini-Mental State Examination [MMSE] score of 10–26).
- **Patients with functional decline and cognitive impairment.**
- Can be considered in **vascular dementia and Lewy body dementia**, but not in **frontotemporal dementia** (may worsen symptoms).

Side Effects and Risk Management

- **Gastrointestinal effects** (nausea, vomiting, diarrhea) are **common,** requiring **slow dose titration.**
- **Bradycardia and syncope** may occur in elderly patients with **pre-existing cardiac conditions.**
- **Rivastigmine transdermal patches** reduce GI side effects and are **preferred in patients with swallowing difficulties.**

Drug	Dosage	Indications	Side Effects
Donepezil	5–10 mg once daily	Mild to moderate Alzheimer's	Nausea, diarrhea, insomnia, bradycardia
Rivastigmine (Oral)	1.5 mg twice daily, titrated to 6 mg twice daily	Mild to moderate Alzheimer's	GI upset, dizziness, weight loss
Rivastigmine (Patch)	4.6 mg/24 hours, titrated to 9.5 mg/24 hours	Mild to moderate Alzheimer's	Skin irritation, nausea
Galantamine	4 mg twice daily, titrated to 12 mg twice daily	Mild to moderate Alzheimer's	GI disturbances, headache

Commonly Used Cholinesterase Inhibitors

4.4.2 NMDA Antagonists

NMDA (N-methyl-D-aspartate) receptor antagonists **help manage moderate to severe Alzheimer's disease** by reducing **excessive glutamate-induced excitotoxicity**, which contributes to **neuronal degeneration.**
Mechanism of Action

- **Memantine blocks NMDA receptors**, preventing excessive **calcium influx** into neurons.
- This **protects neurons from glutamate-mediated excitotoxicity**, slowing disease progression and improving **cognition and daily activities.**

Memantine Dosage and Administration

- Starting dose: **5 mg once daily**, increased by **5 mg per week.**
- Target dose: **10 mg twice daily (or 20 mg once daily for extended-release formulation).**
- Requires dose adjustment in renal impairment (CrCl <30 mL/min: 5 mg twice daily).

Indications for Memantine

- Moderate to severe Alzheimer's disease (MMSE score **<17**).
- Patients intolerant to cholinesterase inhibitors or those with **worsening symptoms despite therapy.**

Side Effects and Risk Management

- **Dizziness and confusion** are common, requiring **cautious dose escalation.**
- **Constipation and headache** may occur, managed with **increased fluid and fiber intake.**
- **May be used in combination with donepezil** for enhanced cognitive benefits.

Combination Therapy

In **moderate to severe Alzheimer's disease, combination therapy with a cholinesterase inhibitor and memantine** provides **better symptom control** than monotherapy.

1. **Donepezil + Memantine Combination**

- Shown to **slow cognitive decline and maintain daily functioning** in advanced stages.
- Used when **cholinesterase inhibitors alone are insufficient.**

2. **Clinical Benefits of Combination Therapy**

- **Greater preservation of memory and executive function.**
- **Reduced behavioral symptoms**, such as agitation and aggression.

Lower rates of nursing home placement compared to monotherapy

Review Questions

1. Describe the classification of seizures in epilepsy.
2. Discuss the differences between focal, generalized, and absence seizures and provide examples of clinical presentations for each type.
3. Explain the pathophysiological basis of epilepsy.
4. How do imbalances between excitatory and inhibitory neurotransmission contribute to seizure generation?
5. Discuss the mechanism of action of sodium channel blockers such as Phenytoin and Carbamazepine in the treatment of epilepsy.
6. Explain how sodium channel blockers modulate neuronal excitability.
7. Outline the mechanism by which GABA enhancers like Valproate and Clonazepam help control seizures.
8. Describe how enhancement of inhibitory neurotransmission can reduce seizure activity.
9. What are the challenges associated with drug-resistant epilepsy and what alternative treatment options are available?
10. Discuss the role of epilepsy surgery and the ketogenic diet in managing refractory epilepsy.
11. Explain the mechanism of action of Levodopa-Carbidopa in the treatment of Parkinsonism.
12. How does carbidopa enhance the efficacy of levodopa and what are the common side effects, including dyskinesia?
13. Discuss the use of dopamine agonists such as Ropinirole and Pramipexole as adjunctive therapy in Parkinsonism.
14. What benefits do dopamine agonists provide and what are their limitations?
15. Describe the role of COMT inhibitors such as Entacapone in Parkinson's disease management.
16. How do COMT inhibitors work to prolong the effect of levodopa therapy?
17. Outline the acute management of stroke with thrombolytic therapy.
18. Discuss the use of Alteplase in stroke management, including its therapeutic window and contraindications.
19. Compare the roles of aspirin and anticoagulants in the acute management of stroke.

20. When is aspirin indicated and when are anticoagulants indicated in stroke management?
21. Discuss the importance of physical and occupational therapy in stroke rehabilitation.
22. How do physical and occupational therapies contribute to functional recovery after a stroke?
23. Explain the mechanism of action of cholinesterase inhibitors such as Donepezil and Rivastigmine in Alzheimer's disease.
24. What are the common gastrointestinal side effects associated with cholinesterase inhibitors?
25. Describe how NMDA antagonists like Memantine work in moderate to severe Alzheimer's disease.
26. Discuss the benefits and limitations of memantine therapy in Alzheimer's disease.
27. How do antiepileptic drugs differ in their mechanisms of action and why is this important for individualized therapy?
28. Compare the mechanisms of sodium channel blockers and GABA enhancers.
29. Discuss the importance of monitoring therapeutic outcomes and side effects in patients receiving antiepileptic drugs.
30. How can clinicians adjust antiepileptic therapy based on efficacy and adverse effect profiles?
31. What factors determine the choice of an antiepileptic drug for a given patient?
32. Explain the rationale behind using a ketogenic diet in drug-resistant epilepsy.
33. What is known about the mechanism by which the ketogenic diet reduces seizure frequency?
34. Describe the clinical criteria for initiating surgical intervention in patients with drug-resistant epilepsy.
35. What pre-surgical evaluations are necessary before epilepsy surgery?
36. Outline the benefits and limitations of levodopa-carbidopa therapy in Parkinsonism.
37. How do side effects such as dyskinesia impact long-term management of Parkinsonism?
38. Discuss the role of adjunctive therapies in Parkinson's disease.
39. How do dopamine agonists and COMT inhibitors complement levodopa therapy in Parkinsonism?

MCQS

1. **Which type of seizure is characterized by focal onset?**
   A) Generalized
   B) Focal
   C) Absence
   D) Myoclonic
   Correct Answer: B

2. **Generalized seizures affect:**
   A) Only one hemisphere
   B) Both hemispheres simultaneously
   C) Only the temporal lobe
   D) Only the motor cortex
   Correct Answer: B

3. **Absence seizures are best characterized by:**
   A) Brief loss of consciousness
   B) Prolonged convulsions
   C) Focal motor activity
   D) Sudden muscle weakness
   Correct Answer: A

4. **Phenytoin exerts its antiepileptic effects by:**
   A) Enhancing GABA activity
   B) Blocking sodium channels
   C) Inhibiting calcium channels
   D) Activating potassium channels
   Correct Answer: B

5. **Carbamazepine is classified as a:**
   A) GABA enhancer
   B) Sodium channel blocker
   C) Calcium channel blocker
   D) NMDA receptor antagonist
   Correct Answer: B

6. **Valproate primarily works by:**
   A) Blocking sodium channels
   B) Enhancing GABAergic transmission
   C) Inhibiting dopamine receptors

D) Activating serotonin receptors

Correct Answer: B

7. **Clonazepam is used as an antiepileptic due to its ability to:**
    A) Block sodium channels
    B) Enhance GABA activity
    C) Inhibit NMDA receptors
    D) Increase glutamate release
    Correct Answer: B

8. **Drug-resistant epilepsy may be managed with:**
    A) Increasing the dose of the same AEDs indefinitely
    B) Epilepsy surgery and the ketogenic diet
    C) Switching to antibiotics
    D) Using only benzodiazepines
    Correct Answer: B

9. **The ketogenic diet in epilepsy management is thought to work by:**
    A) Increasing carbohydrate intake
    B) Producing ketone bodies that have anticonvulsant effects
    C) Enhancing sodium channel function
    D) Stimulating GABA synthesis directly
    Correct Answer: B

10. **Levodopa is converted to dopamine in the brain. Carbidopa is given to:**
    A) Enhance the conversion in the periphery
    B) Prevent peripheral metabolism of levodopa
    C) Inhibit dopamine receptors
    D) Increase the half-life of dopamine in the brain
    Correct Answer: B

11. **A common side effect of long-term levodopa-carbidopa therapy is:**
    A) Hypotension
    B) Dyskinesia
    C) Bradycardia
    D) Hyperglycemia
    Correct Answer: B

12. **Ropinirole is classified as a:**
    A) COMT inhibitor
    B) Dopamine agonist
    C) Anticholinergic agent
    D) MAO-B inhibitor

Correct Answer: B

13. **Pramipexole is used in Parkinson's disease primarily for its:**
    A) Anticholinergic effects
    B) Dopamine agonist activity
    C) COMT inhibition
    D) Direct levodopa replacement
    Correct Answer: B

14. **Entacapone is an adjunct therapy in Parkinson's disease that works by inhibiting:**
    A) Dopamine receptors
    B) COMT (Catechol-O-methyltransferase)
    C) MAO-B (Monoamine oxidase B)
    D) GABA receptors
    Correct Answer: B

15. **In the acute management of ischemic stroke, Alteplase is used for:**
    A) Anticoagulation
    B) Thrombolysis
    C) Blood pressure control
    D) Neuroprotection
    Correct Answer: B

16. **Aspirin is used in stroke management primarily for its:**
    A) Thrombolytic properties
    B) Antiplatelet effects
    C) Anticoagulant effects
    D) Neuroprotective properties
    Correct Answer: B

17. **Anticoagulants in stroke management are used to:**
    A) Dissolve clots immediately
    B) Prevent further clot formation
    C) Increase blood pressure
    D) Enhance neuronal regeneration
    Correct Answer: B

18. **Physical therapy in stroke rehabilitation aims to:**
    A) Improve cognitive function only
    B) Restore motor function and mobility
    C) Increase blood clot formation
    D) Replace the need for medical therapy
    Correct Answer: B

19. **Occupational therapy in stroke rehabilitation focuses on:**
    A) Enhancing daily living skills and independence
    B) Treating seizures
    C) Managing pain exclusively
    D) Improving speech without addressing daily activities
    Correct Answer: A

20. **Donepezil is a cholinesterase inhibitor used in Alzheimer's disease to:**
    A) Block dopamine receptors
    B) Increase acetylcholine levels in the brain
    C) Inhibit NMDA receptors
    D) Increase glutamate release
    Correct Answer: B

21. **Rivastigmine, used in Alzheimer's disease, acts by:**
    A) Enhancing serotonin levels
    B) Inhibiting the breakdown of acetylcholine
    C) Blocking dopamine receptors
    D) Inhibiting GABA synthesis
    Correct Answer: B

22. **A common gastrointestinal side effect associated with cholinesterase inhibitors is:**
    A) Constipation
    B) Diarrhea
    C) Hypertension
    D) Bradycardia
    Correct Answer: B

23. **Memantine is an NMDA receptor antagonist used in:**
    A) Mild Alzheimer's disease
    B) Moderate to severe Alzheimer's disease
    C) Parkinson's disease only
    D) Acute stroke management
    Correct Answer: B

24. **The primary role of NMDA antagonists in Alzheimer's disease is to:**
    A) Enhance glutamate release
    B) Prevent excitotoxicity by modulating glutamatergic transmission
    C) Increase cholinesterase activity
    D) Stimulate neurogenesis directly
    Correct Answer: B

25. **Focal seizures originate from:**
    A) Both hemispheres simultaneously
    B) a specific area of the brain
    C) the brainstem exclusively
    D) the cerebellum
    Correct Answer: B

26. **Generalized seizures involve:**
    A) A localized brain region
    B) widespread electrical discharges across the entire brain
    C) only the frontal lobe
    D) only the occipital lobe
    Correct Answer: B

27. **Absence seizures are typically seen in:**
    A) Elderly patients
    B) Children
    C) Adults with brain tumors
    D) Patients with Parkinson's disease
    Correct Answer: B

28. **Which antiepileptic drug is a sodium channel blocker?**
    A) Valproate
    B) Phenytoin
    C) Clonazepam
    D) Lamotrigine (also sodium channel blocker but not listed in outline;
    however, Phenytoin is sufficient)
    Correct Answer: B

29. **Carbamazepine is primarily used to treat:**
    A) Absence seizures
    B) Focal seizures
    C) Generalized tonic-clonic seizures exclusively
    D) Myoclonic seizures
    Correct Answer: B

30. **Valproate is considered a broad-spectrum antiepileptic drug because it is effective against:**
    A) Only focal seizures
    B) Both focal and generalized seizures
    C) Only absence seizures
    D) Only status epilepticus
    Correct Answer: B

31. **Clonazepam is classified as a:**
    A) Sodium channel blocker
    B) Benzodiazepine enhancing GABA activity
    C) Calcium channel blocker
    D) NMDA receptor antagonist
    Correct Answer: B

32. **The ketogenic diet is used in drug-resistant epilepsy because it:**
    A) Provides high carbohydrates
    B) Induces ketosis, which may reduce seizure frequency
    C) Increases sodium levels
    D) Directly blocks sodium channels
    Correct Answer: B

33. **Epilepsy surgery is considered when:**
    A) Seizures are well-controlled with medications
    B) Seizures remain refractory despite optimal medical management
    C) The patient prefers dietary modifications
    D) There is a diagnosis of Alzheimer's disease
    Correct Answer: B

34. **Levodopa is converted to dopamine in the brain; carbidopa prevents its:**
    A) Conversion in the brain
    B) Peripheral metabolism
    C) Excretion in the urine
    D) Binding to dopamine receptors
    Correct Answer: B

35. **A common side effect of levodopa-carbidopa therapy is:**
    A) Bradykinesia
    B) Dyskinesia
    C) Hypersalivation
    D) Hypertension
    Correct Answer: B

36. **Dyskinesia in Parkinson's patients is most often associated with:**
    A) Low doses of levodopa
    B) High or prolonged levodopa use
    C) COMT inhibitor therapy
    D) Dopamine agonist monotherapy
    Correct Answer: B

37. **Dopamine agonists such as ropinirole are used in Parkinson's disease to:**
    A) Inhibit dopamine receptors
    B) Directly stimulate dopamine receptors
    C) Block levodopa conversion
    D) Increase acetylcholine release
    Correct Answer: B

38. **COMT inhibitors like entacapone work by:**
    A) Increasing dopamine degradation
    B) Inhibiting the enzyme that breaks down levodopa
    C) Blocking dopamine receptors
    D) Enhancing serotonin release
    Correct Answer: B

39. **Thrombolytic therapy in stroke is typically administered within:**
    A) 24 hours of symptom onset
    B) 3–4.5 hours of symptom onset
    C) 72 hours of symptom onset
    D) One week of symptom onset
    Correct Answer: B

40. **Alteplase is classified as a:**
    A) Antiplatelet agent
    B) Thrombolytic agent
    C) Anticoagulant
    D) Neuroprotective drug
    Correct Answer: B

41. **Aspirin, used in stroke management, works primarily by:**
    A) Thrombolysis
    B) Inhibiting platelet aggregation
    C) Dissolving clots
    D) Increasing blood viscosity
    Correct Answer: B

42. **Anticoagulants in stroke prevention work by:**
    A) Stimulating clot formation
    B) Preventing the formation of new clots
    C) Directly lysing existing clots
    D) Enhancing platelet function
    Correct Answer: B

43. **Physical therapy in stroke rehabilitation focuses on:**
    A) Improving cognitive skills
    B) Restoring motor function and mobility
    C) Increasing blood pressure
    D) Enhancing language skills only
    Correct Answer: B

44. **Occupational therapy in stroke rehabilitation primarily helps patients to:**
    A) Regain daily living skills and independence
    B) Improve memory
    C) Increase seizure threshold
    D) Lower cholesterol levels
    Correct Answer: A

45. **Donepezil is indicated for the treatment of:**
    A) Parkinson's disease
    B) Alzheimer's disease
    C) Epilepsy
    D) Stroke rehabilitation
    Correct Answer: B

46. **The mechanism of action of cholinesterase inhibitors in Alzheimer's disease is to:**
    A) Decrease acetylcholine breakdown
    B) Block dopamine receptors
    C) Inhibit NMDA receptors
    D) Increase amyloid deposition
    Correct Answer: A

47. **A common gastrointestinal side effect of cholinesterase inhibitors is:**
    A) Constipation
    B) Diarrhea
    C) Dry mouth
    D) Weight gain
    Correct Answer: B

48. **Rivastigmine differs from donepezil primarily in that it:**
    A) Has a shorter half-life
    B) Inhibits both acetylcholinesterase and butyrylcholinesterase
    C) Is administered intravenously
    D) Acts as an NMDA receptor antagonist
    Correct Answer: B

49. **Memantine, an NMDA receptor antagonist, is used in Alzheimer's disease to:**
    A) Enhance cholinergic transmission
    B) Reduce excitotoxicity associated with glutamate
    C) Increase dopamine levels
    D) Lower blood pressure
    Correct Answer: B

50. **Generalized seizures involve:**
    A) Focal onset
    B) Bilateral synchronous electrical discharges
    C) Only motor symptoms
    D) Only absence symptoms
    Correct Answer: B

51. **Focal seizures are characterized by:**
    A) Loss of consciousness from the start
    B) Localized onset with possible secondary generalization
    C) Always resulting in a tonic-clonic seizure
    D) Only affecting the occipital lobe
    Correct Answer: B

52. **Absence seizures are typically seen as:**
    A) Brief lapses in awareness with subtle motor signs
    B) Prolonged convulsions
    C) Focal motor activity
    D) Status epilepticus
    Correct Answer: A

53. **The therapeutic effect of sodium channel blockers in epilepsy is due to their ability to:**
    A) Enhance GABA release
    B) Stabilize neuronal membranes by reducing repetitive firing
    C) Increase synaptic transmission
    D) Stimulate the central nervous system
    Correct Answer: B

54. **GABA enhancers in epilepsy work by:**
    A) Inhibiting glutamate receptors
    B) Increasing inhibitory neurotransmission
    C) Blocking calcium channels
    D) Stimulating sodium channels
    Correct Answer: B

55. **Ketogenic diet's anticonvulsant effect is thought to be mediated by:**
    A) Increased glucose levels
    B) Production of ketone bodies with neuroprotective properties
    C) Direct inhibition of sodium channels
    D) Enhancement of glutamate signaling
    Correct Answer: B

56. **Drug-resistant epilepsy is defined as:**
    A) Seizures controlled by a single antiepileptic drug
    B) Failure to achieve seizure freedom with adequate trials of two or more appropriate AEDs
    C) A type of absence seizure
    D) Epilepsy in the elderly only
    Correct Answer: B

57. **Which of the following is an advantage of using parenteral iron (e.g., Ferric Gluconate) over oral iron therapy?**
    A) Fewer GI side effects
    B) Lower cost
    C) Increased GI side effects
    D) It does not require monitoring
    Correct Answer: A

58. **A low serum ferritin level is indicative of:**
    A) Iron overload
    B) Iron deficiency
    C) Megaloblastic anemia
    D) Hemolytic anemia
    Correct Answer: B

59. **The direct antiglobulin (Coombs) test is used in the diagnosis of:**
    A) Iron deficiency anemia
    B) Autoimmune hemolytic anemia
    C) Megaloblastic anemia
    D) Anemia of chronic disease
    Correct Answer: B

60. **An elevated reticulocyte count in hemolytic anemia indicates:**
    A) Bone marrow suppression
    B) A compensatory increase in red blood cell production
    C) Iron deficiency
    D) Megaloblastic changes
    Correct Answer: B

61. **In the context of venous thromboembolism, the Wells score is used to:**
    A) Confirm a diagnosis of VTE
    B) Stratify clinical risk for VTE
    C) Monitor anticoagulant therapy
    D) Diagnose hemolytic anemia
    Correct Answer: B

62. **A D-Dimer assay is most useful for:**
    A) Confirming VTE in high-risk patients
    B) Ruling out VTE in patients with low to moderate clinical probability
    C) Monitoring heparin levels
    D) Diagnosing iron deficiency
    Correct Answer: B

63. **Unfractionated heparin is monitored by which laboratory test?**
    A) INR
    B) aPTT
    C) D-Dimer
    D) Serum creatinine
    Correct Answer: B

64. **Rivaroxaban is an example of a:**
    A) Vitamin K antagonist
    B) Direct oral anticoagulant (DOAC)
    C) Heparin derivative
    D) Antiplatelet agent
    Correct Answer: B

65. **Compression stockings prevent VTE by:**
    A) Increasing venous stasis
    B) Promoting venous return and reducing stasis
    C) Directly lysing clots
    D) Increasing blood viscosity
    Correct Answer: B

66. **Prophylactic anticoagulation is indicated in which patient population?**
    A) Low-risk outpatients
    B) Hospitalized patients with high VTE risk
    C) Patients with bleeding disorders
    D) Only in surgical patients
    Correct Answer: B

67. **The role of monitoring aPTT in heparin therapy is to:**
    A) Adjust DOAC dosing

B) Ensure that the heparin level is therapeutic

C) Monitor platelet count

D) Assess liver function

Correct Answer: B

68. **In Alzheimer's disease, cholinesterase inhibitors work by:**

A) Blocking NMDA receptors

B) Inhibiting the breakdown of acetylcholine

C) Stimulating dopamine release

D) Enhancing GABA activity

Correct Answer: B

69. **Memantine's mechanism of action involves:**

A) Inhibiting acetylcholinesterase

B) Blocking NMDA receptors to prevent excitotoxicity

C) Enhancing serotonin release

D) Increasing amyloid production

Correct Answer: B

70. **A common GI side effect of cholinesterase inhibitors is:**

A) Constipation

B) Diarrhea

C) Dry mouth

D) Insomnia

Correct Answer: B

71. **Donepezil is primarily indicated for:**

A) Parkinson's disease

B) Alzheimer's disease

C) Epilepsy

D) Stroke rehabilitation

Correct Answer: B

72. **Which antiepileptic drug is most associated with the potential for drug-induced gingival hyperplasia?**

A) Carbamazepine

B) Phenytoin

C) Valproate

D) Clonazepam

Correct Answer: B

73. **In the management of Parkinson's disease, dyskinesia is a side effect most often associated with:**

A) Dopamine agonists

B) Levodopa-carbidopa

C) COMT inhibitors

D) Anticholinergics

Correct Answer: B

74. **Which of the following is a benefit of using adjunctive dopamine agonists in Parkinson's disease?**

   A) They completely replace the need for levodopa

   B) They provide additional dopaminergic stimulation and may reduce levodopa-related fluctuations

   C) They are free of side effects

   D) They inhibit dopamine metabolism directly

   Correct Answer: B

75. **Entacapone is used in Parkinson's disease to:**

   A) Increase dopamine synthesis

   B) Inhibit COMT and prolong the effect of levodopa

   C) Block dopamine receptors

   D) Stimulate GABA release

   Correct Answer: B

76. **A primary contraindication to the use of unfractionated heparin is a history of:**

   A) Iron deficiency anemia

   B) Heparin-induced thrombocytopenia

   C) Megaloblastic anemia

   D) Epilepsy

   Correct Answer: B

77. **The ketogenic diet used in drug-resistant epilepsy is characterized by:**

   A) High carbohydrate and low fat content

   B) High fat and low carbohydrate content

   C) High protein and low fat content

   D) Balanced macronutrient composition

   Correct Answer: B

78. **Which of the following interventions is recommended as a lifestyle modification in patients with PUD?**

   A) Smoking cessation

   B) Increased alcohol consumption

   C) High caffeine intake

   D) High-fat diet

   Correct Answer: A

CHAPTER FIVE

Psychiatric Disorders

5.1.1 Typical Antipsychotics in Schizophrenia

Schizophrenia is a **chronic psychiatric disorder** characterized by **delusions, hallucinations, disorganized thinking, and cognitive dysfunction. Typical (first-generation) antipsychotics** are primarily used for treating **positive symptoms** such as **hallucinations and delusions** by **blocking dopamine D2 receptors** in the mesolimbic pathway.

Mechanism of Action

Typical antipsychotics **block dopamine D2 receptors in the central nervous system,** leading to:

- **No significant effects on negative symptoms (social withdrawal, anhedonia, cognitive decline),** which are linked to **prefrontal cortex dysfunction.**

- **Reduction of dopamine overactivity in the mesolimbic pathway,** alleviating **hallucinations, delusions, and agitation.**
- **Strong dopamine blockade in the nigrostriatal pathway,** which **increases the risk of extrapyramidal side effects (EPS).**

Drug	Potency	D2 Affinity	Sedation	EPS Risk
Haloperidol	High	Strong	Low	High
Chlorpromazine	Low	Weak	High	Low
Fluphenazine	High	Strong	Low	High

Commonly Used Typical Antipsychotics

Haloperidol: The Most Commonly Used Typical Antipsychotic

Efficacy and Uses

- **Highly effective for treating acute psychotic episodes**, particularly in emergency settings.
- **Rapid onset of action** makes it useful for managing **acute agitation and aggression** in schizophrenia.
- Often used in **hospitalized patients, forensic settings, and emergency psychiatric care.**

Dosage and Administration

- Oral therapy:

  - **Starting dose**: 2–5 mg per day, titrated as needed.
  - **Maintenance dose**: 5–10 mg/day.
  - Maximum recommended dose: **20 mg/day.**

- **Intramuscular (IM) for acute agitation:**

- ○ **Initial dose: 5 mg IM every 4–6 hours**, up to a maximum of **20 mg/day**.
- ○ **Onset of action: 15–30 minutes**, making it useful in emergency settings.

- **Depot formulation (long-acting injection):**

- ○ Haloperidol decanoate is administered **once every 4 weeks** for long-term control in **non-compliant patients**.

Side Effects and Risk Management

Typical antipsychotics, especially **high-potency agents like haloperidol**, have a **high risk of extrapyramidal symptoms (EPS)** due to **strong dopamine blockade**.
Extrapyramidal Symptoms (EPS)

- Incidence: **20–40% with high-potency typical antipsychotics**.
- EPS Types and Management:

Other Side Effects

1. Sedation:

- ○ **More common in low-potency agents like chlorpromazine.**
- ○ Managed by **taking doses at night** or switching to **less sedating alternatives.**

2. **Neuroleptic Malignant Syndrome (NMS) (Rare but Life-Threatening)**

- ○ **Symptoms:** Hyperthermia, autonomic instability, muscle rigidity, altered mental status.
- ○ **Mortality rate: 10–20% if untreated.**
- ○ **Management:**

- ▪ **Discontinue antipsychotic immediately.**
- ▪ **Supportive care with IV fluids and cooling measures.**

- Dantrolene (muscle relaxant) and bromocriptine (dopamine agonist) for severe cases.

3. Hyperprolactinemia

- Dopamine inhibition in the tuberoinfundibular pathway leads to increased prolactin levels.
- **Symptoms**: Galactorrhea, gynecomastia, menstrual irregularities, sexual dysfunction.
- **Management**: Switch to a **prolactin-sparing antipsychotic (e.g., aripiprazole)**.

Clinical Considerations for Typical Antipsychotics

- **First-line treatment for acute agitation and psychotic episodes,** especially in **hospitalized patients.**
- **Not preferred for long-term maintenance** due to **high EPS risk and lack of efficacy in treating negative symptoms.**
- **Low-potency antipsychotics (chlorpromazine) cause more sedation** but fewer EPS, whereas **high-potency agents (haloperidol) have more EPS but minimal sedation.**
- Patients on long-term therapy require **regular monitoring for EPS, tardive dyskinesia, and metabolic side effects.**

EPS Type	Symptoms	Onset	Management
Dystonia	Acute muscle spasms, especially in face, neck, and back	Hours to days	Benztropine (2 mg IM), Diphenhydramine (50 mg IM)
Akathisia	Restlessness, inability to sit still	Days to weeks	Beta-blockers (Propranolol 10–20 mg BID), Benzodiazepines (Lorazepam 1 mg BID)
Parkinsonism	Bradykinesia, rigidity, tremors, masked face	Weeks to months	Benztropine 1–2 mg daily, Amantadine 100 mg BID
Tardive Dyskinesia	Involuntary repetitive movements (lip-smacking, tongue protrusion, grimacing)	Months to years	Stop offending drug, switch to atypical antipsychotics, use Valbenazine 40 mg daily

EPS Types and Management:

5.1.2 Atypical Antipsychotics in Schizophrenia

Atypical antipsychotics, also known as **second-generation antipsychotics (SGAs)**, are widely used in **schizophrenia treatment** due to their **dual action on dopamine D2 and serotonin 5-HT2A receptors**. Unlike **typical (first-generation) antipsychotics**, which primarily target dopamine, atypical antipsychotics offer **better efficacy for negative symptoms** while causing **fewer extrapyramidal side effects (EPS)**.

Mechanism of Action

Atypical antipsychotics **block dopamine D2 receptors**, similar to typical antipsychotics, but also **antagonize serotonin 5-HT2A receptors**, which leads to:

- **Enhanced mood-stabilizing effects**, making SGAs useful in **bipolar disorder and depression**.

1. **Reduced dopamine blockade in the nigrostriatal pathway**, lowering EPS risk.
2. **Increased dopamine release in the prefrontal cortex**, improving negative symptoms (e.g., **apathy, social withdrawal, cognitive deficits**).

Drug	Dosage Range	Key Side Effects
Risperidone	1–6 mg/day	Hyperprolactinemia, sedation, moderate weight gain
Olanzapine	5–20 mg/day	Significant weight gain, metabolic syndrome
Quetiapine	50–800 mg/day	Sedation, hypotension
Aripiprazole	10–30 mg/day	Akathisia, low metabolic risk
Clozapine	50–900 mg/day	Agranulocytosis, hypersalivation, seizures

Commonly Used Atypical Antipsychotics

Risperidone

Efficacy and Uses

- Effective for **both positive and negative symptoms** of schizophrenia.
- **First-line choice** in patients with a high risk of **EPS or metabolic side effects.**

Dosage and Administration

- **Starting dose: 1 mg/day,** increased gradually over 1–2 weeks.
- **Target dose: 4–6 mg/day.**
- Available as an **oral tablet, liquid solution, and long-acting injectable** (Risperdal Consta, every 2 weeks).

Side Effects and Risk Management

- Hyperprolactinemia (dose-dependent):

  - Can cause **galactorrhea, gynecomastia, menstrual irregularities, and sexual dysfunction.**
  - **Switch to aripiprazole if prolactin elevation is problematic.**

- **Weight gain and metabolic disturbances:**

  - Less severe than olanzapine but still **increases appetite.**

- **Moderate sedation** and **orthostatic hypotension,** requiring **dose** adjustments in elderly patients.

Olanzapine

Efficacy and Uses

- Highly effective for schizophrenia, especially in patients with agitation, aggression, or sleep disturbances.
- More sedating than risperidone, making it useful for acute psychotic episodes and bipolar mania.

Dosage and Administration

- Starting dose: 5 mg/day, titrated up to 20 mg/day based on response.
- Available in oral tablet, disintegrating tablet (Zyprexa Zydis), and long-acting injection (Zyprexa Relprevv, every 2–4 weeks).

Side Effects and Risk Management

- Significant weight gain:

  - 5–10 kg within 6 months, leading to high risk of obesity, hyperlipidemia, and type 2 diabetes.
  - Requires regular monitoring of BMI, blood glucose, and lipid levels.

- Metabolic syndrome (Hyperglycemia, Dyslipidemia, Hypertension):

  - Occurs in 20–30% of patients, necessitating lifestyle modifications and periodic metabolic screening.

- Sedation and cognitive slowing, which may be beneficial in agitated or aggressive patients but problematic for others.

Advantages of Atypical Antipsychotics

1. Lower risk of EPS and tardive dyskinesia compared to typical antipsychotics.
2. Greater efficacy in treating negative symptoms such as social withdrawal, emotional blunting, and cognitive impairment.
3. Improved tolerability, making them better suited for long-term treatment and relapse prevention.

4. **Broader spectrum of use**, including **bipolar disorder, schizoaffective disorder, and treatment-resistant depression.**

Clinical Considerations for Choosing Atypical Antipsychotics

- **Risperidone is a good first-line option**, balancing **efficacy, tolerability, and side effects.**
- **Olanzapine is preferred in severely agitated patients** but requires **metabolic monitoring.**
- **Aripiprazole has the lowest metabolic risk**, making it **ideal for obese or diabetic patients.**
- **Clozapine is reserved for treatment-resistant schizophrenia** due to its **risk of agranulocytosis.**

5.2.1 Lithium in Bipolar Disorder

Lithium is a **mood stabilizer** widely used in the **treatment and prevention of bipolar disorder**. It is the **first-line treatment for acute mania and maintenance therapy**, effectively reducing the frequency and severity of mood episodes. Despite its efficacy, lithium requires **close therapeutic monitoring due to its narrow therapeutic index and potential toxicity.**

Mechanism of Action

The exact mechanism of lithium is not fully understood, but it is believed to work by:

1. **Modulating neurotransmitter signaling**

   - Inhibits **dopamine and glutamate activity**, reducing excitatory neurotransmission.
   - Enhances **GABAergic transmission**, stabilizing mood.

2. **Affecting intracellular second messenger systems**

- ○ Inhibits **inositol monophosphatase**, reducing phosphatidylinositol (PI) turnover, which **stabilizes neuronal activity.**
- ○ Modulates **cyclic AMP (cAMP) and glycogen synthase kinase-3 (GSK-3), affecting neuroplasticity and neuroprotection.**

3. **Reducing oxidative stress and apoptosis**

- ○ Protects neurons from degeneration, which is beneficial in **neuroprogressive disorders like bipolar disorder.**

Dosage and Administration

Lithium dosing is **individualized based on therapeutic drug monitoring,** as serum levels must be maintained within a narrow **therapeutic range (0.6–1.2 mEq/L)** to balance efficacy and safety.

- **Serum lithium levels should be checked 5–7 days after starting therapy** and regularly during dose adjustments.
- **Peak plasma levels occur 2–4 hours after administration.**
- **Lithium is excreted via the kidneys,** requiring **dose adjustments in renal impairment.**

Indication	Initial Dose	Maintenance Dose	Therapeutic Range
Acute Mania	600–900 mg/day in divided doses	900–1200 mg/day	0.8–1.2 mEq/L
Maintenance Therapy	300–600 mg/day	600–900 mg/day	0.6–1.0 mEq/L

Dosing Guidelines

Side Effects and Risk Management

Lithium has a range of **dose-dependent and long-term side effects** that necessitate regular monitoring.

Common Side Effects

1. **Renal Dysfunction**

- **Polyuria and polydipsia** due to **nephrogenic diabetes insipidus (NDI)** caused by lithium's inhibition of **aquaporin-2 in renal tubules.**
- **Up to 40% of patients** develop **mild renal impairment** with prolonged use.
- **Management:**

  - Maintain adequate hydration.
  - Consider **amiloride (5–10 mg daily)** if symptoms are severe.
  - Avoid **NSAIDs and ACE inhibitors,** which reduce lithium clearance and increase toxicity risk.

2. **Hypothyroidism**

- Lithium **inhibits thyroid hormone synthesis,** leading to **hypothyroidism in 10–20% of patients.**
- **Management:**

  - Monitor **TSH every 6–12 months.**
  - Initiate **levothyroxine therapy (25–50 mcg/day)** if needed.

3. **Weight Gain and Gastrointestinal Distress**

- **Mild weight gain (2–5 kg) is common,** likely due to **fluid retention and metabolic changes.**
- **GI symptoms** (nausea, diarrhea) occur early but improve with continued use.
- **Taking lithium with food reduces GI upset.**

Lithium Toxicity

Lithium has a **narrow therapeutic index,** meaning that **even small increases in serum levels can lead to toxicity.**

Toxicity Levels and Symptoms

Lithium Level (mEq/L)	Toxicity Symptoms
1.5–2.0	Tremors, nausea, diarrhea, dizziness
2.0–2.5	Confusion, muscle twitching, slurred speech
>2.5	Seizures, coma, arrhythmias, renal failure

Toxicity Levels and Symptoms

Management of Lithium Toxicity

- Mild toxicity (1.5–2.0 mEq/L):

  - Hold lithium temporarily and increase fluid intake.

- Moderate toxicity (2.0–2.5 mEq/L):

  - IV hydration with **normal saline to enhance lithium excretion.**
  - Consider **gastric lavage** if ingestion occurred within 1 hour.

- Severe toxicity (>2.5 mEq/L or symptoms like seizures, coma, arrhythmias):

  - **Hemodialysis is the definitive treatment.**
  - Supportive care with airway protection and IV fluids.

Monitoring Guidelines

To ensure **safe and effective lithium therapy,** regular **monitoring of serum lithium levels and organ function is required.**

Parameter	Monitoring Frequency
Serum Lithium Levels	Weekly during initiation, then every 3–6 months
Renal Function (eGFR, Creatinine, BUN)	Baseline, then every 6–12 months
Thyroid Function (TSH, Free T4)	Baseline, then every 6–12 months
Electrolytes (Sodium, Potassium)	Every 6–12 months
ECG (in patients >40 years old)	Annually

Monitoring Guidelines

Clinical Considerations

- Lithium is the most effective medication for preventing suicide in bipolar disorder (reduces suicide risk by 60–70%).
- Not metabolized by the liver, making it safe in hepatic impairment.
- Contraindicated in pregnancy due to teratogenicity (Ebstein's anomaly – a congenital heart defect).
- Should be avoided with thiazide diuretics, NSAIDs, and ACE inhibitors, which increase lithium levels and risk of toxicity.

5.3.1 Short-Term Benzodiazepines in Anxiety Disorders

Benzodiazepines are fast-acting anxiolytics used in the short-term management of anxiety disorders, including generalized anxiety disorder (GAD), panic disorder, and acute anxiety episodes. They are highly effective but should be used cautiously due to the risk of tolerance, dependence, and withdrawal symptoms.

Mechanism of Action

Benzodiazepines **enhance the inhibitory action of gamma-aminobutyric acid (GABA) at GABA-A receptors,** which leads to:

1. **Increased chloride ion influx,** causing **neuronal hyperpolarization and reduced excitability.**
2. **Rapid anxiolytic, sedative, muscle relaxant, and anticonvulsant effects,** making them useful for **acute anxiety relief.**
3. **Suppression of excessive limbic system activity,** which is hyperactive in anxiety disorders.

Unlike **selective serotonin reuptake inhibitors (SSRIs),** benzodiazepines provide **immediate symptom relief** but do **not treat the underlying disorder** and **should not be used for long-term management**

Drug	Half-Life	Usual Dosage	Indications
Lorazepam	10–20 hours	1–3 mg/day (divided doses)	Acute anxiety, panic attacks, agitation
Diazepam	20–50 hours	2–10 mg BID or TID	Severe anxiety, muscle spasms, alcohol withdrawal
Alprazolam	6–12 hours	0.25–0.5 mg BID or TID	Panic disorder, social anxiety
Clonazepam	18–50 hours	0.5–2 mg/day	Chronic anxiety, panic attacks

Commonly Used Benzodiazepines

- Short-acting benzodiazepines (e.g., alprazolam) have a higher risk of withdrawal symptoms.
- Long-acting benzodiazepines (e.g., diazepam, clonazepam) are preferred for sustained effects and reduced withdrawal risk.

Indications for Short-Term Benzodiazepine Use

1. **Acute Anxiety Episodes**

- Used for **rapid relief of severe distress**, especially when **SSRIs or SNRIs take weeks to show effect.**

2. **Panic Attacks**

- Short-acting benzodiazepines (e.g., **alprazolam, lorazepam**) provide **immediate relief.**

3. **Preoperative Anxiety**

- Given before surgeries or medical procedures to induce **calmness and sedation.**

4. **Alcohol Withdrawal Syndrome**

- Long-acting benzodiazepines (e.g., **diazepam, chlordiazepoxide**) prevent **seizures and agitation.**

5. **Muscle Spasms and Seizure Disorders**

- Diazepam is **commonly used as a muscle relaxant** and **emergency seizure control (IV administration).**

Side Effects and Risk Management

1. Sedation and Cognitive Impairment

- **Drowsiness, dizziness, slowed reaction time** can impair driving and daily activities.
- **Elderly patients are at increased risk of falls and confusion.**

2. Tolerance and Dependence

- **Prolonged use (>4 weeks) leads to tolerance,** requiring **higher doses for the same effect.**

◦ **Dependence occurs in 20–30% of patients on long-term therapy,** particularly with **short-acting agents like alprazolam.**

3. **Withdrawal Symptoms**

◦ Abrupt discontinuation can cause **rebound anxiety, irritability, insomnia, muscle tremors, and seizures.**
◦ **Management**: Gradual tapering over **4–6 weeks** to prevent withdrawal effects.

4. **Risk of Overdose and Respiratory Depression**

◦ Overdose risk is **higher when combined with alcohol or opioids.**
◦ **Flumazenil (0.2 mg IV) is the antidote for benzodiazepine overdose**, but should be used cautiously due to risk of withdrawal seizures.

Clinical Guidelines for Safe Benzodiazepine Use

- **Limit use to 2–4 weeks to avoid dependence.**
- **Prescribe lowest effective dose for the shortest duration.**
- **Avoid in elderly patients**, those with **substance use disorders**, and those at risk of **falls or cognitive decline.**
- **Monitor for signs of abuse, withdrawal, or escalating doses.**
- **Consider SSRIs or SNRIs for long-term anxiety management** to prevent reliance on benzodiazepines.

5.3.2 Long-Term SSRIs in Anxiety Disorders

Selective serotonin reuptake inhibitors (SSRIs) are **first-line agents for long-term management of anxiety disorders**, including **generalized anxiety disorder (GAD), obsessive-compulsive disorder (OCD), panic disorder, and social anxiety disorder.** Unlike **benzodiazepines**, which provide **immediate relief but have high dependence potential**, SSRIs require **several weeks to take effect** but offer **sustained symptom** improvement with a lower risk of dependence.

Mechanism of Action

SSRIs work by **blocking the serotonin transporter (SERT) in presynaptic neurons,** which:

1. **Prevents serotonin reuptake,** leading to increased **serotonin availability at synapses.**
2. **Enhances serotonergic neurotransmission in the limbic system,** which is **dysregulated in anxiety disorders.**
3. **Promotes long-term neuroplasticity,** improving **emotional regulation and stress response.**

Unlike older antidepressants (e.g., tricyclic antidepressants), SSRIs are **selective for serotonin** and have **fewer cardiac and anticholinergic side effects,** making them **safer for long-term use.**

Drug	Dosage Range	Indications	Key Side Effects
Fluoxetine	20–40 mg/day	GAD, OCD, panic disorder	Insomnia, agitation, sexual dysfunction
Sertraline	50–200 mg/day	GAD, OCD, PTSD	GI upset, nausea, sweating
Paroxetine	10–50 mg/day	Social anxiety, GAD	Weight gain, sedation, sexual dysfunction
Escitalopram	10–20 mg/day	GAD, panic disorder	Headache, nausea, dizziness
Fluvoxamine	50–300 mg/day	OCD, social anxiety	GI distress, sedation

Commonly Used SSRIs

- **Fluoxetine has a long half-life (4–6 days),** making it **less likely to cause withdrawal symptoms** if a dose is missed.
- **Paroxetine has the highest risk of withdrawal symptoms** due to its shorter half-life.

Indications for SSRI Therapy in Anxiety Disorders

1. Generalized Anxiety Disorder (GAD)

   - First-line treatment, effective in **reducing excessive worry, tension, and restlessness.**
   - Sertraline and escitalopram are commonly used.

2. Obsessive-Compulsive Disorder (OCD)

   - Requires **higher doses** than for depression.
   - **Fluoxetine, fluvoxamine, and sertraline are preferred** due to their efficacy in **reducing compulsions and intrusive thoughts.**

3. Panic Disorder

   - Reduces **panic attack frequency and anticipatory anxiety.**
   - **Paroxetine and fluoxetine are effective** but **require slow dose titration** to prevent initial anxiety worsening.

4. Post-Traumatic Stress Disorder (PTSD)

   - **Sertraline and fluoxetine are FDA-approved for PTSD.**
   - **Reduces hyperarousal, flashbacks, and emotional numbness.**

5. Social Anxiety Disorder

   - **Paroxetine and sertraline are preferred** due to their ability to reduce social inhibition and performance anxiety.

Onset of Action and Dose Titration

- **SSRIs do not work immediately** and require **2–4 weeks for initial symptom improvement** and **6–8 weeks for full efficacy.**
- **Doses should be started low and increased gradually** to minimize side effects, especially **initial anxiety exacerbation.**

Week	Dosage
Week 1	25 mg/day
Week 2	50 mg/day
Week 4	100 mg/day (if tolerated)
Week 6	150 mg/day (max dose for severe cases)

Example of Dose Titration for Sertraline:

- Higher doses are required for OCD compared to GAD or panic disorder.

Side Effects and Risk Management

1. Gastrointestinal (GI) Upset

   - **Nausea, diarrhea, and bloating** are common in the first 1–2 weeks.
   - **Management**: Take medication **with food** or switch to a **better-tolerated SSRI (e.g., escitalopram).**

2. Sexual Dysfunction

   - **Reduced libido, erectile dysfunction, anorgasmia** occur in **40–60%** of patients.
   - **Management**:

     - **Lower the dose** if possible.
     - **Switch to bupropion,** which has a **lower sexual side effect risk.**
     - **Add sildenafil (Viagra)** for erectile dysfunction.

3. Initial Anxiety Worsening

- ○ Due to **increased serotonin activity in the first few weeks.**
- ○ **Management:**

  - Start with a low dose and titrate slowly.
  - Use short-term benzodiazepines (e.g., lorazepam) for the first **2–4 weeks** if needed.

4. **Weight Gain and Metabolic Effects**

- ○ **Paroxetine has the highest risk of weight gain,** whereas fluoxetine and sertraline have minimal effects.
- ○ **Management:** Encourage **dietary modifications and regular** exercise.

5. **Discontinuation Syndrome**

- ○ Stopping SSRIs abruptly can lead to **withdrawal symptoms** like dizziness, flu-like symptoms, irritability, and brain zaps.
- ○ **Paroxetine has the highest withdrawal risk** due to its **short half-life.**
- ○ **Management:**

  - Taper the dose gradually over 4–6 weeks before discontinuation.
  - Fluoxetine is least likely to cause withdrawal symptoms due to its long half-life.

Class	Drugs	Advantages	Disadvantages
SSRIs	Fluoxetine, Sertraline, Escitalopram	First-line treatment, well-tolerated	Delayed onset (2–4 weeks), sexual dysfunction
SNRIs	Venlafaxine, Duloxetine	Effective in **GAD and** panic disorder	Increased blood pressure, withdrawal symptoms
Benzodiazepines	Lorazepam, Diazepam	Immediate relief of acute anxiety	Risk of **dependence and** withdrawal
Buspirone	Buspirone	No sedation or dependence	Takes 2–4 weeks to work, less effective than SSRIs
Beta-Blockers	Propranolol	Useful for performance anxiety	Not effective for generalized anxiety

Comparison of SSRIs with Other Anxiety Treatments

5.4 Sleep Disorders

Sleep disorders significantly impact **mental health, cognitive function, and overall well-being**. The two most common disorders, **insomnia and obstructive sleep apnea (OSA)**, require targeted pharmacological and non-pharmacological interventions.

5.4.1 Insomnia

Insomnia is characterized by **difficulty initiating or maintaining sleep, early morning awakenings, or non-restorative sleep**, leading to **daytime fatigue and impaired functioning**. It can be **acute (transient) or chronic** (lasting >3 months, occurring ≥3 times per week).

Z-Drugs for Insomnia

Z-drugs (non-benzodiazepine hypnotics) are **first-line pharmacological treatment for insomnia** due to their **selective binding to GABA-A receptors**, resulting in **sedative effects with fewer residual side effects than benzodiazepines**.

Mechanism of Action

- Selectively bind to the **omega-1 subunit of GABA-A receptors**, enhancing **GABAergic inhibition** and promoting **sleep initiation**.
- Compared to benzodiazepines, Z-drugs have **less muscle relaxation and anxiolytic effects**, reducing **hangover sedation**.

Drug	Dosage	Onset of Action	Half-Life	Key Side Effects
Zolpidem	5–10 mg at bedtime	15–30 min	2–3 hours	Dizziness, drowsiness, risk of dependence
Zopiclone	3.75–7.5 mg at bedtime	20–30 min	5–7 hours	Metallic taste, dry mouth, cognitive impairment

Efficacy and Clinical Use

- **Zolpidem is effective for sleep initiation** and is available in both immediate-release **(IR) and extended-release (ER) formulations.**
- **Zopiclone has a longer half-life**, making it useful for **sleep maintenance** but increasing the risk of **morning drowsiness.**

Safety Considerations

- **Short-term use (<4 weeks) is recommended** due to the risk of **tolerance and dependence.**
- **Elderly patients** are at higher risk of **falls, cognitive impairment, and paradoxical agitation.**
- **Avoid alcohol and CNS depressants,** which can **potentiate sedation and respiratory depression.**
- **Rebound insomnia** may occur if stopped abruptly, requiring **gradual tapering.**

Non-Pharmacological Management of Insomnia

Cognitive-Behavioral Therapy for Insomnia (CBT-I) is the **gold-standard treatment for chronic insomnia** and includes:

1. **Sleep hygiene education**

   - Maintain a **consistent sleep schedule.**
   - Avoid **caffeine, nicotine, and heavy meals before bedtime.**

2. **Stimulus control therapy**

   - Use the **bed only for sleep** (avoid TV, phone usage).
   - If unable to sleep within **20 minutes, leave the bed and engage in a relaxing activity.**

3. **Relaxation techniques**

- Deep breathing, progressive muscle relaxation, and meditation.

4. **Sleep restriction therapy**

- Initially **limit total sleep time** to reduce **sleep fragmentation.**

CBT-I is **more effective long-term than Z-drugs** and has **no risk of dependence.**

5.4.2 Sleep Apnea

Obstructive Sleep Apnea (OSA) is a **sleep disorder characterized by** repetitive airway obstruction, leading to **interrupted breathing, oxygen desaturation, and excessive daytime sleepiness.** It is commonly associated with **obesity, hypertension, and metabolic syndrome.**

Continuous Positive Airway Pressure (CPAP) Therapy

CPAP is the **first-line treatment for moderate to severe OSA,** delivering **continuous airflow to keep the upper airway open** during sleep.

Mechanism of Action

- Maintains **positive pressure in the upper airway,** preventing **collapsing of pharyngeal muscles.**
- Reduces **hypoxia, microarousals, and excessive daytime sleepiness.**

Indications for CPAP Use

- **Moderate to severe OSA** (Apnea-Hypopnea Index [AHI] ≥15 events/ hour).
- Patients **with excessive daytime sleepiness, loud snoring, and witnessed apnea episodes.**
- **Hypertensive or obese patients** with coexisting cardiovascular risks.

Benefits of CPAP Therapy

- **Reduces cardiovascular complications** (hypertension, atrial fibrillation, stroke).
- **Improves sleep quality and daytime alertness.**
- **Lowers risk of motor vehicle accidents** due to improved reaction time.

Adjunctive Pharmacotherapy for Residual Sleepiness in OSA

Some OSA patients experience **persistent daytime sleepiness despite optimal CPAP adherence.**

Drug	Dosage	Mechanism	Indications	Side Effects
Modafinil	200 mg in the morning	Enhances dopaminergic and orexinergic activity	Residual sleepiness in OSA	Headache, insomnia, increased BP

Modafinil as a Wakefulness-Promoting Agent

- **Modafinil does not treat airway obstruction** but **improves wakefulness and cognitive function.**
- **Not a substitute for CPAP therapy** but can be used in **non-adherent patients or those with persistent fatigue.**

Lifestyle Modifications for OSA Management

1. **Weight Loss**

    - **Obesity is the most significant modifiable risk factor** for OSA.
    - **Even a 10% weight loss** can reduce **AHI severity by 26%.**

2. **Positional Therapy**

    - Sleeping in the **supine position increases airway collapse.**
    - **Encourage side-sleeping** or use **positional therapy devices.**

3. **Avoidance of Alcohol and Sedatives**

   - **Alcohol relaxes airway muscles,** worsening OSA symptoms.
   - **Sedative medications (e.g., benzodiazepines, opioids) should be avoided.**

4. **Oral Appliance Therapy**

   - **Mandibular advancement devices (MADs)** reposition the jaw **forward,** increasing airway space.
   - **Useful in mild to moderate OSA** or **patients intolerant to CPAP.**

Condition	First-Line Treatment	Alternative Options
Acute Insomnia	Zolpidem, Zopiclone	CBT-I, melatonin, antihistamines
Chronic Insomnia	CBT-I	Low-dose trazodone, doxepin
OSA	CPAP therapy	Weight loss, mandibular devices
OSA with Residual Sleepiness	CPAP + Modafinil	Lifestyle modifications

Comparison of Treatments for Sleep Disorders

REVIEW QUESTIONS

1. Discuss the role and clinical importance of typical antipsychotics in the treatment of schizophrenia.
2. Explain how Haloperidol works in schizophrenia and describe its main side effects.
3. Compare typical and atypical antipsychotics regarding their mechanisms of action and side effect profiles.
4. Discuss the metabolic side effects associated with atypical antipsychotics such as Risperidone and Olanzapine.
5. Describe the role of Lithium in managing bipolar disorder and explain what is meant by its "narrow therapeutic index."
6. List and explain the common side effects of Lithium therapy, including renal dysfunction and hypothyroidism.
7. Compare the use of anticonvulsants (e.g., Valproate and Lamotrigine) as mood stabilizers in bipolar disorder with Lithium therapy.
8. Explain how Valproate works as a mood stabilizer and identify its key adverse effects.
9. Describe the role of Lamotrigine in bipolar disorder, particularly in preventing depressive episodes.
10. Discuss the rationale for using short-term benzodiazepines in the treatment of anxiety disorders.
11. Compare Lorazepam and Diazepam in terms of their use in anxiety management.
12. Explain how SSRIs function in the long-term treatment of anxiety disorders, including OCD and generalized anxiety disorder.
13. Discuss the advantages and potential side effects of long-term SSRI therapy in anxiety disorders.
14. Describe the mechanism of action of Z-drugs (Zolpidem and Zopiclone) in the management of insomnia.
15. Explain the safety concerns associated with the long-term use of Z-drugs for insomnia.
16. Outline the role of CPAP in the treatment of obstructive sleep apnea.
17. Discuss potential adjunctive pharmacotherapy for sleep apnea and the clinical scenarios in which it may be used.

18. Describe how psychosocial interventions complement pharmacotherapy in the treatment of schizophrenia.

19. Explain the importance of monitoring therapeutic outcomes and side effects in patients receiving antipsychotic or mood stabilizer therapy.

20. Discuss the factors that influence the choice of an antipsychotic agent for a patient with schizophrenia.

21. Explain the clinical monitoring required for safe Lithium therapy in bipolar disorder.

22. Describe the role of risk–benefit analysis in deciding between benzodiazepines and SSRIs for anxiety disorders.

23. Discuss how individualized therapeutic plans are developed in psychiatric practice, with examples from schizophrenia and bipolar disorder.

24. Reflect on the impact of drug side effects on patient adherence and overall treatment success.

25. Summarize how integrated treatment strategies across schizophrenia, bipolar disorder, anxiety, and sleep disorders optimize patient outcomes in psychiatric practice.

MCQS

70 Multiple-Choice Questions (MCQs)

1. Which of the following is a typical antipsychotic used in schizophrenia?
   A) Risperidone
   B) Olanzapine
   C) Haloperidol
   D) Clozapine
   Correct Answer: C) Haloperidol

2. Haloperidol is associated with a high risk of which side effect?
   A) Weight gain
   B) Extrapyramidal symptoms
   C) Sedation
   D) Hyperglycemia
   Correct Answer: B) Extrapyramidal symptoms

3. Atypical antipsychotics are preferred over typical antipsychotics in some patients due to a lower risk of:
   A) Cardiac arrhythmias
   B) Extrapyramidal side effects
   C) Hepatotoxicity
   D) Renal dysfunction
   Correct Answer: B) Extrapyramidal side effects

4. Which atypical antipsychotic is particularly associated with significant weight gain and metabolic disturbances?
   A) Risperidone
   B) Olanzapine
   C) Quetiapine
   D) Ziprasidone
   Correct Answer: B) Olanzapine

5. Risperidone is known to cause metabolic side effects such as:
   A) Hypoglycemia
   B) Weight gain
   C) Hypotension

D) Bradycardia

Correct Answer: B) Weight gain

6. **Lithium is primarily used as a mood stabilizer in the treatment of bipolar disorder.**

    A) True

    B) False

    Correct Answer: A) True

7. **A narrow therapeutic index in Lithium therapy means that:**

    A) The drug is very safe at any dose

    B) Therapeutic and toxic doses are very close

    C) It requires no monitoring

    D) It has a wide safety margin

    Correct Answer: B) Therapeutic and toxic doses are very close

8. **A common adverse effect of long-term Lithium use is:**

    A) Hepatotoxicity

    B) Renal dysfunction

    C) Extrapyramidal symptoms

    D) Weight loss

    Correct Answer: B) Renal dysfunction

9. **Hypothyroidism is a known potential side effect of Lithium therapy.**

    A) True

    B) False

    Correct Answer: A) True

10. **Valproate is used as a mood stabilizer in bipolar disorder.**

    A) True

    B) False

    Correct Answer: A) True

11. **Lamotrigine is particularly effective in preventing which type of episode in bipolar disorder?**

    A) Manic

    B) Depressive

    C) Psychotic

    D) Anxiety

    Correct Answer: B) Depressive

12. **Which anticonvulsant is commonly used as a mood stabilizer in bipolar disorder?**

    A) Diazepam

    B) Valproate

C) Zolpidem

D) Haloperidol

Correct Answer: B) Valproate

13. **Benzodiazepines such as Lorazepam are primarily used for:**

    A) Long-term management of anxiety

    B) Short-term relief of acute anxiety symptoms

    C) Mood stabilization

    D) Treatment of psychosis

    Correct Answer: B) Short-term relief of acute anxiety symptoms

14. **Tolerance and dependence are significant risks associated with prolonged use of:**

    A) SSRIs

    B) Benzodiazepines

    C) Atypical antipsychotics

    D) Mood stabilizers

    Correct Answer: B) Benzodiazepines

15. **Which of the following is an example of an SSRI used in anxiety disorders?**

    A) Diazepam

    B) Fluoxetine

    C) Haloperidol

    D) Lithium

    Correct Answer: B) Fluoxetine

16. **SSRIs are first-line treatments for which anxiety disorders?**

    A) Obsessive-compulsive disorder (OCD)

    B) Generalized anxiety disorder (GAD)

    C) Both A and B

    D) Neither A nor B

    Correct Answer: C) Both A and B

17. **Zolpidem is classified as a:**

    A) Benzodiazepine

    B) Z-Drug

    C) SSRI

    D) Antipsychotic

    Correct Answer: B) Z-Drug

18. **The primary mechanism of action of Z-drugs like Zolpidem is:**

    A) Blocking dopamine receptors

    B) Enhancing GABA-A receptor activity

C) Inhibiting serotonin reuptake

D) Activating NMDA receptors

Correct Answer: B) Enhancing GABA-A receptor activity

19. **A common risk with long-term use of Z-drugs is:**

    A) Dependency and tolerance

    B) Extrapyramidal symptoms

    C) Weight loss

    D) Hepatotoxicity

    Correct Answer: A) Dependency and tolerance

20. **CPAP is the standard treatment for:**

    A) Insomnia

    B) Obstructive sleep apnea

    C) Narcolepsy

    D) Restless legs syndrome

    Correct Answer: B) Obstructive sleep apnea

21. **CPAP works by:**

    A) Delivering pressurized air to keep the airway open during sleep

    B) Sedating the patient

    C) Reducing REM sleep

    D) Stimulating muscle relaxation in the legs

    Correct Answer: A) Delivering pressurized air to keep the airway open during sleep

22. **Adjunctive pharmacotherapy in sleep apnea is used to treat:**

    A) Primary airway obstruction

    B) Residual daytime sleepiness

    C) Chronic insomnia

    D) Hypertension

    Correct Answer: B) Residual daytime sleepiness

23. **Typical antipsychotics are associated with a higher risk of:**

    A) Metabolic syndrome

    B) Extrapyramidal symptoms

    C) Weight gain

    D) Sedation

    Correct Answer: B) Extrapyramidal symptoms

24. **Atypical antipsychotics have a lower risk of extrapyramidal symptoms because they:**

    A) Have higher dopamine receptor affinity

    B) Have a greater affinity for serotonin receptors relative to dopamine receptors

    C) Do not cross the blood–brain barrier

    D) Are given at much lower doses

    Correct Answer: B) Have a greater affinity for serotonin receptors relative to dopamine receptors

25. **Weight gain and metabolic disturbances are common side effects of:**

    A) Typical antipsychotics

    B) Atypical antipsychotics such as Olanzapine

    C) Benzodiazepines

    D) SSRIs

    Correct Answer: B) Atypical antipsychotics such as Olanzapine

26. **Lithium's narrow therapeutic index necessitates:**

    A) No monitoring

    B) Occasional monitoring once a year

    C) Frequent monitoring of serum levels

    D) Dose increases without monitoring

    Correct Answer: C) Frequent monitoring of serum levels

27. **Monitoring Lithium therapy typically includes assessment of:**

    A) Serum levels, renal function, and thyroid function

    B) Only liver function

    C) Only blood pressure

    D) Only complete blood count

    Correct Answer: A) Serum levels, renal function, and thyroid function

28. **In bipolar disorder, which anticonvulsant is used as a mood stabilizer?**

    A) Diazepam

    B) Valproate

    C) Zolpidem

    D) Haloperidol

    Correct Answer: B) Valproate

29. **Lamotrigine is particularly beneficial for bipolar disorder in preventing:**

    A) Acute mania

    B) Depressive episodes

    C) Psychosis

    D) Anxiety

    Correct Answer: B) Depressive episodes

30. **Benzodiazepines provide rapid relief of anxiety symptoms because they:**

A) Have a slow onset of action

B) Act immediately by enhancing GABA activity

C) Inhibit serotonin reuptake

D) Stabilize mood over the long term

Correct Answer: B) Act immediately by enhancing GABA activity

31. **The development of tolerance and dependence is a major limitation of:**

A) SSRIs

B) Benzodiazepines

C) Antipsychotics

D) Mood stabilizers

Correct Answer: B) Benzodiazepines

32. **SSRIs, such as Fluoxetine, work by:**

A) Inhibiting dopamine reuptake

B) Inhibiting serotonin reuptake

C) Blocking GABA receptors

D) Stimulating norepinephrine release

Correct Answer: B) Inhibiting serotonin reuptake

33. **SSRIs are first-line treatments for which conditions?**

A) Obsessive-compulsive disorder

B) Generalized anxiety disorder

C) Both A and B

D) Neither A nor B

Correct Answer: C) Both A and B

34. **Zolpidem is indicated primarily for the treatment of:**

A) Anxiety

B) Insomnia

C) Bipolar disorder

D) Schizophrenia

Correct Answer: B) Insomnia

35. **The primary mechanism of action of Z-drugs such as Zolpidem is to:**

A) Block dopamine receptors

B) Enhance GABA-A receptor activity

C) Inhibit serotonin reuptake

D) Activate adrenergic receptors

Correct Answer: B) Enhance GABA-A receptor activity

36. **A potential adverse effect of long-term Z-drug use is:**

A) Tolerance and dependence

B) Extrapyramidal symptoms

C) Significant weight gain

D) Hepatotoxicity

Correct Answer: A) Tolerance and dependence

37. **CPAP is the standard treatment for:**

A) Insomnia

B) Obstructive sleep apnea

C) Narcolepsy

D) Restless legs syndrome

Correct Answer: B) Obstructive sleep apnea

38. **The main purpose of CPAP therapy is to:**

A) Increase total sleep time

B) Maintain airway patency during sleep

C) Sedate the patient

D) Stimulate deep sleep exclusively

Correct Answer: B) Maintain airway patency during sleep

39. **Adjunctive pharmacotherapy in sleep apnea is primarily used to address:**

A) Primary apnea

B) Residual daytime sleepiness

C) Snoring only

D) Hypertension

Correct Answer: B) Residual daytime sleepiness

40. **Schizophrenia treatment typically includes both pharmacotherapy and:**

A) Physical therapy

B) Psychosocial interventions

C) Dietary modifications only

D) Surgical procedures

Correct Answer: B) Psychosocial interventions

41. **The higher risk of extrapyramidal symptoms with typical antipsychotics is due to:**

A) Their high dopamine receptor blockade in the nigrostriatal pathway

B) Their effect on serotonin receptors

C) Their peripheral anticholinergic activity

D) Their low potency

Correct Answer: A) Their high dopamine receptor blockade in the nigrostriatal pathway

42. **Long-term Lithium therapy requires careful monitoring because of its narrow therapeutic index. This necessitates:**

    A) Annual laboratory testing

    B) Frequent monitoring of serum levels, renal, and thyroid functions

    C) No laboratory testing

    D) Only clinical observation

    Correct Answer: B) Frequent monitoring of serum levels, renal, and thyroid functions

43. **Valproate, used in bipolar disorder, is associated with which potential adverse effect?**

    A) Renal failure

    B) Hepatotoxicity

    C) Extrapyramidal symptoms

    D) Hypothyroidism

    Correct Answer: B) Hepatotoxicity

44. **Lamotrigine is particularly beneficial in bipolar disorder for:**

    A) Managing acute mania

    B) Preventing depressive episodes

    C) Treating psychosis

    D) Immediate anxiety relief

    Correct Answer: B) Preventing depressive episodes

45. **Benzodiazepines are effective for immediate relief of anxiety due to their:**

    A) Slow onset

    B) Rapid onset of action

    C) Long-term mood stabilization

    D) Minimal side effects

    Correct Answer: B) Rapid onset of action

46. **A major limitation of long-term benzodiazepine use is the development of:**

    A) Tolerance and dependence

    B) Hepatotoxicity

    C) Weight loss

    D) Renal dysfunction

    Correct Answer: A) Tolerance and dependence

47. **SSRIs improve anxiety symptoms primarily by:**

    A) Inhibiting dopamine reuptake

B) Inhibiting serotonin reuptake

C) Blocking GABA receptors

D) Enhancing norepinephrine release

Correct Answer: B) Inhibiting serotonin reuptake

48. **A common side effect of SSRIs in anxiety disorders is:**

A) Weight loss

B) Gastrointestinal upset

C) Extrapyramidal symptoms

D) Tardive dyskinesia

Correct Answer: B) Gastrointestinal upset

49. **The COMT inhibitor Entacapone is used in Parkinson's disease to:**

A) Directly stimulate dopamine receptors

B) Inhibit the breakdown of levodopa

C) Increase dopamine synthesis

D) Block dopamine reuptake

Correct Answer: B) Inhibit the breakdown of levodopa

50. **In Parkinson's disease, the combination of Levodopa with Carbidopa is used because Carbidopa:**

A) Enhances levodopa's conversion to dopamine in the brain

B) Prevents peripheral metabolism of levodopa

C) Directly stimulates dopamine receptors

D) Blocks COMT activity

Correct Answer: B) Prevents peripheral metabolism of levodopa

51. **Dyskinesia is a common side effect of long-term Levodopa-Carbidopa therapy.**

A) True

B) False

Correct Answer: A) True

52. **Dopamine agonists, such as Ropinirole, function by:**

A) Inhibiting dopamine receptors

B) Directly stimulating dopamine receptors

C) Blocking the conversion of levodopa

D) Enhancing serotonin levels

Correct Answer: B) Directly stimulating dopamine receptors

53. **A potential side effect of dopamine agonists in Parkinson's disease is:**

A) Weight gain

B) Hallucinations

C) Hypotension

D) Bradycardia

Correct Answer: B) Hallucinations

54. **The term "narrow therapeutic index" in relation to Lithium means that:**

    A) There is a wide margin between effective and toxic doses

    B) There is a small margin between effective and toxic doses

    C) It is safe to use without monitoring

    D) It is only effective at very high doses

    Correct Answer: B) There is a small margin between effective and toxic doses

55. **Which laboratory test is critical for monitoring Lithium therapy?**

    A) Serum Lithium levels

    B) Serum calcium levels

    C) Complete blood count

    D) Electrocardiogram

    Correct Answer: A) Serum Lithium levels

56. **Valproate is used as a mood stabilizer and may cause which of the following side effects?**

    A) Hyperthyroidism

    B) Hepatotoxicity

    C) Extrapyramidal symptoms

    D) Renal failure

    Correct Answer: B) Hepatotoxicity

57. **Lamotrigine is especially useful in bipolar disorder for its role in preventing:**

    A) Manic episodes

    B) Depressive episodes

    C) Psychotic episodes

    D) Anxiety symptoms

    Correct Answer: B) Depressive episodes

58. **Short-term benzodiazepine use is indicated for:**

    A) Long-term anxiety management

    B) Immediate relief of acute anxiety

    C) Mood stabilization in bipolar disorder

    D) Treating schizophrenia

    Correct Answer: B) Immediate relief of acute anxiety

59. **Long-term treatment of anxiety disorders with SSRIs is preferred over benzodiazepines because SSRIs:**

A) Have a rapid onset

B) Have a lower risk of dependence

C) Cause more sedation

D) Are more likely to cause tolerance

Correct Answer: B) Have a lower risk of dependence

60. **Zolpidem is indicated for the management of:**

A) Anxiety disorders

B) Insomnia

C) Bipolar disorder

D) Schizophrenia

Correct Answer: B) Insomnia

61. **The mechanism of action of Z-drugs is primarily through modulation of:**

A) Dopamine receptors

B) GABA-A receptors

C) Serotonin receptors

D) NMDA receptors

Correct Answer: B) GABA-A receptors

62. **A known adverse effect of prolonged use of Z-drugs is:**

A) Increased risk of dependency

B) Extrapyramidal symptoms

C) Weight gain

D) Hyperglycemia

Correct Answer: A) Increased risk of dependency

63. **CPAP is used as the first-line treatment for:**

A) Chronic insomnia

B) Obstructive sleep apnea

C) Narcolepsy

D) REM sleep behavior disorder

Correct Answer: B) Obstructive sleep apnea

64. **The primary function of CPAP is to:**

A) Sedate the patient

B) Maintain airway patency during sleep

C) Increase deep sleep duration

D) Stimulate REM sleep

Correct Answer: B) Maintain airway patency during sleep

65. **Adjunctive pharmacotherapy in sleep apnea is sometimes used to address:**

A) Primary airway obstruction

B) Residual daytime sleepiness

C) Hypertension

D) Chronic insomnia unrelated to apnea

Correct Answer: B) Residual daytime sleepiness

66. **Which of the following best describes the integration of pharmacotherapy and psychosocial interventions in schizophrenia treatment?**

    A) Pharmacotherapy alone is sufficient

    B) A combined approach optimizes patient outcomes

    C) Psychosocial interventions are only used if medications fail

    D) They are mutually exclusive

    Correct Answer: B) A combined approach optimizes patient outcomes

67. **The Wells score is used in the evaluation of venous thromboembolism (VTE) to:**

    A) Provide a definitive diagnosis

    B) Stratify patients based on clinical risk factors

    C) Monitor anticoagulant therapy

    D) Measure platelet function

    Correct Answer: B) Stratify patients based on clinical risk factors

68. **Unfractionated heparin therapy is monitored using which laboratory test?**

    A) INR

    B) aPTT

    C) D-Dimer

    D) Serum creatinine

    Correct Answer: B) aPTT

69. **Direct oral anticoagulants (DOACs) such as Rivaroxaban and Apixaban are characterized by:**

    A) The need for routine coagulation monitoring

    B) Predictable pharmacokinetics that allow fixed dosing without routine monitoring

    C) Intravenous administration only

    D) A high risk of bleeding requiring frequent dose adjustments

    Correct Answer: B) Predictable pharmacokinetics that allow fixed dosing without routine monitoring

70. **In the context of Lithium therapy, a "narrow therapeutic index" means that:**

A) There is a wide margin between therapeutic and toxic doses

B) There is a small margin between therapeutic and toxic doses

C) It is effective at any dose

D) It requires no serum monitoring

Correct Answer: B) There is a small margin between therapeutic and toxic doses

CHAPTER SIX

Pain Management

6.1 Pain Pathways

Pain is a **complex neurophysiological process** involving **peripheral sensory neurons, central nervous system processing, and descending modulation**. It serves as a **protective mechanism** but can become **pathological in chronic pain conditions**. Understanding pain pathways helps guide the **selection of appropriate analgesic therapies**.

Neurotransmitters in Pain Modulation

Pain perception involves **both peripheral and central pathways,** mediated by various neurotransmitters.

Peripheral Pain Pathways

1. **Nociceptors**

   - Specialized **sensory neurons** located in **skin, muscles, joints, and viscera.**
   - Activated by **mechanical, thermal, or chemical stimuli**, leading to pain transmission.

2. **Neurotransmitters in Peripheral Pain Transmission**

Neurotransmitter	Role in Pain Transmission
Substance P	Enhances pain signal transmission from nociceptors to the spinal cord.
Glutamate	Activates **NMDA receptors in the dorsal horn**, amplifying pain signals.
Bradykinin	Promotes **inflammation and nociceptor sensitization**, leading to increased pain perception.
Prostaglandins	Sensitize nociceptors, increasing pain intensity.

Mechanism of Sensitization

- Repeated nociceptor activation leads to hyperalgesia (increased pain sensitivity).
- Peripheral sensitization occurs due to inflammatory mediators (prostaglandins, cytokines).
- Central sensitization results from prolonged NMDA receptor activation, contributing to chronic pain conditions.

Central Pain Pathways

Pain signals travel to the **dorsal horn of the spinal cord**, where they undergo **modulation before being transmitted to the brain.**

1. Ascending Pain Pathways

   ◦ **Spinothalamic Tract:** Carries pain signals to the **thalamus and somatosensory cortex,** allowing **conscious pain perception.**
   ◦ **Spinoreticular Tract:** Involved in **emotional and autonomic responses to pain** (e.g., increased heart rate).

2. Descending Pain Modulation

The brainstem has **inhibitory pain pathways** that regulate pain intensity through neurotransmitters:

Neurotransmitter	Function
Endorphins & Enkephalins	Activate **opioid receptors**, inhibiting pain transmission.
Serotonin (5-HT)	Modulates pain via descending pathways from the **raphe nuclei**.
Norepinephrine	Enhances **spinal pain inhibition via the locus coeruleus**.
GABA	Inhibits excitatory pain signals at the spinal level.

Inhibitory pain pathways

Opioid analgesics (e.g., morphine) mimic endogenous opioids, suppressing pain perception.

Tricyclic antidepressants (e.g., amitriptyline) enhance serotonin and norepinephrine levels, improving chronic pain control.

Role of COX Enzymes in Inflammatory Pain

Pain caused by **inflammation** is primarily mediated by **prostaglandins**, which are synthesized via the **cyclooxygenase (COX) pathway**.

Cyclooxygenase (COX) Pathway

1. **COX-1**

   ◦ Constitutive enzyme involved in **gastric mucosal protection, platelet function, and renal blood flow**.
   ◦ **Inhibition leads to GI irritation and increased bleeding risk.**

2. **COX-2**

   ◦ Inducible enzyme, activated during **inflammation, injury, and infection.**
   ◦ Produces **pro-inflammatory prostaglandins**, leading to **pain, swelling, and fever.**
   ◦ Selective **COX-2 inhibitors reduce inflammation while sparing COX-1 functions.**

Drugs Targeting COX Enzymes

NSAIDs inhibit both COX-1 and COX-2, reducing prostaglandin synthesis and alleviating pain and inflammation.

Drug	Mechanism	Dosage	Indications	Side Effects
Ibuprofen	Non-selective COX inhibitor	400–800 mg TID	Musculoskeletal pain, arthritis, headache	GI irritation, nephrotoxicity
Diclofenac	Non-selective COX inhibitor	50–75 mg BID	Osteoarthritis, post-operative pain	GI ulceration, renal impairment
Aspirin	Irreversibly inhibits COX-1 & COX-2	325–650 mg every 4–6 hours	Pain, fever, cardiovascular prevention	Bleeding risk, gastric irritation

Non-Steroidal Anti-Inflammatory Drugs (NSAIDs)

- **NSAIDs are effective for mild to moderate pain but carry risks of GI bleeding, renal impairment, and cardiovascular effects.**

Selective COX-2 Inhibitors

Selective COX-2 inhibitors provide **anti-inflammatory effects with reduced GI toxicity.**

Drug	Mechanism	Dosage	Indications	Side Effects
Celecoxib	Selective COX-2 inhibitor	100–200 mg BID	Osteoarthritis, rheumatoid arthritis	Cardiovascular risk, renal impairment
Etoricoxib	Selective COX-2 inhibitor	60–120 mg once daily	Chronic inflammatory pain	Hypertension, fluid retention

6.2 Neuralgias

Neuralgias refer to **chronic neuropathic pain syndromes** caused by **nerve damage, irritation, or dysfunction.** Unlike **nociceptive pain**, which results from tissue injury, **neuropathic pain** originates from abnormal nerve signaling. It is characterized by **burning, stabbing, or electric shock-like sensations**, often resistant to conventional analgesics.

Gabapentinoids: Mechanism and Role in Neuropathic Pain

Gabapentinoids, including **gabapentin and pregabalin**, are **first-line agents for neuropathic pain**. They **modulate calcium channel activity in the CNS**, reducing excessive excitatory neurotransmission.

Mechanism of Action

1. **Bind to the α2δ subunit of voltage-gated calcium channels in the CNS**, preventing excessive neuronal firing.
2. **Reduce calcium influx**, thereby decreasing the release of pain-mediating neurotransmitters such as:

   - **Glutamate** (primary excitatory neurotransmitter).
   - **Substance P** (enhances nociceptive transmission).
   - **Norepinephrine** (involved in pain perception).

3. **Enhance GABAergic inhibition**, further dampening nerve excitability.

By **modulating abnormal nerve signaling**, gabapentinoids **interrupt neuropathic pain transmission at the spinal level.**

Indications for Gabapentinoids

Gabapentinoids are **highly effective in neuropathic pain syndromes**, particularly:

1. **Diabetic Neuropathy**

   - **Peripheral nerve damage due to prolonged hyperglycemia.**
   - Characterized by **burning pain, tingling, and numbness** in the **feet and hands.**

2. **Post-Herpetic Neuralgia (PHN)**

- Persistent nerve pain following herpes zoster (shingles) infection.
- Pain presents as **burning, electric shocks, and hypersensitivity to touch.**

3. **Trigeminal Neuralgia**

- **Sudden, severe, shock-like facial pain** triggered by **chewing, talking, or light touch.**
- Gabapentinoids help by **stabilizing nerve hyperexcitability.**

4. **Fibromyalgia**

- **Widespread musculoskeletal pain with central sensitization.**
- Pregabalin is FDA-approved for **fibromyalgia management.**

5. **Radiculopathy and Sciatica**

- **Compression of spinal nerve roots** leading to **radiating nerve pain** in the back and legs.

Drug	Dosage	Half-Life	Onset of Action	Key Side Effects
Gabapentin	300 mg/day, titrated to 1800–3600 mg/day	5–7 hours	2–4 weeks	Sedation, dizziness, fatigue
Pregabalin	75 mg BID, titrated to 300 mg/day	6–8 hours	Faster (1–2 weeks)	Weight gain, peripheral edema

Comparison of Gabapentin and Pregabalin

- **Pregabalin has a more predictable pharmacokinetic profile,** allowing **faster titration and earlier pain relief.**
- **Gabapentin has a slower onset,** requiring **longer dose escalation (over weeks)** to achieve therapeutic effects.

Efficacy in Neuropathic Pain

- **50–70% of patients experience significant pain relief with gabapentinoids.**
- **Pregabalin is slightly more potent than gabapentin,** but both have comparable efficacy when titrated to optimal doses.
- **Combination therapy (e.g., gabapentinoids + antidepressants)** improves pain control in resistant cases.

Side Effects and Risk Management

1. Sedation and Dizziness

   - **Common during dose titration,** but improves with continued use.
   - **Start with low doses and titrate gradually** to minimize drowsiness.

2. Weight Gain and Peripheral Edema

   - **More pronounced with pregabalin** than gabapentin.
   - **Encourage dietary modifications and exercise** to counteract weight gain.

3. Cognitive Impairment

   - Some patients report **brain fog, memory issues, or difficulty concentrating.**
   - **Use lower doses in elderly patients** to reduce cognitive side effects.

4. Potential for Misuse

   - Pregabalin and gabapentin **can produce euphoria at high doses,** leading to **off-label abuse.**
   - **Avoid in patients with a history of substance use disorder.**

Clinical Considerations in Gabapentinoid Therapy

- Gabapentinoids are best initiated at low doses and gradually titrated to avoid side effects.
- **Pregabalin provides faster pain relief**, but **gabapentin is more cost-effective** for long-term use.
- **Adjust doses in renal impairment**, as both drugs are **renally excreted**.
- **Combine with antidepressants (e.g., duloxetine, amitriptyline) for enhanced efficacy** in refractory neuropathic pain.

REVIEW QUESTIONS

1. Define pain and describe the physiological process of pain perception.
2. Explain the role of neurotransmitters in pain modulation.
3. Describe the major ascending and descending pain pathways and their significance in pain management.
4. Discuss the role of COX enzymes in inflammatory pain.
5. How do non-steroidal anti-inflammatory drugs (NSAIDs) relieve pain?
6. Explain the mechanism of action of gabapentinoids in the management of neuropathic pain.
7. Define neuralgia and differentiate it from other types of pain.
8. Discuss the importance of understanding pain pathways in the development of effective analgesic therapies.
9. Describe how the balance between excitatory and inhibitory neurotransmitters influences pain perception.
10. Explain the mechanism by which triptans alleviate acute migraine attacks.
11. What are the common adverse effects and contraindications associated with triptan use?
12. Describe the rationale behind using beta-blockers for migraine prophylaxis.
13. Discuss the mechanism of action of topiramate in migraine prophylaxis.
14. Compare the mechanisms of action of triptans and NSAIDs in the management of migraine.
15. Outline the role of the descending inhibitory pain pathway.
16. Discuss the concept of central sensitization and its implications in chronic pain.
17. Explain the term "allodynia" and its relevance in neuropathic pain.
18. How do gabapentinoids alter neuronal excitability in neuropathic pain?
19. Describe the mechanism by which NSAIDs reduce inflammatory pain.
20. Discuss the clinical significance of differentiating between inflammatory and neuropathic pain.
21. Outline the therapeutic goals in the acute management of migraine.
22. Discuss the long-term management strategies for migraine prophylaxis.
23. Explain how patient-specific factors influence the selection of pain management strategies.

24. Discuss the importance of a multidisciplinary approach in pain management.
25. What are the challenges in managing neuropathic pain compared to inflammatory pain?
26. Summarize current trends and future directions in pain management research.

MCQS

1. **Which of the following best defines pain?**
   A) A purely psychological phenomenon
   B) An unpleasant sensory and emotional experience associated with tissue damage
   C) A process occurring only in chronic conditions
   D) A reflex action only
   Correct Answer: B

2. **The ascending pain pathway carries pain signals from:**
   A) The brain to the spinal cord
   B) Peripheral tissues to the brain
   C) The brain to the muscles
   D) The spinal cord to the peripheral tissues
   Correct Answer: B

3. **Which neurotransmitter is most closely associated with pain transmission in the spinal cord?**
   A) Dopamine
   B) Substance P
   C) Serotonin
   D) Acetylcholine
   Correct Answer: B

4. **Glutamate functions in pain modulation as an:**
   A) Inhibitory neurotransmitter
   B) Excitatory neurotransmitter
   C) Neuromodulator only
   D) Hormone
   Correct Answer: B

5. **GABA's role in pain modulation is to:**
   A) Enhance pain signaling
   B) Inhibit pain signaling
   C) Increase excitatory activity
   D) Facilitate COX production
   Correct Answer: B

6. **COX enzymes are responsible for producing which substance that contributes to inflammatory pain?**

    A) Endorphins

    B) Prostaglandins

    C) Cytokines

    D) Leukotrienes

    Correct Answer: B

7. **NSAIDs relieve inflammatory pain primarily by:**

    A) Blocking GABA receptors

    B) Inhibiting COX enzymes

    C) Reducing dopamine synthesis

    D) Blocking calcium channels

    Correct Answer: B

8. **COX-2 is primarily induced during inflammation and leads to the production of:**

    A) Homeostatic prostaglandins

    B) Inflammatory prostaglandins

    C) Platelet aggregators

    D) Gastroprotective agents

    Correct Answer: B

9. **Which COX enzyme is constitutively expressed for normal physiological functions?**

    A) COX-1

    B) COX-2

    C) COX-3

    D) COX-4

    Correct Answer: A

10. **Gabapentinoids are used to treat neuropathic pain by:**

    A) Blocking sodium channels only

    B) Modulating calcium channel activity

    C) Inhibiting COX enzymes

    D) Enhancing opioid receptor activation

    Correct Answer: B

11. **Gabapentinoids exert their effect by binding to which subunit of voltage-gated calcium channels?**

    A) Alpha-1

    B) Beta

    C) Alpha-2-delta

D) Gamma

Correct Answer: C

12. **Neuralgia is best defined as pain along the distribution of:**

    A) Muscle tissue

    B) A nerve

    C) Bone

    D) Skin

    Correct Answer: B

13. **Gabapentinoids help alleviate neuralgic pain by:**

    A) Increasing synaptic transmission

    B) Reducing excitatory neurotransmitter release

    C) Enhancing prostaglandin production

    D) Blocking opioid receptors

    Correct Answer: B

14. **Migraine is classified as a:**

    A) Secondary headache disorder

    B) Primary headache disorder

    C) Tension-type headache

    D) Cluster headache

    Correct Answer: B

15. **Triptans act primarily as agonists at which receptors?**

    A) 5-HT1B/1D receptors

    B) 5-HT2 receptors

    C) Dopamine receptors

    D) GABA receptors

    Correct Answer: A

16. **The mechanism of action of triptans includes:**

    A) Dilating cranial blood vessels

    B) Constricting cranial blood vessels and inhibiting neuropeptide release

    C) Blocking sodium channels

    D) Enhancing COX activity

    Correct Answer: B

17. **A common side effect of triptan use is:**

    A) Hypotension

    B) Chest tightness

    C) Sedation

    D) Weight loss

Correct Answer: B

18. **Beta-blockers in migraine prophylaxis work by:**
    A) Directly reducing neuronal excitability
    B) Modulating vascular tone and sympathetic activity
    C) Enhancing serotonin release
    D) Inhibiting COX enzymes
    Correct Answer: B

19. **Topiramate is used for migraine prophylaxis because it:**
    A) Blocks sodium channels and stabilizes neuronal firing
    B) Increases dopamine synthesis
    C) Acts as a potent analgesic
    D) Enhances prostaglandin synthesis
    Correct Answer: A

20. **The descending inhibitory pain pathway primarily functions to:**
    A) Amplify pain signals
    B) Modulate and suppress pain transmission
    C) Transmit pain signals to the brain
    D) Increase inflammatory mediator release
    Correct Answer: B

21. **Which neurotransmitter is a key component of the descending inhibitory pathway?**
    A) Substance P
    B) Serotonin
    C) Glutamate
    D) Acetylcholine
    Correct Answer: B

22. **Inhibiting COX enzymes with NSAIDs leads to a reduction in:**
    A) Neuropeptide release
    B) Prostaglandin synthesis
    C) Nerve conduction velocity
    D) Calcium influx in neurons
    Correct Answer: B

23. **Which of the following is an example of a non-pharmacological pain management approach?**
    A) Gabapentinoids
    B) Cognitive-behavioral therapy (CBT)
    C) Triptans
    D) Beta-blockers

Correct Answer: B

24. **The primary goal of acute migraine treatment is to:**
    A) Prevent future migraine attacks
    B) Quickly relieve the current headache symptoms
    C) Maintain long-term prophylaxis
    D) Increase serotonin levels permanently
    Correct Answer: B

25. **In neuropathic pain, "allodynia" is defined as pain due to:**
    A) Tissue damage only
    B) Normally non-painful stimuli
    C) Excessive muscle contraction
    D) High levels of inflammation
    Correct Answer: B

26. **Inflammatory pain is primarily due to:**
    A) Nerve injury
    B) Tissue inflammation and release of inflammatory mediators
    C) Psychological factors only
    D) Neuropathic damage
    Correct Answer: B

27. **NSAIDs reduce inflammatory pain by inhibiting:**
    A) Opioid receptors
    B) COX enzymes
    C) Voltage-gated sodium channels
    D) NMDA receptors
    Correct Answer: B

28. **Gabapentin is primarily used to treat:**
    A) Inflammatory pain
    B) Neuropathic pain
    C) Acute migraine attacks
    D) Tension-type headaches
    Correct Answer: B

29. **Which of the following is NOT a typical feature of neuropathic pain?**
    A) Burning or tingling sensation
    B) Sharp, stabbing pain
    C) Pain in response to normally non-painful stimuli
    D) Pain exclusively due to tissue inflammation
    Correct Answer: D

30. **Central sensitization in chronic pain results in:**
    A) A reduced pain response
    B) Hyperalgesia and allodynia
    C) Decreased neuronal excitability
    D) Increased inhibitory neurotransmission
    Correct Answer: B

31. **The balance between excitatory and inhibitory neurotransmitters in pain modulation determines:**
    A) The intensity of pain perception
    B) Only the duration of pain
    C) The location of pain
    D) The type of inflammatory response
    Correct Answer: A

32. **Triptans relieve migraine pain primarily by:**
    A) Blocking GABA receptors
    B) Constricting cranial blood vessels via 5-HT1B/1D receptor activation
    C) Inhibiting sodium channels
    D) Enhancing COX enzyme activity
    Correct Answer: B

33. **Beta-blockers help prevent migraines by modulating:**
    A) Vascular tone and sympathetic activity
    B) Glutamate release directly
    C) GABA receptor sensitivity
    D) Sodium channel function
    Correct Answer: A

34. **Topiramate is beneficial in migraine prophylaxis because it:**
    A) Increases neuronal excitability
    B) Stabilizes neuronal firing and reduces hyperexcitability
    C) Enhances serotonin reuptake
    D) Stimulates prostaglandin synthesis
    Correct Answer: B

35. **Gabapentinoids are most effective in managing which type of pain?**
    A) Inflammatory pain
    B) Neuropathic pain
    C) Acute migraine
    D) Tension headache
    Correct Answer: B

36. **Prostaglandins, which contribute to inflammatory pain, are produced by the action of:**
    A) COX enzymes
    B) Sodium channels
    C) Calcium channels
    D) GABA receptors
    Correct Answer: A

37. **The descending inhibitory pain pathway utilizes which neurotransmitter to modulate pain?**
    A) Glutamate
    B) Substance P
    C) Serotonin
    D) Dopamine
    Correct Answer: C

38. **Neuralgia is best characterized by pain that is:**
    A) Dull and diffuse
    B) Sharp and localized along a nerve distribution
    C) Only present during movement
    D) Associated with deep tissue inflammation
    Correct Answer: B

39. **In migraine, an aura is best described as:**
    A) The headache phase itself
    B) A sensory disturbance that precedes the headache
    C) A type of nausea
    D) A form of prophylactic treatment
    Correct Answer: B

40. **Triptans are contraindicated in patients with:**
    A) Migraine with aura
    B) Coronary artery disease
    C) Tension-type headache
    D) Controlled hypertension
    Correct Answer: B

41. **The term "prophylaxis" in migraine management refers to:**
    A) Treatment during a migraine attack
    B) Preventive therapy to reduce attack frequency and severity
    C) Emergency intervention
    D) Symptomatic relief only
    Correct Answer: B

42. **Propranolol is an example of a beta-blocker used for:**
    A) Acute migraine relief
    B) Migraine prophylaxis
    C) Neuropathic pain
    D) Inflammatory pain
    Correct Answer: B

43. **Topiramate is used in migraine prophylaxis because it:**
    A) Increases neuronal excitability
    B) Stabilizes neuronal firing and reduces hyperexcitability
    C) Acts as a serotonin antagonist
    D) Enhances prostaglandin synthesis
    Correct Answer: B

44. **Gabapentinoids, such as gabapentin, work by binding to the:**
    A) GABA-A receptor directly
    B) Alpha-2-delta subunit of voltage-gated calcium channels
    C) NMDA receptor
    D) Dopamine receptor
    Correct Answer: B

45. **NSAIDs reduce pain primarily by:**
    A) Inhibiting voltage-gated sodium channels
    B) Inhibiting COX enzymes and reducing prostaglandin synthesis
    C) Blocking GABA receptors
    D) Enhancing calcium influx
    Correct Answer: B

46. **Triptans are most effective when administered during the:**
    A) Premonitory phase
    B) Aura phase
    C) Headache phase
    D) Postdrome phase
    Correct Answer: C

47. **Beta-blockers in migraine prophylaxis work by reducing:**
    A) Heart rate exclusively
    B) Sympathetic nervous system activity and vascular instability
    C) GABAergic transmission
    D) Pain receptor sensitivity
    Correct Answer: B

48. **The side effect profile of triptans may include:**
    A) Increased appetite

B) Chest tightness or discomfort

C) Sedation

D) Weight gain

Correct Answer: B

49. **Central sensitization leads to chronic pain by:**

    A) Raising the pain threshold

    B) Lowering the pain threshold and causing hyperalgesia

    C) Inhibiting neurotransmitter release

    D) Decreasing neuronal activity

    Correct Answer: B

50. **Which of the following best describes the effect of gabapentinoids on neuropathic pain?**

    A) They enhance excitatory neurotransmission

    B) They reduce neuronal hyperexcitability

    C) They block opioid receptors

    D) They increase COX-2 expression

    Correct Answer: B

51. **Central sensitization in chronic pain is characterized by:**

    A) Decreased neuronal response to stimuli

    B) Increased responsiveness of central neurons, leading to hyperalgesia

    C) Improved pain inhibition

    D) Reduced neurotransmitter release

    Correct Answer: B

52. **Prostaglandins are primarily produced by:**

    A) COX enzymes

    B) Lipoxygenase

    C) Dopamine receptors

    D) Voltage-gated sodium channels

    Correct Answer: A

53. **The descending inhibitory pathway modulates pain using:**

    A) Glutamate

    B) Substance P

    C) Serotonin

    D) Acetylcholine

    Correct Answer: C

54. **GABA's role in pain modulation is to:**

    A) Enhance pain signals

B) Inhibit pain transmission

C) Increase excitatory neurotransmission

D) Stimulate COX enzymes

Correct Answer: B

55. **Triptans relieve migraine pain by:**

    A) Activating 5-HT1B/1D receptors to cause cranial vasoconstriction

    B) Blocking GABA receptors

    C) Inhibiting COX enzymes

    D) Enhancing glutamate release

    Correct Answer: A

56. **Beta-blockers used for migraine prophylaxis help reduce migraine frequency by:**

    A) Increasing heart rate variability

    B) Reducing sympathetic nervous system activity

    C) Enhancing glutamate neurotransmission

    D) Stimulating dopamine receptors

    Correct Answer: B

57. **Topiramate is beneficial in migraine prophylaxis because it:**

    A) Increases neuronal excitability

    B) Stabilizes neuronal firing and reduces hyperexcitability

    C) Inhibits serotonin receptors

    D) Acts as a strong sedative

    Correct Answer: B

58. **Neuropathic pain is often characterized by:**

    A) Sharp, localized pain

    B) Burning, tingling, or electric shock-like sensations

    C) Pain that responds well to NSAIDs alone

    D) Pain only during physical activity

    Correct Answer: B

59. **The term "allodynia" in neuropathic pain refers to pain from:**

    A) Normally non-painful stimuli

    B) Severe tissue damage

    C) Increased inflammatory markers

    D) Spontaneous muscle contraction

    Correct Answer: A

60. **Acute migraine treatment with triptans aims to:**

    A) Prevent future attacks

    B) Rapidly relieve the current headache

C) Provide long-term prophylaxis

D) Increase cerebral blood flow permanently

Correct Answer: B

61. **NSAIDs alleviate inflammatory pain by:**

    A) Blocking sodium channels

    B) Inhibiting prostaglandin synthesis via COX inhibition

    C) Activating opioid receptors

    D) Enhancing GABA release

    Correct Answer: B

62. **Gabapentinoids are most effective in treating:**

    A) Inflammatory pain

    B) Neuropathic pain

    C) Acute migraine

    D) Tension-type headache

    Correct Answer: B

63. **Central sensitization contributes to:**

    A) Hypoalgesia

    B) Hyperalgesia and allodynia

    C) Reduced pain perception

    D) Increased inhibitory control

    Correct Answer: B

64. **Substance P facilitates pain transmission by:**

    A) Inhibiting glutamate release

    B) Enhancing excitatory signaling in the spinal cord

    C) Blocking GABA receptors

    D) Stimulating opioid release

    Correct Answer: B

65. **Triptan therapy is contraindicated in patients with:**

    A) Controlled hypertension

    B) Coronary artery disease

    C) History of migraine with aura alone

    D) Tension-type headaches

    Correct Answer: B

66. **Migraine prophylaxis is indicated for patients experiencing:**

    A) Occasional mild headaches

    B) Frequent, debilitating migraine attacks

    C) Only tension-type headaches

    D) Sinus headaches

Correct Answer: B

67. **Beta-blockers, such as propranolol, are used in migraine prophylaxis because they:**
    A) Have potent analgesic properties
    B) Reduce sympathetic activity and stabilize vascular tone
    C) Directly block pain transmission
    D) Act as sedatives
    Correct Answer: B

68. **Topiramate may be preferred for migraine prophylaxis because it is associated with:**
    A) Weight gain
    B) Weight loss
    C) Sedation only
    D) No side effects
    Correct Answer: B

69. **The descending inhibitory pain pathway is important because it:**
    A) Amplifies pain signals
    B) Suppresses pain transmission
    C) Increases inflammatory mediator release
    D) Has no role in pain modulation
    Correct Answer: B

70. **Which of the following is a key benefit of a multidisciplinary approach in pain management?**
    A) Sole reliance on pharmacotherapy
    B) Integration of medications, physical therapy, and psychological support
    C) Exclusive use of surgical interventions
    D) Avoidance of patient-specific treatment plans
    Correct Answer: B

71. **In migraine, an aura typically involves:**
    A) A visual or sensory disturbance preceding the headache
    B) The headache phase itself
    C) Only gastrointestinal symptoms
    D) A phase of increased alertness
    Correct Answer: A

72. **Prophylactic migraine treatment aims to:**
    A) Immediately abort a migraine attack
    B) Reduce the frequency, severity, and duration of migraine attacks

C) Eliminate the need for any acute treatments

D) Increase the intensity of migraine symptoms

Correct Answer: B

73. **The inhibition of COX enzymes by NSAIDs results in decreased production of:**

    A) Substance P

    B) Prostaglandins

    C) Glutamate

    D) Serotonin

    Correct Answer: B

74. **Which of the following best describes allodynia?**

    A) Pain from normally painful stimuli

    B) Pain from stimuli that are not normally painful

    C) A type of inflammatory pain

    D) Pain exclusively due to tissue injury

    Correct Answer: B

75. **The primary target of triptans in migraine therapy is to:**

    A) Block dopamine receptors

    B) Activate 5-HT1B/1D receptors

    C) Inhibit GABA receptors

    D) Stimulate COX enzymes

    Correct Answer: B

76. **A common adverse effect of triptan therapy is:**

    A) Increased appetite

    B) Chest discomfort or tightness

    C) Weight loss

    D) Sedation

    Correct Answer: B

77. **In pain management, a multidisciplinary approach is recommended because it:**

    A) Relies solely on medications

    B) Combines pharmacological, physical, and psychological therapies for optimal outcomes

    C) Eliminates the need for any pharmacotherapy

    D) Focuses only on surgical options

    Correct Answer: B

78. **Prophylactic treatment for migraine aims to:**

    A) Treat the headache only once it begins

B) Reduce the frequency, severity, and duration of migraine attacks over time

C) Replace all acute therapies immediately

D) Increase cerebral blood flow permanently

Correct Answer: B

CHAPTER SEVEN

Evidence-Based Medicine

7.1 Introduction to Evidence-Based Medicine

Evidence-Based Medicine (EBM) is a **systematic approach to clinical decision-making** that integrates **scientific research, clinician expertise, and patient preferences.** It helps ensure that medical interventions are safe, effective, and supported by high-quality evidence.

Definition and Principles of EBM

EBM is defined as **the conscientious, explicit, and judicious use of the best current evidence in making decisions about the care of individual patients.** It incorporates three essential components:

1. **Best Available Evidence**

   - Derived from **clinical trials, systematic reviews, and meta-analyses.**
   - Higher levels of evidence are **more reliable** for clinical decision-making.

2. **Clinical Expertise**

   - The **experience, skills, and knowledge** of healthcare providers in interpreting and applying evidence.

3. **Patient Values and Preferences**

○ Informed decision-making based on patient beliefs, concerns, and expectations.

By balancing these three factors, EBM **improves patient care and minimizes unnecessary treatments.**

Five-Step Process of EBM

The **EBM cycle** follows five essential steps:

1. Ask a Clinical Question

Formulating a clear, focused question using the PICO framework

PICO Element	Description	Example
P (Patient/Problem)	Define the patient or condition	Type 2 diabetes, uncontrolled hypertension
I (Intervention)	The treatment or test under consideration	Metformin, ACE inhibitors
C (Comparison)	Alternative treatment or placebo	Metformin vs. sulfonylureas
O (Outcome)	Desired result	HbA1c reduction, cardiovascular risk prevention

PICO framework

- Example clinical question: **"In patients with type 2 diabetes, does metformin reduce cardiovascular events compared to sulfonylureas?"**

2. Acquire Evidence

- **Search for high-quality research** using medical databases like:

  ○ PubMed, Cochrane Library, Embase, Google Scholar.
  ○ **Clinical practice guidelines** from **WHO, NICE, ADA, AHA.**
  ○ **Randomized controlled trials (RCTs) and meta-analyses** provide the most reliable evidence.

3. Appraise the Quality of Evidence

- **Not all studies provide reliable results.** Evaluate research using:

  - Study design (RCTs > observational studies > case reports).
  - Sample size, bias control, and statistical significance (p-value <0.05).
  - Risk-benefit analysis for clinical application.

4. Apply the Findings in Clinical Practice

- **Incorporate research into patient care** while considering:

  - Individual patient characteristics (age, comorbidities, preferences).
  - Availability and cost of interventions.
  - **Ethical considerations and shared decision-making.**

5. Assess the Outcomes of Decisions

- Monitor patient response and **evaluate clinical effectiveness.**
- Adjust treatment based on:

  - Therapeutic success (e.g., HbA1c reduction, BP control).
  - **Adverse effects and patient-reported outcomes.**

7.2 Hierarchy of Evidence

Evidence-Based Medicine (EBM) relies on a **hierarchical structure of evidence** to guide clinical decision-making. **Not all studies provide the same level of reliability,** and understanding the hierarchy helps **distinguish high-quality evidence from lower-tier sources.**

Pyramid of Evidence

The **hierarchy of evidence** is commonly visualized as a **pyramid,** with the **most reliable and least biased sources at the top** and **lower-quality evidence at the bottom.**

? Hierarchy of Clinical Evidence (Top to Bottom)

1. Systematic Reviews and Meta-Analyses

   - **Highest level of evidence**, synthesizing data from multiple high-quality studies.
   - Provide **comprehensive insights and reduce bias.**
   - Example: **A systematic review on the cardiovascular benefits of SGLT2 inhibitors in diabetes patients shows a 25% reduction in heart failure hospitalizations.**

2. Randomized Controlled Trials (RCTs) – Gold Standard

   - **Prospective studies with randomization,** ensuring minimal bias.
   - **Essential for evaluating new drug efficacy.**
   - Example: **A double-blind RCT comparing second-generation antipsychotics (e.g., aripiprazole) with traditional agents like haloperidol found fewer extrapyramidal side effects with newer drugs.**

3. Cohort Studies (Observational, Prospective or Retrospective)

   - Follow groups over time to **compare disease outcomes based on exposure to a risk factor or treatment.**
   - Example: **A cohort study following hypertensive patients for 10 years found a 40% reduction in stroke risk with ACE inhibitors.**

4. Case-Control Studies (Retrospective)

   - Compare **patients with a disease (cases) to those without (controls).**
   - Good for studying **rare diseases or long-term drug effects.**
   - Example: **A case-control study found an increased risk of venous thromboembolism in women using oral contraceptives.**

5. Cross-Sectional Studies (Snapshot Data Collection)

   - Evaluate **prevalence** of a condition at a **single point in time.**
   - Example: **A cross-sectional study on depression prevalence found that 12% of medical students had undiagnosed clinical depression.**

6. Case Reports and Case Series

- **Lowest level of evidence**, describing **individual patient cases.**
- Useful for **rare diseases or adverse drug reactions.**
- Example: **A case report of agranulocytosis caused by clozapine led to regulatory changes requiring blood monitoring.**

7. Expert Opinions & Mechanistic Studies

- Based on **theoretical knowledge, lab studies, and expert recommendations.**
- **Least reliable due to lack of real-world validation.**

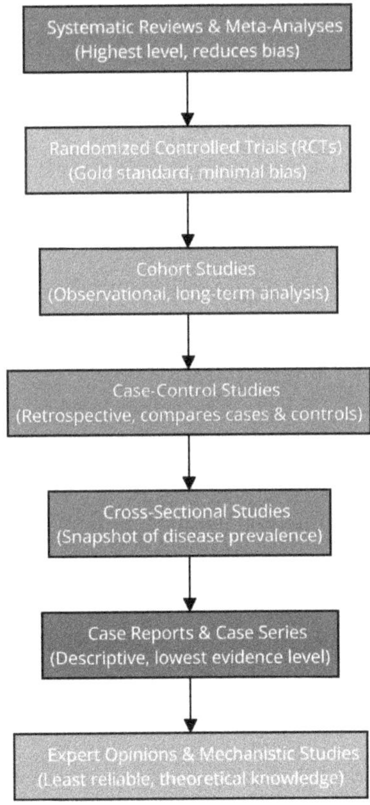

Pyramid of Evidence

Comparing Study Designs and Their Uses

Study Design	Purpose	Advantages	Limitations
Systematic Reviews & Meta-Analyses	Summarize multiple studies	High reliability, reduces bias	Requires high-quality studies
RCTs	Compare interventions	Best for causality, controlled environment	Expensive, ethical limitations
Cohort Studies	Observe exposure-disease relationships	Establish temporal association	Susceptible to confounding
Case-Control Studies	Study rare diseases	Quick and cost-effective	Recall bias, cannot determine causality
Cross-Sectional Studies	Measure disease prevalence	Fast and cheap	No cause-effect relationship
Case Reports	Report unique cases	Highlights new findings	Cannot generalize results
Expert Opinions	Provide guidance	Useful in new fields	Highly subjective

Comparing Study Designs and Their Uses

7.3 Application of Evidence-Based Medicine in Pharmacotherapeutics

The application of **Evidence-Based Medicine (EBM)** in **pharmacotherapeutics** ensures that drug therapies are chosen based on the **best available evidence**, balancing **efficacy, safety, and patient-centered considerations**. Clinicians integrate EBM into **clinical decision-making, drug selection, dose adjustments, and monitoring** to improve patient outcomes.

Clinical Decision-Making Using EBM

Evidence-based pharmacotherapeutics helps healthcare providers:

- **Select the most effective and safest drug therapy for a given condition.**

- Tailor treatment to individual patient characteristics.
- Assess the risk-benefit ratio based on clinical trial data.
- Adjust therapy according to real-world effectiveness and patient response.

Formulating Patient-Specific Questions Using EBM

A structured approach to **clinical queries** helps in identifying the best treatment. **The PICO framework** is widely used in formulating patient-specific EBM questions.

Example Clinical Question in Diabetes Management

"In a diabetic patient with hypertension, what is the most effective treatment to reduce cardiovascular risk?"

Using the **PICO framework**:

Component	Details	Example in Pharmacotherapy
P (Patient/Problem)	Define the patient population or condition.	Type 2 diabetes with hypertension
I (Intervention)	The proposed treatment or drug therapy.	SGLT2 inhibitors (e.g., empagliflozin, dapagliflozin)
C (Comparator)	Alternative treatment or standard care.	Sulfonylureas (e.g., glibenclamide, gliclazide)
O (Outcome)	Expected clinical benefit or risk reduction.	Reduction in cardiovascular mortality

Stepwise Application of EBM in Drug Selection

1. **Define the Clinical Problem**

   ○ Example: A patient with **Type 2 Diabetes Mellitus (T2DM)** and **established cardiovascular disease** requires an **optimal antihyperglycemic agent.**

2. **Search for the Best Available Evidence**

- ○ Sources:

  - ▪ **Randomized Controlled Trials (RCTs)** (e.g., EMPA-REG OUTCOME trial for SGLT2 inhibitors).
  - ▪ **Meta-analyses and systematic reviews** (e.g., Cochrane reviews).
  - ▪ **Guidelines from authoritative bodies** (e.g., ADA, AHA, NICE).

3. **Critically Appraise the Evidence**

   - ○ Compare efficacy and safety outcomes of **SGLT2 inhibitors vs. sulfonylureas.**
   - ○ **Evidence from EMPA-REG trial:**

     - ▪ **Empagliflozin reduces cardiovascular death by 38%** compared to placebo.
     - ▪ **Sulfonylureas increase hypoglycemia risk but have no cardiovascular benefit.**

4. **Apply the Evidence to Clinical Practice**

   - ○ **Individualize treatment based on comorbidities, renal function,** and patient preferences.
   - ○ **Consider contraindications** (e.g., renal impairment for SGLT2 inhibitors).

5. **Monitor and Evaluate Treatment Outcomes**

   - ○ Assess HbA1c reduction, cardiovascular risk improvement, and adverse effects.
   - ○ **Adjust therapy if necessary** (e.g., switch to GLP-1 receptor agonist if weight loss is needed).

Examples of EBM-Based Pharmacotherapeutic Decisions

Example 1: Hypertension Management in High-Risk Patients

- Clinical Question:
  In patients with hypertension and heart failure, should an ACE inhibitor or a beta-blocker be the first-line treatment?
- EBM Answer:

  - ACE inhibitors (e.g., enalapril, ramipril) reduce mortality by 27% in heart failure patients (HOPE trial).
  - Beta-blockers (e.g., bisoprolol) improve survival but should be used with ACE inhibitors for maximal benefit.

Example 2: Anticoagulation in Atrial Fibrillation

- Clinical Question:
  Is apixaban superior to warfarin in preventing stroke in atrial fibrillation?
- EBM Answer (ARISTOTLE trial):

  - Apixaban reduces stroke risk by 21% and major bleeding by 31% compared to warfarin.
  - Warfarin requires INR monitoring, whereas apixaban has a fixed dosing regimen.

EBM-Based Guidelines for Pharmacotherapy Selection

EBM-Based Guidelines for Pharmacotherapy Selection.

Condition	First-Line Therapy (EBM-Based)	Alternative Based on Evidence
Hypertension (with heart failure)	ACE inhibitors (e.g., enalapril)	Beta-blockers (e.g., bisoprolol)
Type 2 Diabetes (with CVD)	SGLT2 inhibitors (e.g., empagliflozin)	GLP-1 receptor agonists
Atrial Fibrillation (Stroke Prevention)	DOACs (e.g., apixaban, rivaroxaban)	Warfarin (requires INR monitoring)
Neuropathic Pain	Pregabalin, gabapentin	TCAs (e.g., amitriptyline)
Major Depressive Disorder	SSRIs (e.g., fluoxetine, sertraline)	SNRIs (e.g., venlafaxine)

EBM-Based Guidelines for Pharmacotherapy Selection

Interpreting Research Data in Evidence-Based Medicine

Interpreting clinical research data is essential for **making informed pharmacotherapeutic decisions. Key statistical measures** help assess treatment efficacy, risk reduction, and clinical impact.

Key Metrics in Clinical Research

1. Relative Risk (RR)

    ◦ Measures the likelihood of an event occurring in the treatment group compared to the control group.

$$RR = \frac{\text{Incidence in Treatment Group}}{\text{Incidence in Control Group}}$$

Formula for Relative Risk

Example:
In a study evaluating the effect of **statins on myocardial infarction (MI)**:
Statin group: 5% incidence of MI.
Placebo group: 10% incidence of MI.

$$RR = \frac{5\%}{10\%} = 0.5$$

Interpretation: Patients taking statins have **50% of the risk of MI** compared to those not taking statins.

Clinical Implication:

- RR <1 → Treatment reduces risk.
- RR >1 → Treatment increases risk.

1. **Odds Ratio (OR)**

   - Compares the **odds of an outcome occurring in the treatment group versus the control group.**
   - Commonly used in **case-control studies.**

$$OR - \frac{\text{Odds of Event in Treatment Group}}{\text{Odds of Event in Control Group}}$$

Odds Ratio (OR)

Example:

- A study on **smoking and lung cancer** found:

  - **Lung cancer cases:** 80 smokers, 20 non-smokers.
  - **Controls (healthy people):** 40 smokers, 60 non-smokers.

$$OR - \frac{\left(\frac{80}{20}\right)}{\left(\frac{40}{60}\right)} - \frac{4}{0.67} - 6$$

Interpretation: Smokers have **6 times the odds of developing lung cancer compared to non-smokers.**

Clinical Implication:

OR = **1** → No association.

OR **>1** → Increased risk with exposure.

OR **<1** → Protective effect of treatment.

Absolute Risk Reduction (ARR)

Measures the absolute difference in risk between treatment and control groups.

ARR=Incidence in Control Group–Incidence in Treatment Group

Example:

In a study on aspirin for stroke prevention:

Control group stroke incidence: 8%.

Aspirin group stroke incidence: 4%.

Interpretation: Aspirin reduces stroke risk by **4 percentage points.**

Number Needed to Treat (NNT)

Indicates how many patients need to be treated to prevent one adverse event.

Formula:

$$NNT = \frac{1}{ARR}$$

Hazard Ratio (HR)

Compares the time to an event in treatment vs. control groups over a study period.

Used in **survival analysis (Kaplan-Meier curves).**

$$HR = \frac{\text{Hazard rate in Treatment Group}}{\text{Hazard rate in Control Group}}$$

Hazard Ratio (HR)

Statistic	Definition	Formula	Example Interpretation
Relative Risk (RR)	Risk in treatment vs. control group	$RR = \frac{Risk_{treatment}}{Risk_{control}}$	RR = 0.5 → Treatment reduces risk by 50%
Odds Ratio (OR)	Odds of event in cases vs. controls	$OR = \frac{Odds_{treatment}}{Odds_{control}}$	OR = 6 → Smokers are 6 times more likely to develop lung cancer
Absolute Risk Reduction (ARR)	Absolute difference in risk	$ARR = Risk_{control} - Risk_{treatment}$	ARR = 4% → Stroke risk reduced by 4% with aspirin
Number Needed to Treat (NNT)	Patients needed to treat to prevent 1 event	$NNT = \frac{1}{ARR}$	NNT = 25 → 25 patients need aspirin to prevent 1 stroke
Hazard Ratio (HR)	Time to event in treatment vs. control	$HR = \frac{Hazard_{treatment}}{Hazard_{control}}$	HR = 0.5 → 50% reduction in disease progression

Comparison of Key Metrics

7.4 Pharmacist's Role in Evidence-Based Medicine

Pharmacists play a **crucial role in applying Evidence-Based Medicine (EBM)** by **evaluating research, optimizing drug therapy, educating patients, and ensuring adherence to clinical guidelines.** Their expertise in **drug pharmacokinetics, pharmacodynamics, and therapeutic monitoring** allows them to make informed recommendations in patient care.

Role in Literature Evaluation

Pharmacists must critically assess clinical studies before applying findings to practice. This involves:

1. Appraising Clinical Trials

Evaluating **study design, methodology, and statistical analysis.**

Checking for **randomization, blinding, and allocation concealment** to **reduce bias.**

Ensuring adequate **sample size** to **improve study reliability.**

Study Feature	Significance in EBM
Randomization	Reduces selection bias, ensuring equal distribution of confounders.
Blinding	Prevents observer and participant bias, maintaining objectivity.
Sample Size Calculation	Ensures statistical power, minimizing false conclusions.
Control Groups	Helps compare the effectiveness of interventions.
P-Value and Confidence Intervals	Determines statistical significance of results.

2. Identifying Bias in Clinical Studies

Publication Bias: Favoring **positive results over negative ones,** skewing treatment perception.

Selection Bias: Patients **not randomly assigned,** leading to **differences between treatment and control groups.**

Attrition Bias: Loss of participants from the study affects validity.

Pharmacists should rely on **systematic reviews and meta-analyses** to minimize bias in decision-making.

Implementing EBM in Pharmacy Practice

1. Optimizing Drug Therapy Based on Latest Guidelines

American Diabetes Association (ADA) guidelines: Recommending **SGLT2 inhibitors or GLP-1 receptor agonists** for Type 2 diabetes with cardiovascular risk.

American Heart Association (AHA) guidelines: Using **beta-blockers and ACE inhibitors** for heart failure.

National Comprehensive Cancer Network (NCCN) guidelines: Selecting chemotherapy regimens based on **latest oncological evidence.**

2. Individualized Pharmacotherapy Adjustments

Warfarin dosing adjusted based on INR monitoring.

Renal dosing adjustments for antibiotics (e.g., aminoglycosides in renal failure).

Switching antidepressants based on treatment resistance in depression.

3. Educating Patients on Evidence-Based Therapeutic Options

Explaining **drug efficacy, side effects, and risk-benefit analysis.**

Encouraging **medication adherence** by addressing concerns **with scientific data.**

Assisting in **shared decision-making** between doctors and patients.

Example:

A patient with **hypertension and diabetes** might be prescribed **SGLT2 inhibitors** based on evidence showing **reduced cardiovascular mortality by 38%** (EMPA-REG trial).

7.5 Challenges in Implementing EBM

Despite its benefits, implementing EBM in pharmacy practice faces multiple barriers.

Barriers to EBM Implementation

Limited Access to High-Quality Evidence

In **resource-poor settings**, access to **journals and clinical trial data** is restricted.

Lack of institutional support for continuous medical education.

Time Constraints in Busy Clinical Settings

Pharmacists have **limited time to review new literature** while managing patient care.

Decision-making under time pressure may lead to reliance on outdated practices.

Variability in Patient Preferences and Values

Some patients **prioritize cost over effectiveness.**

Others prefer **alternative medicine despite evidence favoring conventional drugs.**

Solutions to Overcome EBM Barriers

Use of Summarized Evidence Resources

Pharmacists can **quickly access clinical guidelines** from trusted databases such as:

Cochrane Library (systematic reviews).

PubMed Clinical Queries (peer-reviewed studies).

UpToDate (evidence-based clinical summaries).

Mobile applications (e.g., Medscape, Micromedex, Epocrates) provide quick clinical references.

Multidisciplinary Teamwork in Decision-Making

Pharmacists collaborate with **physicians, nurses, and specialists** to optimize EBM-based care.

Regular clinical meetings ensure that all healthcare providers follow the latest guidelines.

Continuing Education and Training

Regular **EBM workshops, journal clubs, and pharmacy training programs** enhance pharmacist competency.

Encouraging **research participation and clinical audits** improves **pharmacist involvement in evidence-based practices.**

7.6 Case Studies in Evidence-Based Medicine

The application of **Evidence-Based Medicine (EBM) in real-world clinical scenarios** ensures that **treatment decisions are guided by high-quality research.** Case studies illustrate how EBM improves **patient outcomes, optimizes pharmacotherapy, and enhances clinical decision-making.**

Example 1: Application of EBM in Managing Stroke

Clinical Question

"Is alteplase effective in elderly patients with ischemic stroke?"

Background

Stroke is the second leading cause of death and disability worldwide.

Thrombolytic therapy with alteplase (tPA) is the standard of care for acute ischemic stroke.

However, concerns exist regarding the safety of thrombolysis in elderly patients (>80 years), particularly the risk of hemorrhage.

Evidence Review

Randomized Controlled Trials (RCTs) Supporting Alteplase in Stroke NINDS Trial (1995):

Showed a **significant improvement in functional outcomes** when alteplase was administered within **3 hours of symptom onset.**

35% more patients had minimal disability at 3 months compared to placebo.

ECASS-3 Trial (2008):

Demonstrated that **alteplase remains effective up to 4.5 hours** after stroke onset.

Increased the odds of **independent living by 34% compared to placebo.**

Real-World Data on Elderly Patients

IST-3 Trial (2012):

Included **3,035 patients,** with **half aged over 80 years.**

Found that **elderly patients benefited from alteplase with similar functional recovery as younger patients.**

However, there was a slightly increased risk of symptomatic intracranial hemorrhage (7% vs. 3% in younger patients).

Conclusion Based on EBM

Alteplase remains the standard of care for acute ischemic stroke, even in elderly patients.

Benefits outweigh risks if administered within 4.5 hours, provided there are no contraindications (e.g., recent hemorrhage, severe hypertension).

Guidelines (AHA/ASA) recommend thrombolysis in patients aged >80 years with close monitoring for bleeding risks.

Example 2: EBM in Managing Chronic Pain

Clinical Question

"Do gabapentinoids improve outcomes in diabetic neuropathy?"

Background

Diabetic neuropathy affects up to 50% of long-standing diabetes patients.

Chronic nerve pain leads to poor sleep, reduced mobility, and diminished quality of life.

First-line treatment includes anticonvulsants (gabapentin, pregabalin) based on their mechanism of action.

Evidence Review

Meta-Analyses Supporting Gabapentinoids for Neuropathic Pain

Cochrane Review (2017) on Pregabalin:

Included **37 RCTs with over 9,000 patients.**

Found that **pregabalin provided at least 50% pain relief in 50-70% of** patients.

Improved sleep quality and reduced pain-related anxiety.

Neurontin Study (2020) on Gabapentin:

Showed that **gabapentin reduced pain scores by 30-50% in diabetic neuropathy patients.**

Higher doses (1,800–3,600 mg/day) were more effective but increased sedation risk.

Real-World Evidence and Long-Term Outcomes

Studies confirm that **gabapentinoids significantly improve neuropathic pain relief** but require **gradual dose escalation to minimize dizziness and sedation.**

Combination therapy with **SNRIs (e.g., duloxetine) enhances pain relief** in resistant cases.

Conclusion Based on EBM

Gabapentinoids (pregabalin, gabapentin) are first-line therapies for diabetic neuropathy based on high-quality RCTs.

Evidence supports their use in reducing neuropathic pain by 50-70%, improving sleep, and enhancing patient quality of life.

Dosing should be individualized to balance efficacy and side effects, with regular monitoring for sedation and weight gain.

Clinical Condition	Treatment Evaluated	EBM Outcome
Acute Ischemic Stroke	Alteplase (tPA)	Reduces disability, benefits outweigh risks in elderly patients.
Diabetic Neuropathy	Gabapentinoids (pregabalin, gabapentin)	50-70% pain relief, effective but requires careful dose titration.

Key Takeaways from EBM Case Studies

REVIEW QUESTIONS

1. Define evidence-based medicine (EBM) and describe its three core components.
   (Discuss the integration of the best available evidence, clinical expertise, and patient preferences and values.)
2. Explain why EBM is critical in improving clinical outcomes and ensuring rational prescribing practices.
3. Outline the 5-step process of EBM and describe the purpose of each step. *(Include: Ask a clinical question, Acquire evidence, Appraise the evidence, Apply findings to practice, and Assess therapeutic outcomes.)*
4. Discuss how formulating a clear clinical question using the PICO framework can guide effective evidence searches.
5. Provide an example of a well-formulated PICO question and explain each component (P, I, C, O).
6. Describe the "Pyramid of Evidence" and explain why systematic reviews and meta-analyses are considered the most robust form of evidence.
7. Compare the strengths and weaknesses of randomized controlled trials (RCTs) versus observational studies in clinical research.
8. What are the limitations of expert opinion and case reports in the hierarchy of evidence?
9. Identify reliable evidence sources (e.g., PubMed, Cochrane Library, clinical guidelines) and explain how they contribute to EBM.
10. Discuss how critical appraisal of evidence (considering study design, randomization, blinding, etc.) impacts clinical decision-making.
11. Explain the significance of clinical outcomes such as Relative Risk Reduction (RRR), Absolute Risk Reduction (ARR), and Number Needed to Treat (NNT) in interpreting study results.
12. How does calculating the Number Needed to Treat (NNT) (using NNT = 1/ARR) help clinicians understand the effectiveness of an intervention?
13. Discuss the pharmacist's role in EBM, particularly in literature appraisal and educating patients about therapy risks and benefits.
14. Explain how collaboration between pharmacists, physicians, and other healthcare professionals can enhance the implementation of EBM in clinical practice.

15. Identify common barriers to implementing EBM in resource-poor or busy clinical settings, and suggest strategies to overcome them.

16. How can decision support tools and clinical guidelines facilitate the integration of EBM into everyday practice?

17. Discuss the importance of incorporating real-world evidence (RWE) alongside RCT data in informing clinical decisions.

18. Explain how artificial intelligence (AI) can be used for evidence synthesis and personalized medicine within the EBM framework.

19. Describe a case study where EBM was applied to select an anticoagulation therapy (e.g., comparing rivaroxaban to warfarin), including the clinical question, evidence, and outcome.

20. Reflect on future directions in EBM. What global trends and technological advancements are likely to shape the evolution of evidence-based practice?

MCQS

1. **EBM stands for:**
   A) Electronic Biopsy Method
   B) Evidence-Based Medicine
   C) Empirical Biostatistical Measurement
   D) Essential Basic Medicine
   Correct Answer: B

2. **The three core components of EBM are:**
   A) Best available evidence, clinical expertise, and patient preferences and values
   B) Research data, cost-effectiveness, and clinical judgment
   C) Clinical experience, hospital policy, and patient insurance
   D) Laboratory tests, expert opinions, and statistical analysis
   Correct Answer: A

3. **The 5-step process of EBM includes all of the following EXCEPT:**
   A) Ask a clinical question
   B) Acquire relevant evidence
   C) Advertise the evidence
   D) Assess therapeutic outcomes
   Correct Answer: C

4. **The "Ask" step in EBM primarily involves:**
   A) Formulating a well-structured clinical question
   B) Searching for evidence
   C) Critically appraising research
   D) Applying findings to patient care
   Correct Answer: A

5. **In the PICO framework, the "I" stands for:**
   A) Investigation
   B) Intervention
   C) Inference
   D) Interpretation
   Correct Answer: B

6. **Systematic reviews and meta-analyses are placed at the top of the evidence hierarchy because they:**

A) Are less expensive to conduct

B) Summarize multiple studies and provide robust conclusions

C) Rely solely on expert opinions

D) Are the easiest type of study to perform

Correct Answer: B

7. **Randomized controlled trials (RCTs) are considered the gold standard because they:**

    A) Allow for observational data collection

    B) Minimize bias through randomization and control

    C) Are less time-consuming than other studies

    D) Rely on historical data

    Correct Answer: B

8. **Expert opinion and case reports are considered the least reliable evidence because they:**

    A) Are often biased and lack systematic analysis

    B) Include large sample sizes

    C) Are derived from systematic reviews

    D) Always follow strict protocols

    Correct Answer: A

9. **A well-formulated clinical question using the PICO format helps to:**

    A) Widen the search for evidence

    B) Focus the literature search on specific aspects of patient care

    C) Replace the need for evidence appraisal

    D) Limit clinical expertise

    Correct Answer: B

10. **Which source is considered highly reliable for obtaining clinical evidence?**

    A) Social media blogs

    B) Cochrane Library

    C) Non-peer-reviewed websites

    D) Patient testimonials

    Correct Answer: B

11. **The process of "appraising" evidence in EBM involves:**

    A) Immediately applying research findings

    B) Critically evaluating the validity and relevance of the evidence

    C) Asking patients for their opinions

    D) Ignoring study limitations

    Correct Answer: B

12. **The formula for Number Needed to Treat (NNT) is:**
    A) NNT = 1 / Relative Risk Reduction
    B) NNT = 1 / Absolute Risk Reduction
    C) NNT = Absolute Risk Reduction / 1
    D) NNT = Relative Risk Reduction x 100
    Correct Answer: B

13. **Which of the following best describes the hierarchy of evidence?**
    A) A ranking from expert opinions to randomized controlled trials
    B) A pyramid with systematic reviews at the top and case reports at the bottom
    C) A list of journals ranked by impact factor
    D) A set of clinical guidelines
    Correct Answer: B

14. **The "apply" step in the EBM process refers to:**
    A) Searching for evidence
    B) Critically evaluating research
    C) Integrating evidence with clinical expertise and patient values in practice
    D) Formulating a clinical question
    Correct Answer: C

15. **Which of the following is a major barrier to implementing EBM in clinical practice?**
    A) Abundance of high-quality evidence
    B) Time constraints in busy clinical settings
    C) Excessive funding for research
    D) Universal access to medical journals
    Correct Answer: B

16. **Real-World Evidence (RWE) is derived from:**
    A) Controlled laboratory experiments only
    B) Observational studies and routine clinical practice data
    C) Randomized controlled trials exclusively
    D) Expert opinions
    Correct Answer: B

17. **Artificial Intelligence (AI) in EBM is primarily used for:**
    A) Replacing clinical expertise entirely
    B) Enhancing evidence synthesis and personalizing medicine
    C) Generating random clinical questions
    D) Reducing the need for patient data

Correct Answer: B

18. **Clinical guidelines help practitioners by:**

    A) Providing unsummarized raw data

    B) Offering evidence-based recommendations for practice

    C) Eliminating the need for clinical judgment

    D) Relying solely on case reports

    Correct Answer: B

19. **The Wells score is an example of a tool used to:**

    A) Formulate clinical questions

    B) Assess risk factors in evidence-based practice

    C) Guide literature searches

    D) Monitor therapeutic outcomes

    Correct Answer: B

20. **The "assess" step in the EBM process involves:**

    A) Formulating the initial clinical question

    B) Applying evidence without further review

    C) Evaluating the impact of the applied intervention on patient outcomes

    D) Acquiring raw data only

    Correct Answer: C

21. **A case study in EBM often involves:**

    A) Ignoring all evidence and relying on tradition

    B) Applying EBM principles to a specific clinical scenario

    C) Using only expert opinions

    D) Focusing solely on statistical analysis

    Correct Answer: B

22. **Which of the following best describes the role of a pharmacist in EBM?**

    A) Dispensing medications without patient counseling

    B) Critically appraising literature and advising on evidence-based therapy

    C) Designing clinical trials exclusively

    D) Replacing the role of the physician

    Correct Answer: B

23. **Decision support tools in EBM are used to:**

    A) Eliminate the need for literature searches

    B) Integrate and summarize evidence for real-time clinical decision-making

C) Increase administrative tasks

D) Replace clinical guidelines

Correct Answer: B

24. **Open-access evidence databases are particularly important because they:**

    A) Restrict access to only high-income settings

    B) Provide free access to high-quality evidence, especially in resource-limited settings

    C) Are only available to academic researchers

    D) Limit the dissemination of clinical guidelines

    Correct Answer: B

25. **A well-formulated PICO question includes all of the following components except:**

    A) Patient/Population

    B) Intervention

    C) Comparator

    D) Cost

    Correct Answer: D

26. **The primary aim of EBM is to:**

    A) Base all decisions on the latest drug advertisements

    B) Integrate scientific evidence with clinical expertise and patient values to improve outcomes

    C) Replace clinical judgment with research findings

    D) Focus only on the statistical significance of studies

    Correct Answer: B

27. **Which of the following is an example of an evidence source that is part of the EBM workflow?**

    A) Cochrane Library

    B) Social media forums

    C) Unpublished anecdotes

    D) Personal blogs

    Correct Answer: A

28. **The integration of real-world evidence (RWE) with traditional RCT data is expected to:**

    A) Limit personalized medicine

    B) Provide a more comprehensive view of treatment effectiveness in diverse populations

    C) Replace the need for RCTs

D) Increase research bias

Correct Answer: B

29. **In a PICO question, the "Comparator" component is used to:**

    A) Identify the patient population

    B) Specify the intervention to be tested

    C) Define the alternative treatment or standard care

    D) Determine the cost-effectiveness

    Correct Answer: C

30. **Future directions in EBM are likely to include:**

    A) A decrease in open-access evidence

    B) The integration of AI for enhanced evidence synthesis and personalized treatment strategies

    C) A reliance solely on expert opinion

    D) Eliminating observational studies from the hierarchy

    Correct Answer: B

www.ingramcontent.com/pod-product-compliance
Lightning Source LLC
Chambersburg PA
CBHW042045150726
48005CB00034B/1869